# Retrieving
# Political Emotion

Barbara Koziak

# Retrieving Political Emotion

*Thumos*, Aristotle, and Gender

The Pennsylvania State University Press
University Park, Pennsylvania

Library of Congress Cataloging-in-Publication Data

Koziak, Barbara, 1961–
    Retrieving political emotion : Thumos, Aristotle, and gender / Barbara
Koziak.
        p.        cm.
    Includes bibliographical references and index.
    ISBN 0-271-01921-2
    1. Aristotle—Contributions in political science. 2. Political science—
Greece—History. 3. Political psychology. 4. Feminist psychology.
5. Emotions. I. Title.
JC71.A7K69    2000
320′.01′1—dc21                                                          98-50151
                                                                              CIP

It is the policy of The Pennsylvania State University Press to use acid-free
paper for the first printing of all clothbound books. Publications on uncoated
stock satisfy the minimum requirements of American National Standard for
Information Sciences—Permanence of Paper for Printed Library Materials,
ANSI Z39.48–1992.

*For my friends*

# Contents

# Acknowledgments

Although books are written while the writer is sitting alone, this book was composed when I could imagine myself surrounded by friends. Two of my dearest friends were writing books at the same time. Miriam Feldblum, kept up steady stream of computer and phone comments, always helping me to clarify my dilemmas. Her intellectual vivacity, from which I continually benefit, graces her work on citizenship politics. Sarah Winter's friendship has continually nurtured my imagination by sharing so generously our common love of the seemingly unrelated matters of Ancient Greek culture, the history of psychological concepts, and modern dance. As I finished this book, her work on Freud and Greek tragedy sat atop my desk as an magnificent exemplar. I thank her for the careful reading and comments on most of the chapters.

I have been no less fortunate in my colleagues, mentors, and teachers. For sheer commitment to the process of intellectual nurturance, none have been so important for me as Steven B. Smith. From my early undergraduate days, Steven's deep erudition have inspired my study of political philosophy. For excellent, extensive comments and the opportunity to teach in the pastoral setting of Bryn Mawr College, I thank Stephen G. Salkever. For other welcome comments, insights, and general support I thank Shelly Burtt, Norma Thompson, Pat Sykes, Dierdre Golash, Jeff Reiman, Michael Boylan, Marissa Golden, Cynthia Freeland, Rogers Smith, Ian Shapiro, Rogan Kersh, Romand Coles, Fred C. Alford, Joel Schwartz, Matty Woodruff, and Russell Rainbolt and the anonymous reviewers for Penn State Press and the *Journal of Politics*. Ken Sharpe, Richard Schuldenfrei, Ross Lence, Donald Lutz, Jane Marcus, Paul Zammito are all teachers who kindled my interest from my early days as an undergraduate. Richard Schuldenfrei first made me understand the problem of integrity in an intellectual and ethical life.

Finally the joy and kinship of my friends and family have nourished my work. My oldest friends, Stephanie Judd and Russell Rainbolt, are invariably loving and wise. I owe my life to them. Dinners have always sparkled whenever they were spent with Miriam Feldblum and her three sons, Ariel, Issac, Noah; Sarah Winter and Panos Zagouras with their daughter Alexia, Laura and Dale Cloud, and Bruce Barrett and Teresa Eke. Thanks are especially due to my parents, Joseph and Kveta Koziak, for their long-standing concern and support for my work and, most importantly, for the immense courage and obstinate hope they showed in Czechoslovakia of 1966.

# Introduction

He began to think of her, of what she was thinking and feeling.
For the first time he really pictured to himself her personal life, her
ideas, her desires; and the notion that she could and should have a
separate life of her own appeared to him so dreadful that he
hastened to drive it away.... To put himself in thought and feeling
into another being was a mental exercise foreign to Karenin. He
considered such a mental exercise harmful and dangerous
romancing.... "The question of her feelings, of what has taken place
or may take place in her heart, is not my affair but the affair of her
conscience, and comes under the head of religion," he said to himself,
feeling relieved at having found the category of regulating
principles to which the newly-arisen situation rightly belonged.
—Tolstoy, *Anna Karenina*

Emotion in politics has no need for retrieval. Among other emotions, anger, envy, compassion, righteousness, grief, sometimes feigned, sometimes sincere, play daily on the world's political stage. While we may clearly see the emotional in politics, a conception of political emotion sorely needs retrieval. Although most political theories imply or suggest some view of the role of emotion in political life, some of which are at the same time deeply hostile to emotion, no general treatment of the emotional has been written in the history of normative political theory.

Reason and the image of the reason-ruled person have long dominated political philosophy, but never completely nor without challenge. What reason and being reason-ruled means has changed from Plato to Locke to Rawls, and so have the passions and nonrational elements infiltrating reason's domain. For Plato, reason is never fully extricated from *eros* and myth; for Locke, reason gives us access to natural law; and for Rawls, cupidity is made to serve reason or even to become the inner drive of reason. With Hegel, reason acquired a history; with Nietzsche, the disrepute of mediocrity.

Reason's incomplete reign is marked by the anxiety over emotion. In political philosophy, the dread of political emotion has ebbed and flowed, writing and rewriting the constructions of the psyche and the symbolic codes of our political worlds. But political philosophy has rarely addressed what it so clearly reveals—that the emotional is no less human and no less political than is the rational. Even in critiques of rationalistic political theory and of "logocentrism" the emotions are barely mentioned.

This is not a book in which I reasonably argue for the overthrow of reason. I recognize the formulation of the concept of rationality as crucial to philosophy's development. Myth and ritual provided interpretations of life, which can be said to constitute philosophies of life. But the arrival of the practice of philosophy and the philosophical life included a skepticism toward appearance, custom, and traditional authority. If anything, philosophy at its beginnings must be identified with the rational (although not merely rational) techniques of criticism, clarification, comparison. While in recent years philosophy has been attacked for its claims to rationality, universality, objectivity and truth, this is to a large extent because philosophy itself has acquired traditional authority.

But I am not so much concerned with the practice of philosophy as with how philosophy figured the human within a political system. Philosophy, seeing within itself what it supposed was the most sublime, or the most reliable, of human capacities, described the political human in its own image—for Aristotle, *logos* or reason makes us political animals. The ambition of Hobbes and Spinoza was to study human emotion "geometrically." The beastly passions could be tamed by the philosopher or social scientist studying them objectively, neutrally, free of their pull. Is there any account of the political life that pays equal respect to reason and emotion and reconsiders the idea of a strict dichotomy between the two?

At this moment, at the mention of emotion, Hume and Rousseau may come to mind. Yet I contend that the better place to look is back to a period that appears to many as a celebration of rationality—ancient Greece. In this study I retrieve Aristotle's treatment of *thumos*, most often translated as "spiritedness," showing how it represents a theory of political emotion available to contemporary challenges to rationalistic explanations of political community. I proceed by first recounting the use of *thumos* in Homer's *Iliad* and in Plato's *Republic*, Aristotle's two most important sources, eventually arguing that he borrows from each but goes substantially beyond both. I then show how Aristotle uses *thumos* in three ways, developing at greatest length the third way, where *thumos* is understood as the capacity for emotion. As a technical term, *capacity,* or *dunamis*, embraces both "activity" and a "characteristic disposition." With the *Nicomachean Ethics* and the *Politics*, I look at the activity of *thumos*—how a person with a good *thumos* acts and in the context of which institutions. With the *Poetics* I look at the characteristic disposition of *thumos*—what patterns and objects typify a person's emotional capacity in the best regime.

Although the greater part of this book is a historical examination that ultimately focuses on Aristotle, this historical argument is set within a framework that introduces recent emotion theory and begins to develop a more comprehensive theory of political emotion. Such a theory is sorely needed because few canonical political philosophers and even fewer contemporary political theorists make use of the possibilities that the Aristotelian treatment of political emotion offered, and because much political philosophy is marred by the marginalization or misrepresentation of emotion. The political realm has often been construed as open only to those who possess reason. In various ways Plato, Aristotle, Hobbes, Locke, and Kant all built their political constructions on a demand for a society governed by reason, apparently maligning emotion. But, as has long been argued, the ancient and modern conceptions of reason are astoundingly different. Whereas for Plato and Aristotle reason is an end in itself, linked to contemplation of the cosmos, in the seventeenth and eighteenth centuries rationality is instrumental, tied to calculation and material self-interest.[1] Likewise, the conception of emotion has hardly remained static. Early modern rational self-interest was formulated as a strategy to withstand the force of dangerous passions.[2] The emotions were indeed typically called "passions," phenomena inherently disruptive of and distinct from reason. So while there was no denial that the political is often emotional, the hope was to create a more rational political realm and to outfox emotion.[3]

Contemporary political theory has not yet substantially left this modern legacy behind. Much contemporary theory is symptomatically bereft of a conception of emotion's political roles. Its proponents seek to persuade by

1. See Charles Taylor, *Sources of the Self: The Making of the Modern Identity* (Cambridge, Mass.: Harvard University Press, 1989).

2. This history is explored in Albert O. Hirschman, *The Passions and the Interests* (Princeton: Princeton University Press, 1978).

3. This is particularly true of liberal political theory; see Stephen Holmes, *Passions and Constraints* (Cambridge, Mass.: Harvard University Press, 1995).

argument directed at rational beings and see political actors as driven chiefly by rational motives such as norms of justice or economic self-interest. That these accounts of motivation are grounded in particular accounts of the psychic structure has usually been hidden. If we identify the kinds of selves theorized, and include an appreciation of emotion, we may end up with different theoretical results. The disregard of emotion has perpetuated certain strands of liberal theory and explanatory political science that rely on the universality and reliability of self-interest. Much of the history of political philosophy has then been neglected.

Of course, challenges to liberal political theory, and to its conceptions of rationality, have been profuse. But while radical democratic, communitarian, conservative, and postmodern theory certainly contribute to the loss of liberal authority on the question of psyche and ontology, they have only peripherally addressed issues of emotion, and have rarely articulated them as key to reconceiving the subject of theorizing.

Perhaps the most serious resulting practical defect of such political philosophy is the unexamined relationship between the oppression of women and of other marginalized groups and cultural views of emotion, a relationship that has been described in feminist research and theory above all. To some extent even in Plato and Aristotle, but particularly since the Enlightenment, women have been depicted as excessively emotional in ways that made them unreliable in the public sphere of politics, intellectual pursuits, and the professions. Hegel, in other ways a critic of Enlightenment philosophy, writes, "The difference between men and women is like that between animals and plants. Men correspond to animals, while women correspond to plants because their development is more placid and the principle that underlies it is the rather vague unity of feeling. When women hold the helm of government, the state is at once in jeopardy, because women regulate their actions not by the demands of universality but by arbitrary inclinations and opinions."[4]

In the epigraph that heads this introduction, Tolstoy describes Karenin's ruminating about his wife's inner life, perfectly displaying the wariness and dread some men and some political thinkers have felt toward the thinking/feeling life of women and of political actors generally. Karenin briefly considers the possibility of a complex inner life, but consigns such a life to the category of religion. So while with Hegel emotional life and women as its symbol become privatized and restricted to

4. Hegel, *The Philosophy of Right* (New York: Oxford University Press, 1967), 263–64.

the familial realm, with Karenin both are estranged to the realm of a privatized religion.

Since so many philosophers across time have purported that women are unequal due to their emotionality, their inability to reason, many feminists are skeptical of this legacy's unflattering portrayal of emotion, including the dichotomy of reason and emotion. If women are not so incapable as some men thought them, then perhaps emotions are not so incapable either.[5] In fact, feminist work has contributed to the contemporary burgeoning of work on the social and moral significance of emotion.[6] But in political theory work has just begun on the normative political role of emotion.[7] My claim, in this essay, is that a well-founded feminist politics should address how to incorporate and educate the emotional capacities of citizens.[8] This need arises because gender structures the emotions

5. Mary Daly, *Gyn / Ecology: The Metaethics of Radical Feminism* (Boston: Beacon, 1978) and *Pure Lust: Elemental Feminist Philosophy* (Boston: Beacon, 1984); Susan Griffin, *Woman and Nature* (New York: Harper and Row, 1980); Joan Cocks: "Wordless Emotions: Some Critical Reflections on Radical Feminism," *Politics and Society* 13, no. 1 (1984); Alison Jaggar, "Love and Knowledge: Emotion in Feminist Epistemology," in *Gender / Body / Knowledge: Feminist Reconstructions of Being and Knowing*, ed. Jaggar and Susan Bordo (New Brunswick: Rutgers University Press, 1989); Arlene Russell Hochschild, *The Managed Heart: Commercialization of Human Feeling* (Berkeley and Los Angeles: University of California Press, 1983); Genevieve Lloyd, *The Man of Reason: "Male" and "Female" in Western Philosophy*, 2d ed. (Minneapolis: University of Minnesota Press, 1993).

6. See, for example, Robert C. Solomon, *The Passions: The Myth and Nature of Human Emotion* (Garden City, N.Y.: Anchor Press, 1977); William Lyons, *Emotion* (London: Cambridge University Press, 1980); Amelie Rorty, ed., *Explaining Emotions* (Berkeley and Los Angeles: University of California Press, 1980); Cheshire Calhoun and Robert Solomon, eds., *What Is an Emotion? Classic Readings in Philosophical Psychology* (New York: Oxford University Press, 1984); Rom Harre, ed., *The Social Construction of Emotions* (Oxford: Basil Blackwell, 1986); Carol A. Stearns and Peter N. Stearns, *Emotion and Social Change: Toward a New Psychohistory* (New York: Holmes and Meier, 1988); Ronald de Sousa, *The Rationality of Emotion* (Cambridge: MIT Press, 1990); Justin Oakley, *Morality and the Emotions* (New York: Routledge, 1992). Joel Pfister and Nancy Schnog, eds., *Inventing the Psychological: Towards a History of Emotional Life in America* (New Haven: Yale University Press, 1997).

7. See for example Susan Okin, "Reason and Feeling in Thinking about Justice," *Ethics* 99, no. 2 (1989): 229–49; Joan Tronto, *Moral Boundaries* (New York: Routledge, 1993); Morwenna Griffiths, *Feminisms and the Self: The Web of Identity* (New York: Routledge, 1995); Robert Solomon, *A Passion for Justice: Emotions and the Origins of the Social Contract* (Reading, Mass: Addison-Wesley, 1990); Stephen Holmes, *Passions and Constraints*; Albert Hirschman, *The Passions and the Interests*; Michael Ignatieff, *The Needs of Strangers* (New York: Penguin, 1982).

8. Although I will continue to use the words "emotion" and "reason" suggesting two separate capacities, I certainly allow for a great deal of interrelationship or even identity between the two. Whether these categories are philosophically, psychologically or historically adequate, or whether we should significantly blur if not renounce the distinction is a huge question. I can say that in the cognitivist interpretation of emotion, which traces

that matter in political life, including the institutions and practices fostering them. In turn, this structuring justifies the gender divisions we still see in social life. Anger, especially, but also greed or interest have often appeared as the province of men and the animus of political life. The institutions that train and direct these emotions, such as the military for anger and the language and practice of interest politics for greed, delegitimate or inappropriately configure the emotions and practices needed for feminist transformation.

At the end, then, of the present book, centrally dedicated to a historical retrieval of the Aristotelian political emotion, I use an encounter with one branch of feminist political theory, care feminism, to refine why we need a theory of political emotion and how we should theorize about it in the contemporary context. In many ways this book is only the beginning for me. Much could be written on the conceptions of emotional and, more broadly, psychological life as they have shaped the philosophies of various thinkers. Much still can be done on integrating and examining the voluminous literature on emotion itself. Much work could be done in empirical research that used such revisionist work to ask better questions about what we humans need and want in our common life. And finally, I have hardly exhausted even the issues related to emotion or *thumos* in Plato and Aristotle. This book, then, invites political theorists to talk in a more focused way about emotional life as depicted in visions of political philosophers, and ultimately as lived by all of us in both the dreariness and the enthusiasm of political life.

---

its beginnings to Aristotle, emotions are partly distinguished by their rational beliefs whether factual or evaluative. See Lyons, *Emotion,* and de Sousa, *The Rationality of Emotion.*

# 1

# Emotion in Theory

## Emotion, Reason, and Political Theory

Why should how we think about emotion matter to how we conduct politics? Perhaps the clearest way to answer this question is to look at one historical period in which it mattered a great deal how political actors and thinkers thought about emotion. Indeed their approach to emotion not only helped to legitimize the capitalist economic revolution, but also had far-reaching political consequences. By the early modern era, according to Albert Hirschman's elegant book, *The Passions and the Interests*, the aristocratic passion for glory which drove unceasing political conflicts had slowly, but increasingly, been discredited.[1] Rather than aiming for political power as the path to glory, a steadily growing segment of the population pursued the traditionally despised professions of

---

1. Albert O. Hirschman, *The Passions and the Interests* (Princeton: Princeton University Press, 1977).

the merchant and the commercial entrepreneur. "How," asks Hirschman, "did commercial, banking, and similar money-making pursuits become honorable at some point in the modern age after having stood condemned or despised as greed, love of lucre, and avarice for centuries past?"[2] He answers that intellectuals and administrative elites believed that the pursuit of money could become the antidote for the pursuit of glory, that the love of comfort and luxury could supersede the quest for renown and political domination.

Intellectuals argued this case for the elevation of commercial pursuits through an innovative strategy for disciplining human passions. In most Hellenistic and Medieval writers, the passions were held to be universally dangerous, and particularly recalcitrant, so that the only means of countering them was religious, political, or philosophical repression. Dissatisfied with this strategy of repression, early modern intellectuals, such as Spinoza, Montesquieu, and Hume, speculated that one passion, greed, could serve as the means of "countervailing" the destructive passion for glory. More significantly, a series of theorists began to employ the language of interest first to describe the motivation of princes or rulers (state-interest), but later to unite all humans in the universal interest for material self-advancement (self-interest). In another crucial move, interest was accorded the honor of rationality, and rational self-interest was born as the prescription for social and political peace. Thus the emergence of capitalism and its associated political forms were encouraged by a transformation in models of human psychology and especially by the invention of "interest."

This episode of intellectual history had wide implications for the understanding of emotion in political affairs. When interest was discursively invented, employing greed to counteract the passion for glory, its status as an emotion was erased. Most cunningly, the reinvention of greed as rational interest obscured its association with emotion; the emotional origins of interest were effectively lost. Long after the initial formulation by an administrative and intellectual elite, social scientists would find in interest something which appeared more clear, more reliable, more intelligible, and more public than emotion.

Hirschman's story of the invention of a new political and economic psychology should lead one to suspect that the varying formulations of psychology and particularly the place of the emotions among political theorists, and among all of us as political actors, delimit and determine,

2. Ibid., 9.

legitimate and authorize, our sense of effective, desirable, and just political institutions and practices. In Hirschman's example, intellectuals
began with a newly evolved consensus about the danger of the pursuing
glory, and about the inefficacy of traditional restraints on human passions, and then rethought emotional discipline in a way that legitimized
the political encouragement of commercial pursuits. Notice that taking
seriously the emotional assumptions in political theory does not entail
psychologizing politics; one need not reduce politics to expression of various psychological needs and neuroses. Instead talk or discourse about
emotion is one way of conducting politics, exercising power, and creating
and enforcing value.

The canon of western political philosophy likewise incorporates a
wealth of thought on emotion almost entirely unexplored for the purposes of political reflection, except perhaps for Rousseau's contributions.
Rousseau is taken to be the "discoverer of passion and its irresistible
primitive force" and to have "discovered" political compassion.[3] In the
*Discourse of the Origins of Inequality*, Rousseau first famously argues
that natural humans, before they became social and political beings,
possess two basic sentiments–self-love and pity. Claiming not to desire
the extirpation of "passions," since they are fundamentally the work of
nature and God, although social life engenders a panoply of new harmful
passion, Rousseau wants to educate them, aligning them to their natural
forms. Self-love is the "source of all our passions, the origin and principle
of all the other ... a primitive, innate passion."[4] The second pre-social
passion, pity is a "pure movement of nature prior to all reflection" that
"moderates in each individual the activity of love of oneself, contributes
to the mutual preservation of the entire species. It carries us without
reflection to the aid of those whom we see suffer; in the state of nature,
it takes the place of laws, morals, and virtue."[5] Not reason, but this passion or natural virtue can be the sturdy ground for morality. A rational
philosopher can too easily forget the cries of pain outside his window.[6]
With the development of reason and rudimentary societies the most
important social passion of vanity or *amour-propre* eviscerates pity,

3. Ernst Cassirer, *The Question of Jean Jacques Rousseau* (New Haven: Yale University Press, 1989), 83; and Clifford Orwin, "Rousseau and the Discovery of Political Compassion," in *The Legacy of Rousseau*, ed. Clifford Orwin and Nathan Tarcov (Chicago:
University of Chicago Press, 1997).

4. *Emile or On Education*, trans. Allan Bloom (New York: Basic Books, 1979), 212–13.

5. Rousseau, *The First and Second Discourses*, ed. Roger D. Masters, trans. Roger D.
and Judith R. Masters (New York: St. Martin's Press, 1964), 131, 133.

6. Ibid., 132.

and metamorphosizes into greed, envy, contempt, and hypocrisy. In his critique of social life, but especially of modern commercial societies, Rousseau means to awaken grief for losing our simple response to the suffering of others.

But it is especially misleading to start with Rousseau, since he inaugurated an approach to emotion as authentic emanation from the depths of one's inner being.[7] In this period, due especially to Rousseau, "[t]hought and feeling—the psychological—are now confined to minds."[8] Learning to see the emotional outside of Rousseau is learning to see emotion as something other than natural and subjective. In addition, Rousseau's politics owe more to his interpretation of reason than to passion or emotion. The best society will be founded not on the passions but on law as an expression of "general will." Nevertheless, Rousseau writes with all the vibrancy of emotive enthusiasm, one that in this scholarly age would often fail to find sanction, and he, like most political philosophers, cannot fail to script political emotion into his desired society even if the topic is overcome by his overt commitment to the victory of reason.

Even those thinkers who have a reputation for being indifferent or even overtly antagonistic to conventionally desirable emotion, especially to the variety found in Rousseau, were compelled to allow some conception of emotional motivations into their political theories.

In John Locke's early modern conception, the humans found in a state of nature who consent to form political society are motivated explicitly by fear of thieves, thugs, murderers, and rapacious monarchs and by anxiety for a secure livelihood.[9] He mentions the love and want of society and, through a quotation of another author, the aspiration of "Communion and Fellowship with others" as additional motivations, but only secondarily, almost as an aside to comfort us with the assurance that self-interest and property are not necessarily the only concerns of civil society. Still, the explicit purpose of government, the only legitimate government, is above all to protect of property. Looking at the argument as a whole, fear and anxiety surpasses love and want of society[10] as the true motivation for

7. For a nuanced discussion of the role of Locke, Shaftesbury, Hutcheson, and Rousseau in the development of a modern internalized identity, see Taylor, *Sources of the Self.*
8. Ibid., 186.
9. Locke, *The Second Treatise of Government,* in his *Two Treatises of Government,* ed. Peter Laslett (New York: Mentor, 1960), sec. 123.
10. This phrase, "the love and want of society," is indeed Locke's. In section 101 of the *Second Treatise*, referring to the state of nature, he writes: "The inconveniences of that condition, and the love and want of society, no sooner brought any number of them together, but they presently united and incorporated, if they designed to continue together." But does anyone doubt that the *Treatise* is an analysis of the inconveniences?

forming a political government. Like Hobbes before him, Locke justifies his political regime by appeal to a picture of human passion and desire.

Yet the dichotomy of reason and emotion or passion so prevalent in these early modern thinkers serves to inform our conception of government. For example, in the *Federalist Papers*, the authors contending against the suggestion that the people should settle disputes between the three branches of government, declare that such a proposal would engage public prejudices and passions, but that "it is the reason, alone, of the public, that ought to control and regulate the government. The passions ought to be controlled and regulated by the government."[11] The defective Athenian democracy is criticized for its indulgence of the majority's passions: "What bitter anguish would not the people of Athens have often escaped if their government had contained so provident a safeguard against the tyranny of their own passions?"[12]

Even for Marx, who seems to rely least on human psychology, emotion-concepts are central to his work. Alienation for Marx is the central predicament of the economic institutions of capitalism. The portrayal of alienation makes plain the inhumanity of factory labor: "What constitutes the alienation of labour? First that the labour is *external* to the worker, i.e., it does not belong to his essential being; that in his work; therefore, he does not affirm himself but denies himself, does not feel content but unhappy, does not develop freely his physical and mental energy but mortifies his body and ruins his mind. The worker therefore only feels himself outside his work, and in his work feels outside himself. He is at home when he is not working, and when he is working he is not at home."[13] So although grounded in the way in which a worker in the capitalist system is related to his or her work, and also, although not evident in this quotation, to economic distribution and consumption, alienation is also partly a psychological or mental condition.[14]

Tocqueville, on the other hand, is one of the few theorists who continually articulates the character of the democratic regime through reference to emotion-concepts.[15] On his view, the leveling of economic disparity in

11. *The Federalist Papers* (New York: Mentor, 1961), No. 49, p. 317.

12. Ibid., No. 63, p. 384.

13. Marx, *Economic and Philosophical Manuscripts of 1844* in *The Marx-Engels Reader*, 2d ed., ed. Robert C. Tucker (New York: W. W. Norton, 1978), 74.

14. See the discussion of the complex history of this concept in *A Dictionary of Marxist Thought*, ed. Tom Bottomore et al. (Cambridge: Harvard University Press, 1983).

15. In fact, Stephen Salkever has called Tocqueville an Aristotelian social scientist for his attention to the complex details of a particular political context. Rather than theorizing for purely rational beings in the universal abstract mode, Toqueville sets out to "identify those attitudes and practices that have the greatest bearing on the particular

the United States produces particular dispositions, one of which is America's dominant passion for equality, another is a receptivity to the ethic of "self-interest rightly understood." This simple ethic encourages Americans to participate in local politics and civic associations, prompting them to public spiritedness and altruistic action by an appeal to self-interest. While Tocqueville juxtaposes this democratic ethic and the aristocratic ethic of self-sacrifice through magnificent and noble deeds, democratic ethics also differs from those early modern philosophers who claimed that citizens acting on and in their own self-interest will generate a common good. His embrace of self-interest as ultimate justification for benevolent acts should be studied in relation to his reconciliation of gender difference and social equality. One commentator has approvingly argued that Tocqueville theorized the family and women's "special" role in it as one source of virtues that offset democratic individualism.[16]

Not only philosophers but articulate political leaders understand the necessity of emotion in political life. In reflecting on his experience as dissident, state builder, and president, Václav Havel has claimed:

> A moral and intellectual state cannot be established through a constitution, or through law, or through directives, but only through complex, long-term, and never-ending work involving education and self-education. . . . It is not, in short, something we can simply declare or introduce. It is a way of going about things, and it demands the courage to breathe moral and spiritual motivation into everything, to seek the human dimension in all things. Science, technology, expertise, and so-called professionalism are not enough. Something more is necessary. For the sake of simplicity, it might be called spirit. Or feeling. Or conscience.[17]

Despite these examples of how emotion enters into political theories, how pictures of emotional needs and pains legitimate political theories, how political regimes privilege, amplify, stunt, or nurture actual political emotions, recent theory has tended to concentrate on the rational or leave unarticulated its dependence on emotion-concepts. Within all political

---

possibilities that define democratic life." See Salkever, *Finding the Mean* (Princeton: Princeton University Press, 1990), 246.

16. F. L. Morton, "Sexual Equality and the Family in Tocqueville's *Democracy in America*," *Canadian Journal of Political Science* 17 (1984): 310–24.

17. Václav Havel, *Summer Meditations*, trans. Paul Wilson (New York: Alfred A. Knopf, 1992), 20.

principles and theories is the prescription for some emotional relationship between the self and others. But the freedom to address this topic directly, to be able to theorize emotional and institutional relationships has been hampered by a diminished view of emotion in philosophy and in the social sciences. In the renewal of systematic political philosophy, reason is central and ubiquitous, as it continues to be in rational choice explanations of political behavior. The rise of identity politics and the resurgence of nationalism has brought more to mind that in concentrating on formal mechanisms of conflict mediation within democratic states, and on long-range economic and structural forces as determinants of political life, we have missed a crucial nexus of relations between cultural and political paradigms: the emotional inheritances and innovations of individuals, and the political representations through images and practice of social relations between, for example, taxpayers and AFDC (Aid to Families with Dependent Children) recipients. That is, in foregoing serious study of emotion, we have as a result foregone a study of the ties that bind, and knives that sever.

## Aristotle and Contemporary Emotion Theory

Yet recently there has been a sea change in the scholarly understanding of emotion. Philosophers have gone from viewing the passions or emotions as universally wild, irrational, dangerous, subjective bodily phenomena that impair good practical and theoretical judgment, to posing emotions as rational, cognitive, evaluative, and essential to good moral character and action. Historians, sociologists, and anthropologists have increasingly been studying the social sources and effects of our emotions. Feminists have been particularly attracted to revaluing emotional life due to the commonly linked disparagement of women and emotion as unreasoning. In its entirety this revisionist approach to emotion is tremendously exciting research that should prompt a reevaluation of political philosophy's history and contemporary tasks. While political theorists have occasionally eyed the psychological views of canonical philosophers, they have done little to alter the practice and concerns of mainstream theory. Such a transformed view of emotion enables us to take seriously a little-understood feature of traditional political philosophy—the changing models of emotion and their effect on other elements of a political theorist's vision. More important, scholars in this field have often noted the paucity of theory about the relationship between emotion and political affairs. At the same time, many writers imply that their work of unearthing the cultural constitution of emotion has a political intention, an implication that suggests the possibility and need for a normative theory of emotion.

The loose scholarly consensus gathered around the concept of emotion may be dubbed the revisionist approach. Since works in this approach often mention Aristotle as an authoritative ancestor, I will describe the main elements of this approach while comparing them to Aristotle's views. As an introduction to my critical history of *thumos*, the revisionist approach illuminates the ancient history of emotion. Conversely, Aristotle can help to remedy the political shortcomings of the revisionist approach. Few writers have extensively addressed how political life is infused with emotion, or what the political consequences of this reconceptualization of emotions might be. Moreover, those who have addressed these issues have not explored their appearance in the major works of political philosophy.

The revisionist approach has ardently contested two standard approaches to the psychology of emotion. The first, sensation or physiological theory, exemplified in the work of Descartes, Hume, and William James, views emotions as the mere awareness of physiological motions caused by simple perceptions of outside events.[18] For example, to a person in a jungle for the first time, the ocular perception of a pouncing lion causes the bodily commotion that we recognize, or become aware of, as fear. The second type, behavioral, developed by Charles Darwin, John Dewey and Gilbert Ryle, conceives of emotion as a group of gestures and actions. In Ryle's work, for example, anger is the disposition to shout, redden, and engage in verbal abuse.[19] Both these theories tend to reinforce a prevalent view that emotions are essentially biological or physical phenomena, that they are simple responses to external stimuli, that they are subjective and irrational, and that they are individual, asocial, and ahistorical events.

In contrast to these older approaches, revisionist work agrees to a large, but not unanimous, extent on three points: that reason or cognitions in

18. Other names are in use. William Lyons calls these Cartesian theories, Arlene Hochschild calls them "organismatic" theories. See William Lyons, *Emotion* (London: Cambridge University Press, 1980) and Arlie Russell Hochschild, *The Managed Heart: Commercialization of Human Feeling* (Berkeley and Los Angeles: University of California Press, 1983).

19. Cheshire Calhoun and Robert Solomon, *What is an Emotion? Classic Readings in Philosophical Psychology* (New York: Oxford University Press, 1984), 12.

the form of beliefs or evaluations are central to emotion, that emotions play a necessary role in good moral judgment, and that emotions are social rather than merely individual, subjective events and so are historically variable, and culturally shaped or constructed. This third thesis, the most disputed of the three, is sometimes extended in an argument that emotions are social acts rather than passive individual responses to external stimuli.[20]

If we compare Aristotle's views on emotion to the revisionists' first two points, we can see that Aristotle clearly would have few arguments with the idea that emotions have a rational, cognitive dimension, and that they are necessary to good moral judgment. In fact, most writers on these issues of rationality draw their inspiration, if not the details of their theory, from Aristotle. William Lyons, for example, recognizes in Aristotle's work the first "cognitive" theory of emotion, but stresses evaluation rather than merely belief as the key to differentiating emotions.[21] Justin Oakley argues that emotions are complexes of psychic affects (not necessarily always bodily feelings), desires and cognitions of various kinds, whose rationality may be assessed by whether an emotion is based on a true thought or belief, whether it is proportional to its object, and whether its desire is appropriate.[22] Ronald de Sousa argues that emotions can be evaluated for their axiological rationality in contrast to cognitive or strategic rationality.[23]

This cognitive feature of emotion pervades Aristotle's analysis of emotions relevant to political and judicial oratory. In the *Rhetoric*, Aristotle identifies three aspects of an emotion—a thought or belief, a feeling of pain or pleasure, and a desire for some event, action, or situation. For example, anger is a "desire, accompanied by pain, for real or apparent

---

20. See for example, Robert C. Solomon, *The Passions* (New York: Anchor, 1977); Lyons, *Emotion*; Amelie Oksenberg Rorty, ed., *Explaining Emotions* (Berkeley and Los Angeles: University of California Press, 1980); Calhoun and Solomon, *What is an Emotion?*; Carol Z. Stearns and Peter N. Stearns, eds., *Emotion and Social Change: Toward a New Psychohistory* (New York: Holmes and Meier, 1988); Ronald de Sousa, *The Rationality of Emotion* (Cambridge: MIT Press, 1990); Justin Oakley, *Morality and the Emotions* (New York: Routledge, 1992); Rom Harré, ed., *The Social Construction of Emotions* (New York: Basil Blackwell, 1986); Joel Pfister and Nancy Schnog, *Inventing the Psychological: Towards a Cultural History of Emotional Life in America* (New Haven: Yale University Press, 1997); Martha Nussbaum, "Emotions and Women's Capabilities," in *Women, Culture and Development: A Study of Human Capabilities*, ed. Martha Nussbaum and Jonathan Glover (New York: Oxford University Press, 1995), and "Rational Emotions," in *Poetic Justice: The Literary Imagination and Public Life* (Boston: Beacon Press, 1995).

21. Lyons, *Emotion*.

22. See his chapter on the nature of emotion, in *Morality and the Emotions*.

23. Ronald de Sousa, *The Rationality of Emotion*, 173.

revenge for a real or apparent slight affecting a man himself or one of his friends" (*Rhet.* 1378a31–32). In the emotion of friendly feeling (*philia*) the desire is "wishing for him what you believe to be good things, not for your own sake but for his, and being inclined, so far as you can, to bring them about" (*Rhet.* 1380b36–37);[24] the feeling is pleasure; the belief is that the other person is your friend. Thus a belief subject to rational evaluation is central to an emotion; erase the belief and the emotion normally dissipates.

More important, scholars of the revisionist school have contended that emotions are indispensable to good ethical judgment and conduct in several ways. First, emotion has been treated as a necessary form of moral perception. A keen sense of indignation or compassion enables us to render a situation or event as a moral problem.[25] Certain behavior on a playground, for example, could be seen either as a typical and natural bit of rowdiness or as a noxious treatment of a fellow human being. Second, emotions themselves, or the lack of them, have been construed as part of an action or part of a person's character subject to moral evaluation. Feeling impatient and angry, for example, when helping someone, or on the other hand, failing to feel regret when one cannot tend to two conflicting duties similarly may be morally undesirable. Third, emotions have been identified as integral to certain other valued practices and moral qualities, for example, strength of will, love and friendship, and the feeling of self-worth. Writers in feminist moral theory especially have been understandably enthusiastic about apprehending the moral role of emotions. Rationalistic moral theory, on the view of many feminists, has neglected the social relations, such as parenting and intense friendship, typically associated with women. Emotions not only help us as motivators to accomplish what reason tells us is morally right, but they allow us to discover what is morally required.[26]

24. The first passage is from the Loeb translations and the second from the Oxford Revised translation.

25. The first appearance of the perceptive quality of emotions is found in Martha C. Nussbaum, *The Fragility of Goodness: Luk and Ethics in Greek Tragedy and Philosophy* (New York: Cambridge University Press, 1986); more detailed discussion of this aspect can be found in Nancy Sherman, *The Fabric of Character: Aristotle's Theory of Virtue* (New York: Oxford University Press, 1989) and Oakley, *Morality and the Emotions* and especially in Arne Johan Vetlesen's *Perception, Empathy, and Judgment: An Inquiry into the Preconditions of Moral Performance* (University Park: Pennsylvania State University Press, 1994).

26. Virginia Held, *Feminist Morality* (Chicago: University of Chicago Press, 1993), 29–30; Annette Baier, "The Need for More than Justice," *Canadian Journal of Philosophy* suppl. vol. 13 (1987): 19–56.

Many of those who write about these moral capabilities typically draw on Aristotle as the exemplar of this approach, needing only elaboration and refinement or sometimes significant development. Aristotle himself considers it mistaken to define virtues as a state of freedom from emotion, as does Speusippus, the successor to Plato at the Academy (*NE* 2.3.1104b24). Moral virtues are actually habitual ways of both acting and feeling. A courageous person, for example, feels fear neither too much nor too little.

Not only are scholars examining the rational elements of emotion, but they are finding emotional conditions of good practical reasoning. Uniting the concern for moral and ethical life and the interrelation of cognition and emotion, Antonio Damasio draws a remarkable picture of how emotions and practical reason cooperate.[27] In reflecting on a series of studies of brain injuries, he finds that when patients lose the ability to feel emotions, they also lose the ability to reason and make decisions about practical, social, personal, and moral affairs. Damasio starts with the celebrated nineteenth-century case in which a railroad worker named Phineas Gage was struck by a metal rod that cut a hole through his prefrontal lobes. Although he survived, Gage, becoming hostile and asocial, could no longer function in his work. Finding similar patterns of injury, psychological dysfunction, and social failure in contemporary patients, Damasio proposes that emotion guides cognitive, rational capacities. For example, a patient who was asked to choose between two dates for the next appointment conducted an elaborate cost-benefit analysis lasting for a half hour without managing to decide, until Damasio makes the decision for him. Emotions "point us in the proper direction, take us to the appropriate place in a decision-making space, where we may put the instruments of logic to good use."[28] Yet Damasio recognizes that emotions may also damage good reasoning. Indeed, their potential to damage and their role as guides for reason can show up at the same time. When landing in the midst of a dangerous thunderstorm, an airline pilot must suppress the emotion of fear in order to act with calculative rationality while at the same time relying, for motivation to act at all, on emotions underlying the desire to survive and obligations to the passengers.[29] In related studies that generated a popular bestseller, John Mayer and Peter Salovey theorized the existence of "emotional

27. Antonio R. Damasio, *Descartes' Error: Emotion, Reason, and the Human Brain* (New York: G. P. Putnam's Sons, 1994).
28. Ibid., xiii.
29. Ibid., 195.

intelligence."[30] The ideal of the emotionally intelligent person requires that he or she excel at identifying, generating, understanding, and regulating emotion.

Descartes's error in irrevocably splitting the mind and the body, and then in conjunction reason and emotion, would have, as Damasio notes, stirred Aristotle's indignation.[31] As I discuss in Chapter 3, Aristotle conceived of the reasoning capacity as having two aspects, one that is reason proper, and one that listens to or obeys reason. In fact, the idea of brain sections or parts that Damasio himself tries to complicate would hardly appeal to Aristotle, who ends up favoring soul capacities. All in all, then, Aristotle's psychology provides the ancestral model for the revisionist view of the relation of reason and emotion.

Another distinctive but not universal concern of the revisionist school is its increasing call for cultural, historical, contextual understanding of emotions—the way in which cultures, social groups, and historical periods vary in the emotions they name and recognize, in the patterns of individual emotions, in how intensely those who live in them feel emotions, in their whole emotional style, in how they treat emotions generally, even in whether they recognize something called the "psychological." For example, scholars have argued that boredom develops with modernity; the emotion of *amae*, a pleasure in being treated as a childlike dependent, is unique to Japanese culture; and *song,* an indignant anger, differentiates the Polynesian Ifaluk from many Western cultures.[32] One of the first claims about the history of emotion was that in the early modern period affection of parents toward children and affection between husbands and wives increased, while emotional ties between men decreased, so that that both intensity and objects of emotions changed. The new emotional standards of the seventeenth century, they claimed, inaugurated a modern emotional paradigm, a thesis that has survived an array of

---

30. John D. Mayer and Peter Salovey, "What is Emotional Intelligence?" in *Emotional Development and Emotional Intelligence: Educational Implications*, ed. Peter Salovey and David J. Slayter (New York: Basic Books, 1997). For the popular version, see Daniel Goleman, *Emotional Intelligence* (New York: Bantam Books, 1995) which begins with a preface titled "Aristotle's Challenge."

31. Damasio, *Descartes' Error*, 251.

32. Patricia Meyer Spacks, *Boredom* (Chicago: University of Chicago Press, 1996); H. Morsbach and W. J. Tyler, "A Japanese Emotion: *Amae,*" in Harré, *The Social Construction of Emotions*; Catherine Lutz, *Unnatural Emotions: Everyday Sentiments on a Micronesian Atoll and Their Challenge to Western Theory* (Chicago: University of Chicago Press, 1988).

challenges.[33] In eighteenth-century England, the educated upper classes embraced the fashionable culture of sensibility, a literary culture of extravagant pathos, pity, and sympathy.[34] In a recent book, the historian of the emotions Peter Stearns argues that American (U.S.) emotional culture of the middle class moved during the 1920s away from Victorian effusiveness and toward late twentieth-century cool.[35] In the most comprehensive thesis, Nancy Schnog has maintained that even the "psychological" is a "distinctively twentieth-century idea" constituted by a panoply of powers and institutions. And she suggests that the spread of Freudian psychoanalysis has established a "broadly shared skeletal understanding of the nature of the self and its psychodynamic processes."[36]

In the ancient Greek context, Jean-Pierre Vernant has done extensive work on questions of ancient psychology, including the extent to which Athenians considered themselves "individuals," and the idea of will in tragic theater.[37] His work has culminated in a call for a new understanding of the interrelation of history and psychology, a movement away from psychologizing history based on a notion of immutable human nature, to a historical psychology that "admit[s] the possibility of a transformation in human activities" including "forms of feeling and perceptive organization . . . intellectual operations and large complex functions like the person or the will."[38]

Several questions, however, confront this historicist and culturalist work: What verb best describes how culture acts on emotion? Does it

33. Lawrence Stone, *The Family, Sex, and Marriage in England, 1500–1800* (New York: Harper and Row, 1977); Phillipe Ariès, *The Hour of Our Death* (New York: Oxford University Press, 1991); see also Edward Shorter, *The Making of the Modern Family* (New York: Basic Books, 1975). The state of this early historical research is examined in Stearns and Stearns, *Emotion and Social Change* and Peter N. Stearns and Carol Z. Stearns, "Emotionology: Clarifying the History of Emotions and Emotional Standards," *American Historical Review* 90 (1985): 820.

34. This characterization is taken from Adela Pinch, "Emotion and History: A Review Article," *Comparative Studies in Society and History* 37 (1995): 100–109. See also Pinch, *Strange Fits of Passion: Epistemologies of Emotion, Hume to Austen* (Stanford: Stanford Uiversity Press, 1996), and G. J. Barker-Benfield, *The Culture of Sensibility: Sex and Society in Eighteenth-Century England* (Chicago: University of Chicago Press, 1992).

35. Peter Stearns, *American Cool: Constructing a Twentieth-Century Emotional Style* (New York: New York University Press, 1994).

36. Nancy Schnog, "On Inventing the Psychological," in Pfister and Schnog, *Inventing the Psychological*, 8.

37. Jean-Pierre Vernant and Pierre Vidal-Naquet, *Myth and Tragedy in Ancient Greece*, trans. Janet Lloyd (New York: Zone Books, 1990) and Jean-Pierre Vernant, *Mortals and Immortals: Collected Essays*, ed. Froma I. Zeitlin (Princeton: Princeton University Press, 1991).

constitute, create, or does it merely shape and influence the feeling and expression of emotion? Does culture and history do this to all emotions, some emotion, or to some part of all emotions? Is there such a thing as a natural emotion? Joel Pfister offers a good review of some of the important issues and writers concerned with these questions. In the standard, nonrevisionist conception of the interaction of emotion and society, society for good or ill *controls, restrains,* or, on the other hand, *allows,* the free expression of the emotions. Here although emotions are natural, society acts on emotions through regulative rules.[39] In this model emotion is a "psychophysical essence that is manipulated or wrestled with."[40] For all their differences, the three methods of dealing with emotion or passions that Albert Hirschman traces in the early modern period as contributing to the later establishment of capitalism—coercion, harnessing, and countervailing—all share a common sense of controlling a natural though regrettable feature of humans. In the countervailing strategy that triumphed over the coercion and harnessing, some passions, especially greed and covetousness, countervail the supposedly more dangerous passions of glory-seeking. Similarly, in Hobbes's account of the social contract, the fear of death overpowers the desire for domination over others.

In the constructionist conception a different set of verbs is used. Through diverse familial, religious, political, economic, and material practices, society and the environment *shape, channel,* or *configure* or, in a stronger version, *constitute* or *create* emotional life. The verbs used, then, help to distinguish what might be called a strong constructionist from a weak, or as I prefer, moderate, constructionist position.[41] Where strong constructionists would deny any natural basis to emotion, since nature is itself a linguistic, human construction, the moderate constructionist allows for some natural ingredients. Moderate constructionists accept the existence of rudimentary natural emotions such as fear or anger, but argue that these simple emotions may be socially elaborated atop their natural base. Similarly, the more complex emotions, such as regret, may themselves have natural origins and biological elements but still crucially depend on cultural and social belief systems.

---

39. James R. Averill, "The Acquisition of Emotions in Adulthood," in Harré, *The Social Construction of Emotions.*

40. Catherine Lutz, "Engendered Emotion: Gender, Power, and the Rhetoric of Emotional Control in American Discourse," in *Language and the Politics of Emotion,* ed. Lutz and Lila Abu-Lughod (New York: Cambridge University Press, 1990), 72.

41. As does Claire Armon-Jones in "The Thesis of Constructionism," in Harré, *The Social Construction of Emotions,* 32–55.

Thus we distinguish at least three positions on the question of constructionism in terms of emotions. Nonconstructionists believe that society gives no patterns to emotions, that emotions are essentially fully formed at a young age, and that at best society can govern whether or not, and how intensely, some emotion is expressed. Strong constructionists argue that even when ordinary people talk of controlling emotion, this discourse of control creates the very emotions it seeks to manage.[42] Moderate constructionists argue that society and the environment pattern, shape, and codify all emotions. Some authors of course do not neatly fit into these categories—some will mix the verb *constitute* and the word *shape*, while others who clearly prefer the verb *shape* nevertheless do not call themselves even moderate constructionists.[43]

In this debate, Aristotle, I presume, would be cast as an essentialist who sought to define a universal human nature, although he only succeeded in surreptitiously transforming the features of a Greek male aristocrat into universal human features. But this view is a serious misinterpretation. For Aristotle, understanding an emotion requires knowledge of its typical context—the typical frame of mind, the typical grounds or reasons, and the typical objects, especially the kind of people toward whom we feel an emotion. And emotional habits can be changed by virtue of the political regime in which one lives. Recall how Aristotle speaks about the human as a political animal, writing that "there is in everyone by nature an impulse toward this sort of partnership. And yet the one who first constituted [a city] is responsible for the greatest of goods" (*Pol.* 1253a29–31). This cooperation between nature and invention, or human art, is echoed in his discussion of sources of virtue. He notes that: "we are by nature equipped with the ability to receive them [the virtues], and habit brings this ability to completion and fulfillment" (*NE* 1103a24–25). So while humans have a definite nature, it is not a set of determinate and specific passions or drives such as Freud's eros and thanatos, the sex drive and the death drive, which in various forms animate our actions. Rather for Aristotle we have determinate, but rather unformed, capacities for speech and moral argument, for emotions and actions potentially directed toward

---

42. Catherine Lutz, in "Engendered Emotion," makes this very argument about the greater tendency of women to talk of trying to control their emotions. The source of this interpretation is, of course, Michel Foucault, *The History of Sex,* vol. 1: *An Introduction,* trans. Robert Hurley (New York: Vintage Books, 1980).

43. For the first case, see Claire Armon-Jones, "The Thesis of Constructionism"; for the second, see William Reddy, "Against Constructionism: The Historical Ethnograpy of Emotions" *Cultural Anthropology* 38 (June 1997): 327–40.

the noble. These unformed capacities can be both shaped and constituted, neither metaphor used exclusively is correct here. Thus Aristotle is a sort of constructionist, but, as on so many other issues, a moderate constructionist, one who acknowledges and often details the ways in which different cultures and political systems create a certain moral and emotional character out of the amorphous, rudimentary human capacities.

Another issue that has not been adequately confronted in this literature is the political context of emotional life, either the specific political practices that influence emotional life or the normative conclusions that might be drawn from such an analysis. Sometimes one finds references to how the author cannot escape preferring one emotional style over others, yet without sustained reasons for such judgments. Relying on evidence from classic novels, Walter Kern argues that modern love, or at least the literary model of modern love, is more frank, more unconstrained by social strictures, more devoid of a sharp dichotomy between genders, in sum more "authentic" than Victorian love. Although Kern pleads that his purpose is descriptive, he admits that he must favor the transformation of Victorian into modern love: "I have found it impossible not to valorize the direction of that movement."[44] At other times one finds a more direct, although equally undeveloped, statement of normative and political intent. Schnog writes in the introduction to *Inventing the Psychological* that the book's contributors propose "to better understand the reasons why psychological self-definitions ... gain cultural authority and lose explanatory power at particular historical moments" and "how areas of cultural life not typically associated with the production of psychological knowledge—economics, politics, mass media, and the arts—play key roles in helping to create and disseminate professional and popular languages of interior life."[45] In the most explicit political appeal, the book, according to Schnog, will illustrate the "the power of the psychological professions to naturalize *oppressive* standards of social adjustment, to perpetuate *social inequities*, to legitimate *dangerously personalized* visions of pain, and to speak, for better or for worse, to widespread needs for self-disclosure and solace."[46] Such a program assumes some vision of nonoppressive social adjustment, of a socially equitable society, of the proper balance between political and personal answers to human pain, and presumably

---

44. Stephen Kern, *The Culture of Love: Victorians to Moderns* (Cambridge, Mass.: Harvard University Press, 1992), 400.

45. Pfister and Schnog, *Inventing the Psychological*, 3.

46. Ibid., 7, emphasis added.

of the psychological and emotional character adequate for such a political visions.

The historicist and constructivist literature, however, is virtually silent on the value of one emotional repertoire over another, although it cannot escape implicit judgments. Catherine Lutz, for example, compares the Western model of emotion to the Polynesian Ifaluk model, the Western practice of anger to the Iflaluk's. Each time there is a tendency to judge the Iflaluk superior to the Western model, but the grounds are inadequately explored and the possibility of applying any part of the Ifaluk model is unaddressed. Schnog and Pfister suggest that liberation is possible from the tyranny of a certain depth psychology, or from psychologizing entirely. William Reddy complains about this very political inadequacy of historicist or constructivist emotion theory and history. He attributes to strong constructivists the view that the "individual is entirely empty and wholly plastic," a view that for him eliminates the possibility of political judgment—"there is nothing in virtue of which liberation is good." As an alternative to what for him is an entirely relativistic theory, he proposes a theory of "emotives" meant to complement Austin's constatives and performatives. While he repeats several times that his account is meant to be more politically relevant, the example he investigates of the French emotional style of "delicatesse" or delicacy, a cirumlocutionary approach to describing and controlling potentially intense emotions, is unexplored in political terms. For Reddy, "Emotional control is the real site of the exercise of power: politics is just a process of determining who must repress as illegitimate, who must foreground as valuable the feelings and desires that come up for them in given contexts and relationships."[47] Categorical statements such as these that something is the "real site of the exercise of power" or that "politics is just a process" reduce politics to the exercise of power, and further unnecessarily raise its effect on emotions as the crucial political act. While I would like to see theorists take more account of the intertwining of politics and emotions, the act of vetoing a bill, for example, is still a real political act, but not an act necessarily aimed at emotions.

Despite these gestures toward a politics of emotion, few have attempted a focused study on the effects of specifically political institutions, practices, and discourses on the emotional culture of a particular period and vice versa, of the bearing of political philosophy on the question of the

47. Reddy, "Against Constructionism," 335.

politics of emotion, or indeed a normative account of emotional life in politics.[48] On this subject Aristotle provides an essential contribution toward a comprehensive account of political emotion. If politics is understood rightly we need to examine the role of emotion in moral action, evaluate the effect of economic, cultural, and political institutions on emotional habits, and then decide on the best emotional repertoire to encourage in our regime and in the best regime possible for us. These at least are the arguments of the following chapters.

Aristotle alone, however, is not enough. I am certain that I would not be writing this account of political emotion without the impetus of late twentieth-century feminist thought. Indeed, feminist writers really are indispensable to theorizing the political meaning of emotional life. As early as the eighteenth century, women observed the creation of and simultaneous disparagement of female emotionality. Mary Wollstonecraft noted sadly, "It would be an endless task to trace the variety of meanness, cares, and sorrows, into which women are plunged by the prevailing opinion, that they were created rather to feel than reason, and that all the power they obtain, must be obtained by their charms and weakness."[49] Canonical male philosophers usually approved this division between the sexes for its sweet complementarity. Instead, Wollstonecraft angrily urged education, the access to reason, to be opened to women.

Nearly two hundred years later, some feminists demanded access to reason less often than to reimagined emotion. Shulamith Firestone's *The Dialectic of Sex: The Case for Feminist Revolution* is best known for her call to abolish the nuclear family and overcome biology by embracing artificial reproduction. But Firestone also looks to the cultural institutions of emotion that legitimate the family—the "phenomenon" of love, especially romantic love, or romanticism in general. "For love," she writes, "perhaps even more than childbearing, is the pivot of women's oppression today. . . .

48. In the collection *Inventing the Psychological*, Catherine Lutz describes the effect of Cold War military practices and ideology on our cultural understanding of psychological life. Some other examples include Susan Okin, "Reason and Feeling in Thinking About Justice," *Ethics* 99, no. 2 (1989): 229–49; Morwenna Griffiths, *Feminisms and the Self: The Web of Identity* (New York: Routledge, 1995); Robert Solomon, *A Passion for Justice: Emotions and the Origins of the Social Contract* (Reading, Mass.: Addison-Wesley, 1990); Stephen Holmes, *Passions and Constraints* (Chicago: University of Chicago Press, 1995); Hirschman, *The Passions and the Interests*; Michael Ignatieff, *The Needs of Strangers* (New York: Penguin, 1982); Roberto Managabeira Unger, *Passion: An Essay on Personality* (New York: Free Press, 1984). Less direct discussions of emotion in politics can be found in care feminism, examples of which I analyze in Chapter 6.

49. Quoted in Adela Pinch, *Strange Fits of Passion: Epistemologies of Emotion, Hume to Austen* (Stanford: Stanford University Press, 1996).

The panic felt at any threat to love is a good clue to its political significance. . . . *[W]omen and love are underpinnings. Examine them and you threaten the very structure of culture.*"[50] Here, Firestone represents a good number of later feminists who, while they may have differed with her on particular issues, nevertheless concluded that the gender system is intimately connected to a system of emotional norms affecting both men and women. And encompassing this particular emotion norm of romantic love are the general norms and practices for emotion as such in which men according to Firestone exhibit a hypertrophied rationalism.[51] Not only was feminism about emotion, about the ideologies of emotion that damaged women, but its strategies could be seen to work partly through emotion or on emotion: "revolutionary feminism is the only radical program that immediately cracks through to the emotional strata underlying 'serious' politics, thus reintegrating the personal with the public, the subjective with the objective, the emotional with the rational—the female principle with the male."[52] Firestone's early second-wave feminist radicalization of the critique of women's inequality was developed by others along four main lines: radical feminists who valorized emotion over reason; psychoanalytic and object relations psychological accounts of gendered personality; critiques of traditional masculinist conceptions of reason; and theories of ethics and politics inspired by women's traditions of nurturance in the private sphere.[53] The last group includes the

50. Shulamith Firestone, *The Dialectic of Sex: The Case for Feminist Revolution* (New York: William Morrow, 1970), 121.

51. Ibid., 193.

52. Ibid., 196.

53. Early radical feminist work that valorized passion and emotion includes Mary Daly, *Gyn / Ecology: The Metaethics of Radical Feminism* (Boston: Beacon Press, 1978), and *Pure Lust: Elemental Feminist Philosophy* (Boston: Beacon Press, 1984); Susan Griffin, *Woman and Nature* (New York: Harper and Row, 1980). A politically engaged critic of this early writing is Joan Cocks, "Wordless Emotions: Some Critical Reflections on Radical Feminism," *Politics and Society* 13, no. 1 (1984): 27-57. See also Elizabeth Rapaport, "On the Future of Love: Rousseau and the Radical Feminists," in *Women and Philosophy: Toward a Theory of Liberation*, ed. Carol C. Gould and Marx W. Wartofsky (New York: G. P. Putnam's Sons, 1976), 185-205; Morwenna Griffiths, "Feminism, Feelings and Philosophy," in *Feminist Perspectives in Philosophy*, ed. Morwenna Griffiths and Margaret Whitford (Bloomington and Indianapolis: Indiana University Press, 1988), 131–51. The second line is represented by Dorothy Dinnerstein, *The Mermaid and the Minotaur: Sexual Arrangements and Human Malaise* (New York: Harper and Row, 1976); Nancy Chodorow, *The Reproduction of Mothering: Psychonalysis and the Sociology of Gender* (Berkeley and Los Angeles: University of California Press, 1978); Jessica Benjamin, *The Bonds of Love: Psychoanalysis, Feminism, and the Problem of Domination* (New York: Pantheon Books, 1988). A recent Kleinian psychoanalytic perspective on the subject of passions in political theory is Cynthia Burack, *The Problem of the Passions: Feminism, Psychoanalysis, and*

extensive literature on the "ethic of care" and political care feminism as well as accounts of "emotional work" and "sex-affective labor."[54]

Whatever particular disagreements these feminists thinkers might have, their work supplies three elements for a theory of political emotion. First, it suggests that curiosity is well-placed about the depreciated other(s) of reason, emotion being chief among them. Although there is no cause to believe that standing the dichotomy on its head, and identifying with "feminine" qualities or practices will be an adequate response, starting from that position may lead to more new insights than staying with the old rationalist beginnings. Second, this literature has correctly warned against the divide itself, leading to question of whether emotion and reason are interwoven, or somehow work in conjunction, or whether perhaps these two psychic capacities are falsely described as mutually distinct, even if in some or all cases they infiltrate each other. Third, this literature reveals what is politically at stake when we theorize about emotion. Gender relations and identity are partly constituted out of the practices, norms, and symbolics of emotional life. That is to say that one of the ways that a woman might identify herself and be identified by others is by her displaying the marks of loving sentiment—wearing a heart-shaped pendant, cooing at the sight of a child, crying in the movie theater at the end of a tragic love story. If gender is partly so formed, a political theorist must ask: Can I write a truly liberatory political theory without examining the role of emotional culture in replicating or exacerbating inequality among men and women and contributing to distorted lives for both, and retarding whatever progress has been made through older political concepts such as rights or equality itself? Although I hope to provide a more comprehensive analysis of this literature at some other time, in Chapter 6 I shall look at the some of the work associated with women's nurturance.

So Aristotle and feminist theory are be the crucial entrée points for a comprehensive history of the treatment of the politics of emotion in

---

*Social Theory* (New York: New York University Press, 1994). The third line, the reevaluation of reason and epistemology, includes Louise M. Antony and Charlotte Witt, eds., *A Mind of One's Own: Feminist Essays on Reason and Objectivity* (Boulder: Westview Press, 1992); Genevieve Lloyd, *The Man of Reason: "Male" and "Female" in Western Philosophy*, 2d ed. (Minneapolis: University of Minnesota Press, 1993); Lorraine Code, *What Can She Know? Feminist Theory and the Construction of Knowledge* (Ithaca: Cornell University Press, 1991); Susan R. Bordo, *The Flight to Objectivity: Essays on Cartesianism and Culture* (Albany: State University of New York Press, 1987); Evelyn Fox Keller, *Reflections on Gender and Science* (New Haven: Yale University Press, 1985).

54. For citations, see Chapter 6.

political philosophy. They offer the beginnings of a normative theory of political emotion and thereby helpfully expand the range of revisionist emotion theory. But revisionist theory in turn can help to reconstruct Aristotle's treatment of political emotion. Perhaps the first useful concept advanced by emotion theory is that of the *paradigm scenario*. Developed by Ronald de Sousa in his study of the rationality of emotion, paradigm scenarios refer to dramatic narratives learned in childhood, reinforced by oral and printed stories, and by visual art, refined by literature, teaching us when and how to feel which emotions. Each scenario will have definite objects and typical responses. Although humans have some innate emotional gestures such as the smile, these are named, contextualized, and structured by familial and cultural education. If they are not, children may lose their initial innate abilities or their emotional life may remain relatively elementary. Each scenario can be revised in light of new emergent and competing paradigms. Indeed, it is in reference to paradigm scenarios that emotions are rational or not.

A slightly different terminology but a similar concept appears in Catherine Lutz's work on the people of Ifaluk, a Pacific atoll. Across cultures, she claims, emotions are socially inculcated through "scenes" (or scenarios). "In each cultural community," she writes, "there will be one or more 'scenes' identified as prototypic or classic or best examples of particular emotions."[55] These narrative pieces constitute social life: "The scenes each emotion concept evokes are most typically social scenes involving relations between two or more individuals. The emotions can be seen as sociocultural achievements in the fundamental sense that they characterize and create a relationship between individuals and groups." The scene for *song*, or justifiable anger, is one in which there is a rule or value violation, it is pointed out by someone, who simultaneously calls for the condemnation of the act, and the perpetrator reacts in fear to that anger, amending his or her ways.[56]

De Sousa and Lutz write of scenarios, or scenes, for individual emotions, but I would like to expand the helpful term to cover what any culture thinks of emotionality in general. Each culture will have paradigm scenarios not just of particular, relatively distinct emotions, but also of an emotional person and perhaps an emotional situation. I call such a general scenario a *governing scenario of emotion*. For some authors and cultures women engaged in cradling a child, crying during a traumatic

55. Lutz, *Unnatural Emotions*, 211.
56. Ibid., 157.

situation, screaming and cowering in fear in a dangerous situation have functioned as the chief characters in such scenarios of emotion. A different scenario, the governing scenario of political emotion, may rule in the public domain. The angry crowd full of nationalist zeal or perhaps religious zeal has functioned as the scenarios of political emotion. Recently in American politics, so dominated by the affairs of the legal trials of prominent political and entertainment figures, the courtroom in which the victims and their families are allowed to describe their suffering, is becoming, at least for journalists, the paradigm scenario of public emotion. These scenarios are the vivid images through which we recall quickly, and even unconsciously, what it means to be emotional or to observe an emotional event.

In the third concept for understanding emotional life in general and the history of *thumos* in particular, a set of paradigm scenarios for individual emotions composes a paradigm *emotional repertoire*.[57] Not all emotions that one culture can identify will have paradigm scenarios in another culture, and one culture may have more specified and differentiated paradigm scenarios related to one emotion. Tahitians, for example, have an extensive cultural discourse around anger and various refined versions of it, but have little or no discourse around sadness.[58] As a result, they treat sadness as a physical malady, rather than as an emotion proper.

Such scenarios of emotion will also imply a separate but related notion of *emotional style*. While all people probably experience emotion, the cultural markers of emotion will differ. Although individuals within a culture will surely differ in their emotional constitutions—their styles, repertoires, and the cultural scenarios they use as reference points— cultures, by which I also mean subcultures differing by class, gender, profession, or sexual orientation, do tend to inculcate an identifying emotional style. Exuberant, flashing, vocal emotional displays may divide one culture or subculture from another more reticent, shy, and outwardly restrained, but nevertheless inwardly still feeling emotion. Although this divide of outward display versus inner restraint most commonly differentiates emotional styles, other qualities are possible. The problem is to focus on understanding this character of cultural life, and to attempt to transcend the easy, conventional contrasts.

57. Both Ronald de Sousa and Carol Z. Stearns and Peter N. Stearns mention or use the words "emotional repertoire," but do not extensively define the term.

58. See Robert Levy, "Emotion, Knowing, and Culture," in *Culture Theory: Essays on Mind, Self, and Emotion* (New York: Cambridge University Press, 1984), 214–37.

Finally, I should say something more about *political emotion*. Though this phrase does not appear in the revisionist literature, from the analytic and the cultural approaches it is possible to see how there is a distinctive class of political emotion. By political emotion, I do not mean that some emotions are exclusively political. Although patriotism will probably come to mind as the name of a uniquely political emotion, it is in fact a variant of love, with a paradigm scenario that focuses on the political community as object. That we would probably think only of patriotism or nationalist fervor when asked to identify political emotions only points to the poverty of our theories and their origin in the era of the modern nation-state. So although there do not exist exclusively political emotions, there exist paradigm scenarios of political involvement and affect. Interpreting these scenarios gives us an important insight into how political regimes work, how they generate loyalty, how they create images of the relationship between citizens, how they manage what goods we expect from political community, and what we are willing to give to community and other individuals. My example here will be the analysis of welfare debates. In addition, the concept of political emotion refers to the influence of political culture on the experience of some emotions in relatively nonpolitical spheres. For instance, as Lute notes, Americans tend to amalgamate indignation and other kinds of anger. Since Americans have a strong sense of personal right to do what they desire, anger is usually expressed as the frustration of individual desire. So the culture of rights diminishes the complexity of anger. Certainly the demarcation between what is political and what is nonpolitical should be understood as especially porous, especially by those who want to understand the power exercised through gender. In many instances my use of the term political emotion will refer to those emotions enacted through such typically political institutions as citizenship and the federal legislature, but I do not mean to exclude more expansive understandings of the political. In Firestone's early critique of romantic love, the conventions of the emotion have helped to disempower and distort women's lives. This makes the final point implicit in my concept of political emotion. "Private" and "personal" emotions may themselves be political in the sense that they carry repercussions for people's lives in terms of freedom, opportunity, equality, and participation in public institutions.

The concepts of *paradigm scenario, governing scenario of emotion, emotional repertoire, emotional style,* and *political emotion* help to explain both the history of *thumos* from Homer to Plato to Aristotle and to elucidate Aristotle's own work on the needs of a good regime, on rhetoric, and on tragedy. In effect, the *Iliad* contains many of the original paradigm scenarios for individual emotions, the governing emotion scenario, and the accompanying emotional repertoire for Ancient Greek male culture. Plato, after all, calls Homer the "teacher of Greece," and young boys were required to memorize Homer in learning how to read and write. It is easy to see that the chief subject of these scenarios was anger and so *thumos* as the inner life of the hero could easily be mistaken for anger itself. Plato concentrates on a scenario with this character because the threat in politics that he perceived came from those who were often unreservedly attached to this scenario of honor and outrage.

Aristotle's examination of emotions in book 2 of the *Rhetoric* details sixteen paradigm scenarios. So although Aristotle did not use the term "paradigm scenarios," this way of relating individual psychological events to socially learned narratives does not, I believe, distort Aristotle's meaning while it offers a compelling term for analysis and for differentiating Homer, Plato, and Aristotle.

And in the *Ethics* and *Politics*, Aristotle sees the threat primarily more as an absence or as a too narrow application of some emotions—for example, *philia*—rather than as Plato did the presence of too much undisciplined anger (and too many unruly appetites). He aims to expand the emotional repertoire, and revise governing scenarios, by emphasizing the integrative emotions any polis needs to achieve the good life.

# Theorizing *Thumos*

Until recently, few works addressed Aristotle's view of emotion and fewer still even mentioned how this view influenced his political theory. In an early book-length treatment, *Aristotle on Emotion*, W. W. Fortenbaugh argues that a new psychology leads to essentially two changes in political theory.[59] First, Aristotle's grouping of emotions and desire in one part of the soul grounds an improved educational theory. Habituation in the proper loves and hates through enjoyment of good characters and noble deeds in musical education starts early for young children. This may appear to resemble Plato's concern in his rewriting of permissible poetry, but Fortenbaugh maintains that the tripartition of the soul does not

---

59. W. W. Fortenbaugh, *Aristotle On Emotion: A Contribution to Philosophical Psychology, Rhetoric, Poetics, Politics, and Ethics* (London: Duckworth, 1975).

support education as presented in the *Republic*.[60] In contrast, Aristotle's bipartition is expertly suited to support early childhood training. Second, Aristotle's new division of the soul helps to explain and justify the position, relative to mature men, of young men, women, and slaves. Fortenbaugh's work is a valuable beginning, but hardly all that could be said on the subject. Fortenbaugh appears to consider only what changes are wrought by the new structure of the soul, not what is the role of emotion in politics. More recently, Martha Nussbaum's and Nancy Sherman's work has been invaluable in revealing the ethical wisdom of Aristotle, including his friendly view of emotion.[61] Explicitly feminist work has also begun to appear that praises Aristotle on the role of emotion. Although other scholars also acknowledge Aristotle's work as the first cognitive theory of emotion, and friendship is an occasional topic in ethical and political theory writings, little is done with the distinctiveness of Aristotle's approach, in particular the interdependence of his new understandings of the soul, of emotion, and of ethical and political action.

The best way to recover these interconnections and to explore the political effect of Aristotle's theory of emotion is to spotlight one particularly elusive word in Greek literature and philosophy. Translated sometimes as "spiritedness," sometimes as "heart" or "passion," and sometimes as "anger," the word *thumos* (or *thymos*) occurs in the *Iliad* alongside *psuche⁻* and *nous* as a term for one element of inner life. The epic's heroes are characteristically "high-hearted," or possessing great *thumos*. In the *Republic*'s famous account of the tripartite soul, it appears as the middle part between desire and reason, while in the corresponding account of the just regime, its predominance in a personality is the main criterion for a citizen's admittance to the auxiliary class. Aristotle, in his account of the best regime, contends that both *thumos* and *logos* are necessary to political activity.

By choosing one English word over another, the translators already interpret how Greeks understood emotion, just as the concept *thumos* in Greek culture already interprets how emotions work in the psyche. There is enough material around to show how cultural and philosophical treatments of emotion vary, so that we should be careful to avoid assuming that we know what Homer, Aristotle, or Plato meant. One perplexity

60. Ibid., 45.

61. Nussbaum, *The Fragility of Goodness* and *The Therapy of Desire*; Nancy Sherman, *The Fabric of Character: Aristotle's Theory of Virtue* (New York: Oxford University Press, 1989), and *Making a Necessity of Virtue: Aristotle and Kant on Virtue* (New York: Cambridge University Press, 1997).

occasioned by the typical translations is this: it is especially odd that the translation of *thumos* should hover between the broad concept, spiritedness, and the narrow concept, anger. This perplexity should have led commentators to question what the relationship of the broader interpretation to the narrower one might be, to ask why anger should be the narrow concept, and to ascertain whether the word's meaning had ever fluctuated. When Plato calls a third of the soul *"thumos,"* it is difficult to see how the word could mean only anger or even spiritedness. If *thumos* were only anger and spiritedness, where in the soul do love, joy, or sorrow occur?

The most politically relevant work on the meaning of *thumos* for political philosophy has been done by a group of scholars influenced by the writings of Leo Strauss on classical political philosophy. According to these commentators, *thumos*, translated as "spiritedness," is a universal psychic disposition, typically expressed as anger against violations of one's honor or as a desire for recognition. These interpreters associate it with the desire to protect one's family and property, with justice, and manliness, and identify it as the fundamental political impulse.[62] Indeed, the psychological disposition identified by the Greek word *thumos* has been credited with the East European revolutions of 1989, touted as a possible source of renovation in American politics, and defended from the attack of feminists as the "central *natural* passion" of men's souls. In *The End of History and the Last Man*, Francis Fukuyama explains the expansion of democracy by the spread of *thumos*. While industrialization and modern science originate in the emancipation of materialistic desire, democracy satisfies the popular desire expressed in *thumos*.[63] Citing Hegel as the greatest modern explicator, Fukuyama understands *thumos* as the "desire for recognition" standing in contrast to both reason and low desires for material wealth. As a universal human impulse, in its "humble" form it appears as the belief in one's moral dignity, in the courage to assert moral integrity and honesty in the face of threats of repression. In its darker form it desires superiority over others, and the struggle of war

---

62. Laurence Berns, "Spiritedness in Ethics and Politics: A Study in Aristotelian Psychology," *Interpretation* 12 (1984): 335–48; Allan Bloom, "Interpretive Essay," in *The Republic of Plato*, trans. Allan Bloom (New York: Basic Books, 1968); Ann Charney, "Spiritedness and Piety in Aristotle," in *Understanding the Political Spirit*, ed. Catherine Zuckert (New Haven: Yale University Press, 1990); Carnes Lord, "Aristotle's Anthropology," in *Essays on Aristotelian Political Science*, ed. Carnes Lord and David K. O'Connor (Berkeley and Los Angeles: University of California Press, 1992), 49–73; Catherine Zuckert, "On the Role of Spiritedness in Politics," in *Understanding the Political Spirit*, 1–29.

63. Francis Fukuyama, *End of History and the Last Man* (New York: Free Press, 1990), 204–6.

over the pale pleasures of peace. Similarly, both Catherine Zuckert and Allan Bloom look to the propagation of *thumos* to countervail the ignoble pursuit of economic self-interest. And Bloom and Carnes Lord attach it specifically to masculinity. In his best-selling attack on collegiate culture, *The Closing of the American Mind*, Bloom asserts the hopelessness of alleged attempts by feminists to make men docile and caring. They will fail because of the natural male passion—*thumos*.[64] All these authors criticize post-war political science for conceiving rational action as driven by the pursuit of self-preservation, wealth and bodily gratification, while entirely neglecting the role of *thumos* in political life. *Thumos* appears to be the missing phenomenon of post-war political science.

While I am sympathetic to this critique of political science, and happy for the attention to the understudies *thumos*, my account differs from these treatments of *thumos* in these ways. First, I have supposed at the start that *thumos* should be understood against the general background of concepts of emotion. Putting *thumos* in this wider frame enables me to show how it is one formulation of the place of emotion in the soul that the ancient Greeks envisioned. Students of philosophy know the history of the formulations of reason while remaining predominantly unaware of the history of the formulations of emotion. Since I concur with the general conclusions of the revisionist approach to emotion, and since in many ways Aristotle is a key predecessor to this approach, I will use its fundamental orientation to understand ancient *thumos*.

Second, I am initially skeptical that *thumos* is a universal psychic phenomenon or as universally accessible in the same form. As I mentioned, Zuckert recognizes both an ancient and a modern form of spiritedness, and Lord notes Aristotle's connection between culture and climate and the possession of spiritedness. Despite these recognitions, the whole discussion retains the air of a discovery of some drive homogeneous in essence, while variable mainly in degree, across cultural and historical difference.

Third, following on the first two points, I rely on modern work concerning emotion to show the possibility of treating the variability of emotion-concepts not just in degree or in their objects, but in themselves and in the way in which they are associated with other parts of the psyche. Finally, since I aim to problematize the meaning of *thumos*, I do not translate it as "spiritedness," rather I continue to use the Greek.

64. Allan Bloom, *The Closing of the American Mind* (New York: Simon and Schuster, 1987), 129.

This formulation of the task for a serious appreciation of the Greeks provides impetus for a question this study poses—to what extent has *thumos* been misunderstood due to a belief in the transparency of Greek psychological ideas and the simple universality of human psychology? To what extent have our political choices been limited by the lack of an appreciation of key alternative formulations of the human psyche?

# Plan of the Book

To begin my revised history, I trace in Chapter 2 the meaning of *thumos* in Homer's *Iliad*, outlining its repercussions in Plato's *Republic*. Although the *Iliad* is typically considered by Plato and often by modern commentators as the source of the martial aggressive *thumos*, I argue that Homer, imagining *thumos* as a quasi-bodily organ, places within it a variety of emotions including grief and love. The typical internal disposition of the Homeric warrior is not *thumos* itself, but a *thumos* configured by social habits and institutions of war to feel predominantly anger. While Plato constructs a tripartite *psuchē*, or soul, out of the more dispersed internal psychic organs of Homeric psychology, Plato narrows the meaning of *thumos* by emphasizing both its aggressive anger and its primitive sense of justice.

In Chapter 3, I delineate Aristotle's three diverse uses of *thumos*. The first and second, *thumos* as the emotion anger and as the aggressive martial *thumos*, do not differ from Plato's conception, as recent commentators have argued. His third use, however, *thumos* as the general capacity for emotion, constitutes an innovation over the formulations in the *Iliad* and the *Republic*. This last use appears most straightforwardly in the *De Anima*, but I believe informs Aristotle's treatment of the emotional features of practical, including political, virtue. In Chapter 4, I examine the political action that a rightly configured *thumos* enables. With a close reading of Aristotle's claim that a citizen of the best regime will need both *logos* and *thumos*, I draw out the political *thumos*'s support of benefaction toward fellow citizens. The configuration or characteristic disposition of this political *thumos* I explicate in Chapter 5. Aristotle's criticism of the hostility toward strangers typical of Plato's thumotic guardians reverberates in his approach to the theme of strangers and recognition in the *Poetics*'s treatment of Euripides' *Iphigenia in Tauris*.

Finally, in Chapter 6, I argue that Aristotle and feminist theory complement each other because both take emotion seriously. The first shows how to connect emotion to ethical practices and political institutions; the second guards against structuring political institutions around social practices that resonate with masculinized emotional constitutions, whose danger lies in silencing whole segments of psychological social experience. One sign of this silence has been the marginalized, fragile status of emotion in philosophy. In particular, I examine three examples of political care feminism both for their contribution to a theory of political emotion and for their shortcomings from the perspective of an Aristotelian-inspired account of political emotion. In order to focus my examination, I use an interpretation of recent United States Senate debates about welfare reform, comparing liberal, Aristotelian, and feminist care approaches.

# 2

# Homeric and Platonic *Thumos*

The tongue of man is a twisty thing, there are plenty of words
there of every kind, the range of words is wide, and their variance.
The sort of thing you say is the thing that will be said to you.
—Homer, *Iliad*

Two important early Western accounts of the human psychic interior appear in Homer's *Iliad* and Plato's *Republic*, one an epic poem, the other a philosophical dialogue. Homer's version is a strange collection of interior elements, some neither purely organic nor purely psychic—*kardia* and *ētor* meaning heart, *phrenes* meaning lungs, or diaphragm, or mind, *noos* meaning mind, plan, or purpose, *psuchē* meaning a breath that flees the body at the point of death, and *thumos*, my object of investigation. Much later Plato uses *psuchē* as the whole that encompasses three divisions—the reasoning, spirited (thumotic) and appetitive. Whereas in the *Iliad*'s psychology no element is identified as the true self nor are the elements hierarchically arranged, in the *Republic* when the soul is appropriately organized, reason rules. Plato's version of the human psychic interior is more familiar, if only because we have a bounded view of our "self," but perhaps also because Freud's ego, superego, and id echo the Platonic divisions. To unearth the early history of the place of emotion in psychology, politics, and in the formation of gender, and to prepare for reading Aristotle, these two works are indispensable. They set the terms and issues on which Aristotle works and innovates, and through the tangled history of later appropriation of Plato and Aristotle, how we experience what our "self" is and what motivates us. This chapter is not a comprehensive account of Homer's or Plato's psychology, but concentrates on the most politically relevant feature common to Homer, Plato, and Aristotle: *thumos*. In examining this one feature, as I argued in Chapter 1, we have the key to understanding their philosophical psychology of politics.

On the typical view among political theorists, anger is the "simple" meaning of *thumos*, but simple often translates into central or prototypical. If Achilles is the paradigmatic thumotic man, and the *Iliad* the best-known story of Achilles, then there is some truth to this view. A *thumos* filled with anger opens the epic and remains its recurring theme. The *Iliad*, after all, as its first line announces, narrates the "wrath of Achilles." However, several features of *thumos* complicate the typical picture. For one, as classicists know, *thumos* is not an emotion itself, but a seat or organ of emotional feeling, so that it moves with many other emotions. One less familiar feature of Homeric *thumos* is that female characters also possess a *thumos*, but their social and narrative position entails the emotions of grief or sorrow rather than anger. Moreover, *thumos* participates in deliberation, a feature so strange to modern readers that they have launched a contentious debate about whether Homeric characters can be said to make decisions or even to reason. All this suggests the ill fit between the concept of spiritedness and *thumos*, a discrepancy that requires explanation through how the political and social context crucially shapes the *thumos* or emotional life of Iliadic characters.

Yet the *Iliad* is ultimately about anger itself, and the narrative has something to tell us about emotional dispositions or the state of the *thumos*. At first, Achilles embodies the interdependence of aristocratic warrior society and dominance of anger in the male characters. Using the terms developed in Chapter 1, the story of Achilles as Greek hero and icon is the paradigm scenario of anger and the governing paradigm scenario of political emotion in Homeric society. Yet in Homer's *Iliad*, Achilles' narrative predicament undermines the prominence of anger and breaks the hold of these scenarios. Achilles' anger at an affront to his honor, his realization that the warrior system will not always reward the deserving, and his grief at the death of Patroclus leads to a stunning denouement. He welcomes, eats, drinks, and shares sorrow and pity with the leader of his adversaries. His thumotic anger is countered by thumotic sorrow.

So when we view the subject more broadly, asking how the *Iliad*'s narrative treats *thumos*, it becomes apparent that how we understand the meaning of *thumos* depends on how we interpret the poem as a whole. On my view, even if the poem glorifies heroic society and its ethics, *thumos* is not entirely or simply anger, but harbors other emotions. But based on attention to the predicament of Achilles and its resolution in book 24 during the meeting between Achilles and the Trojan king, Priam, a view of the epic as a critique of heroic ethics turns on a change in the central emotion of Achilles and, therefore, on the conception and constitution of the *thumos*. Where Achilles was liable to the pathologies inherent in the dominating emotion of anger among heroic warriors, in the last book a calm settles over the harshness of the Trojan war and the belligerence of Achilles' emotions. Now a surprisingly empathetic compassion, a sharing of sorrows turns Achilles' *thumos* and a temporary reenactment of domestic activities of eating and sleeping proffers the peace of city/political life. Not the anger of a militarized, overly masculinized, heroic personality, but compassion and shared sorrow, pity and mutual fear, may drive humans into the political life of the polis.

Homer's poetic depiction of warrior emotions is challenged and epic psychology is substantially altered in Plato's *Republic*. In the first extended philosophical psychology, Plato's *Republic* gives an especially meaty role to *thumos* but entirely bypasses *phrenes, ētor,* and *kardia*. Through his discussion of the guardians and their poetic reeducation, Plato concentrates almost exclusively on the experience of anger. His corrections of poetry, in fact, serve to expunge sympathetic emotions. Apparently, for Plato, there is no good model of emotional response other than that of the angry person in civil defense and war. Poetry cannot educate the emotions, on the contrary, it fuels a rage of indiscriminate desires and emotions and so must be controlled by the state.

In this account Plato creates a warrior character that arguably was not even in the *Iliad* itself. Furthermore, in this creation he confines *thumos* to anger without the *Iliad*'s variety of possible emotional expressions. At the same time, he increases its importance by ordering and limiting the numbers of soul parts, but also by attaching it to one particular way of life. Despite Plato's feminist sounding arguments in book 5, through his contrasting female imagery of excessive emotionality and male imagery of invulnerability, he creates a manliness and womanliness as emotional stances requiring disciplinary inculcation. Plato and his modern day interpreters often script *thumos* into a submersed narrative of anger, justice, manliness, and the military life. In so doing, they raise questions about the gendered motivations of political life. When Homer explicitly tells a tale of anger and war, he has a far more expansive understanding of *thumos*, one that is *not* yet tied to manliness. So, although Plato invents the study of political psychology, he severely narrows the Homeric conception of *thumos*. Ostensibly, his preferred model of political engagement, his governing scenario of political emotion is the story of the philosopher-ruler, raised through the ranks of warrior auxiliaries, schooled through a rigorous program of mathematics and geometry to gain distance from the changing world of appearances. I say ostensibly because I agree with those who contend that the surface or literal reading of the *Republic* is inadequate. The irony, the metaphors, the images, the dialogue form all suggest we cannot easily be sure of Plato's intention. But if, as I agree, we must ultimately focus on Plato's questions rather than his answers, he still is limited in his understanding of political emotion. True, Plato initiates the theoretical question of the relationship between emotion and politics, but the question is posed more broadly and answered quite differently by Aristotle.

# Homeric *Thumos*

## Anger and Other Emotions

The prevailing view among political theorists is right about one thing: anger often appears as, or with, *thumos*, but this is because anger itself is the central emotional subject of the *Iliad*. The listener, and now reader, is meant to focus on anger from the poem's famous first line: "Sing, goddess, the anger of Peleus's Son Achilleus."[1] Achilles' anger, as it turns out, is only a reaction to the anger of Agamemnon, whose own anger is a reaction to Apollo's anger. The genealogy of anger could be continued. For Apollo only becomes angry after the Greeks became angry after Menelaus became angry after Hera became angry. Anger in ancient Greek folklore moves wavelike through the annals of its gods, goddesses, and heroes. Without telling the whole story, let me recapitulate the tale from the point of Apollo's anger. The Greeks, encamped on the beaches near the city of Troy, are in the tenth year of their war against the Trojans.

---

1. For the Greek text I have consulted Homer, *The Iliad*, trans. A. T. Murray, Loeb Classical Library (Cambridge, Mass.: Harvard University Press, 1978). All translations are from Homer, *The* Iliad *of Homer*, trans. Richmond Lattimore (Chicago: University of Chicago Press, 1951) and are identified by chapter and line number.

Agamemnon has angered a priest of Apollo by capturing and enslaving his daughter Chryseis and then refusing ransom for her. When the priest successfully appeals to him, Apollo showers arrows and plague upon the Greek soldiers. This is the situation then as the epic opens.

When the seer Kalchas reveals how Apollo's divine anger may be assuaged, Agamemnon's anger in turn erupts and: "the heart within filled black to the brim with anger" (1.103). He demands a woman to replace the one he must return. Since it is Achilles' slave woman he covets, Achilles' anger rises and threatens to end in violence. Athena stays the most violent part of this anger, but when Agamemnon refuses to compromise, instead ordering the seizure of the slave woman, the animosity between the two warriors continues. Homer then tells the story of an emotional wave and its material consequences.

In this early sequence, Achilles' reaction to Agamemnon's threatened seizure of Briseis connects *thumos* and anger. Here is Lattimore's rendering:

> So he spoke. And the anger came on Peleus's son, and within his
> shaggy breast the heart was divided two ways, pondering
> whether to draw from beside his thigh the sharp sword, driving
> away all those who stood between and kill the son of Atreus,
> or else to check his spleen [*thumos*] within and keep down his
>     anger.
> Now as he weighed in mind [*phrenes*] and spirit [*thumos*] these
>     two courses,
> and was drawing from its scabbard the great sword, Athene
>     descended
> from the sky. (1.188–95).

Achilles' anger rises; his "mind" is divided; he considers whether to restrain his *thumos*. Restraining anger is directly linked to restraining *thumos*. So the epic's introductions of Agamemnon, Achilles, and Apollo consistently reveal them to be men and a god of anger—anger at affronts to their honor. The association of anger with *thumos* occurs fairly often, as when Achilles is moved by "*menos* [anger] and overweening *thumos*" (20.174), and when he roars at Hector, "I wish somehow my *menos* and *thumos* impelled me to slice you up and eat your meat raw, for things you did" (22.346–47). *Thumos* is related to the impulse needed to fight. In the midst of battle the heroes will often rouse their men to fight harder, as when Ajax and Hector, on their opposite sides, "stirred up the *thumos* and strength in each man" (11.291; 15.500, 514). The hoary Nestor recounts past triumphs saying, "[M]y hard-enduring heart [*thumos*] in its daring drove me to fight" (7.152–53).

Yet anger is not the only emotion associated with *thumos*. Many other emotions, both pleasurable and painful, happen in, to, with *thumos*. Agamemnon's delegation, sent to entice Achilles back into battle, finds the warrior playing his lyre, singing tales of heroes and so delighting his *thumos* (9.189). A huge eagle, an omen from Zeus, gladdens the *thumoi* (plural) of Trojan citizens when Priam sets out to ransom Hector's body (24.320). Priam, speaking of Achilles' father, says that when the father hears of the son he is gladdened in his *thumos* (24.491). Achilles claims that he "loved this one [Briseis] from my *thumos*, though it was my spear that won her" (9.343). Similarly, Phoenix, Achilles' old former tutor, loves the young warrior out of his *thumos* (9.486).

Not only the desirable, pleasurable emotions of delight, gladness, and love, but also the troubling, painful emotions of sorrow, shame, and fear are connected with *thumos*. Beseeching Hector to stay within the city gates rather than fight Achilles alone, Priam talks of his other sons whom he cannot discern on the battlefield: "But if they are dead already and gone down to the House of Hades, it is sorrow to our hearts [*thumoi*]" (22.53–54). When Zeus sends a message to Thetis, she laments, "What does he, the great god, want with me? I feel shamefast / to mingle with the immortals, and my heart [*thumos*] is confused with sorrows" (24.89–91). Achilles in his extraordinary meeting with Priam is described as taking "the aged king by the right hand / at the wrist, so that his heart [*thumos*] might have no fear" (24.672).

So many emotions are found in *thumos*—indeed, almost all emotional descriptions involve *thumos*, that we could tentatively agree to calling *thumos* the "neutral bearer of emotion."[2] Quite frequently anger infuses *thumos*, but other emotions just as naturally may be said to be thumotic. Is this bearer of emotion, however, peculiar to the male characters? Is it somehow especially manly so that a woman with *thumos* must be said to be transgressing the gender code for femininity?

---

2. Caroline Casswell, *A Study of Thumos in Early Greek Epic* (Leiden: E. J. Brill, 1990), 50. Casswell's study is the most thorough review of the word's usage and semantic associations in Homer without, however, handling the ethical and political themes, as I seek to do. Her conclusions add to but do not substantially change my contention that *thumos* encompasses many emotions, as well as participating in thought.

## Interior Part

But here the reader may begin to suspect something more is amiss with the old interpretations of *thumos* than merely the purported association with anger. After all, Homer speaks of emotions "in," of emotions occurring "out of," *thumos*; and *thumos* is often the object of transitive verbs of feeling: people delight and gladden their *thumos*. In fact, in English we must often translate passages with a definite article: we must write *the thumos*. Although sometimes an emotion or a drive appropriately translates *thumos*, more often *thumos* is the site, location, the interior mental but quasi-physical part where emotions happen. That is why the translation "heart" often makes sense, except that the Greeks had other words for the organ that pumps blood through the body. As an interior part, *thumos* is not alone. Within both the mortals and the immortals of the *Iliad* move many somatic-psychic parts including *phrenes, noos, kardia,* and *psuchē*. All of these words should be approached with delicacy; not only do scholars debate their meanings, some advise understanding Greek psychology in its own terms.[3]

Not only are the words themselves disputed but so is their relationship. Do the parts make up an intelligible whole? So many of these parts fill the human interior that Bruno Snell famously claimed that Homer and his characters had no sense of a unified physical body or even a coherent mental self.[4] A. W. H. Adkins agreed: "Homeric man, then, not only has a psychology and a physiology in which the parts are more in evident than the whole: he believes that the gods may act directly upon him or some aspect of him to affect his actions for good or ill."[5] That Homeric characters lacked either a unified body or a soul also meant, according to Snell, that they could not be said to decide or choose their actions. For Adkins, these absences meant that early Greeks lacked a sense of responsibility and duty, and that they were immersed in an overwhelming competitive system of values with little or no cooperative virtues.

3. The best treatment of Homeric and tragic psychobiology is Ruth Padel, *In and Out of the Mind: Greek Images of the Tragic Self* (Princeton: Princeton University Press, 1992). Padel resists categorizing and solidifying English meanings for each of these words. Instead, she evokes their multiple shades of meaning. On this issue in regard to *thumos*, see John P. Lynch and Gary B. Miles, "In Search of *Thumos*: Toward an Understanding of a Greek Psychological Term," *Prudentia* 12 (1980): 3–9; and Casswell, *A Study of Thumos in Early Greek Epic*, who writes "I have not found a word or phrase which could serve as an adequate universal equivalent" (2).

4. Bruno Snell, *The Discovery of the Mind: The Greek Origins of European Thought*, trans. T. G. Rosenmeyer (New York: Harper and Row, 1960).

5. A. W. H. Adkins, *From the Many to the One* (Ithaca: Cornell University Press, 1970), 26.

While influential, these contentions have been strongly disputed, most recently by Bernard Williams in the service of counseling a return to the moral cosmos of Homer and the tragedians.[6] For Williams, epic and tragic characters share with twentieth-century Westerners notions of the self, will, responsibility, and the capacity for decision making: "Beneath the terms that mark differences between Homer and ourselves lie a complex net of concepts in terms of which particular actions are explained, and this net was the same for Homer as it is for us."[7]

So Homer represents either a primitive, rudimentary state in Western thinking, or he is more or less like us in the essentials. For Snell and Adkins, the former is true, whereas for Williams, Homer is more or less just like us. Perhaps a more satisfactory third position is preferable. Rather than alienating or assimilating Homer, we might try to balance the familiar and the foreign. Ruth Padel does just this in arguing that Homer's humans are characterized by "unity in multiplicity."[8] These characters experience disorientation and self-conflict, something we post-Freudians can understand, but there remain important differences. The main difference is that Greeks do not speak metaphorically; they neglect to dissociate image and reality when describing their physical and mental interior. In contrast, late modern Westerners "tolerate extraordinary dissociations between what we think is inside us and what we imply is inside us when we speak of our feelings. We, not they, are the cultural oddity. We inherit Greek vocabulary and imagery about thought and feeling but do not share the ideas about innards that inform their usage in the fifth century."[9] For my purposes, the most important element of the strangeness of Homeric language means that our own analytic distinctions cannot be easily made. Indeed, we are handicapped by our long cultural history. As Padel notes, "No word has a total monopoly over thinking or feeling. Concrete physical inner organs belong with ideas of psychological agency. Intellectual activity is inseparable from emotional activity."[10] Homer can provide a picture of an alternative psychology, although we need not suppose it is a finished psychological theory. We can consider at a later point what the *Iliad* as a whole, as a narrative, means to say about the role of anger in the social community.

---

6. Bernard Williams, *Shame and Necessity* (Berkeley and Los Angeles: University of California Press, 1993).

7. Ibid., 34.

8. Padel, *In and Out of the Mind*, 46.

9. Ibid., 35.

10. Ibid., 39.

The role of *thumos* as an interior part is most in evidence in its relationship with *phrenes*. After *thumos*, which appears over seven hundred times in the *Iliad* and the *Odyssey*, the most important and most often used word to describe an interior human part is *phrenes*. "Diaphragm," "lungs," and "pericardium" have all been proposed as translations of *phrenes*, yet according to Shirley Darcus Sullivan, it has an exclusively physical meaning in only three passages and even then the general chest cavity is the most fitting translation.[11] Sullivan concludes that in 376 passages, *phrenes* bears a far more psychological than physical meaning. *Thumos* and *phrenes* are equally elusive, reminding us that they may be concrete physical organs while acting as abstract mental concepts. As a physical space, *phrenes* normally encloses the *thumos*, but the *thumos* may move out and return, as it may move out of the body during fainting or a falling into unconsciousness near death. Thus the *thumos* and the *phrenes* are intimately involved although not just as physical spaces or parts. Just like the *thumos*, the *phrenes* may contain or experience emotion. Apollo rejoices in his *phrenes* (1.474); characters often ponder simultaneously in *phrenes* and *thumos*. In fact, the relationship of enclosure signals when *thumos* is acting properly; when *phrenes* encloses *thumos*, *thumos* acts appropriately.[12] For example, a coward characteristically is unable to keep his *thumos* within his *phrenes* (13.279–83). Thus it would be inappropriate to say that only a bold warrior had *thumos* (or, more appropriately, a *thumos*), since a coward has one also. In fact, everyone—both terrifying warrior and coward—has a *thumos*. The question is, in what condition is the *thumos*? In the cowardly person, it is overcome by fear and escapes the *phrenes*. The condition of the good warrior's *thumos* is much harder to describe. The picture of the appropriately thumotic warrior can only emerge after we look at deliberation, moral evaluation, and the particular story of Achilles.

## Women and *Thumos*

Typically unexamined by either classicists or political theorists is how the women of the *Iliad* relate to *thumos*. Even with a cursory reading it

11. Shirley Darcus Sullivan, *Psychological Activity in Homer: A Study of Phren* (Ottawa, Canada: Carleton University Press, 1988). *Phrenes* is the plural form of *phren*. Homer commonly uses this plural, yet it can have both a plural and singular meaning. For simplicity I will also use the plural form with the singular meaning and so will join it with singular English verbs.

12. On the relationship of *phrenes* and *thumos,* see Sullivan, *Psychological Activity in Homer*, 83; and Casswell, *A Study of Thumos in Early Greek Epic*, 43–44, 50.

becomes clear that although mortal women appear in very few passages, when they do they certainly have *thumoi*, so sex is no bar from having a *thumos*. Upon closer inspection, however, a woman's *thumos* is associated more with sorrow or grief than with anger. While all humans may be moved and inspirited by the gods rather than actively choosing and feeling, the *Iliad*'s women particularly are passive in the midst of war. When Achilles hears of Patrocles' death, the narrator tells us that "the hand-maidens Achilleus and Patroklos had taken / captive, stricken at heart [*thumos*] cried out aloud, and came running out of doors about valiant Achilles" (18.28–30). In grief Briseis speaks to Patrocles' body: "Patrok-los, far more pleasing to my *thumos* in its sorrows, / I left you here alive when I went away from the shelter" (19.287–88). During his meeting with Andromache on the ramparts of Troy, Hector asks his wife, "Why does your *thumos* sorrow so much for me?" (6.486).

But while the "handmaidens" and Andromache are women who only suffer, Helen has more actively controlled her life by running away with Paris. Yet at this point in her story, her emotions are also expressions of her passivity. At first when Helen appears in book 3, her emotions are the longing of homesickness and sexual desire: "Speaking so, the goddess left in her heart [thumos] sweet longing [*himeros*] after her husband of time before, and her city and her parents" (3.139–40). But when meeting Priam on the ramparts of Troy, Helen reproaches herself and tells him: "now I am worn with weeping" (3.176). Later the goddess Aphrodite, who first brought Helen and Paris together in the entanglement that led to the Trojan War, saves Paris from imminent death by snatching him from the battlefield and depositing him in his bedroom. She then mercilessly demands that Helen return to his arms: "So she spoke, and troubled the *thumos* in Helen's bosom" (3.395). Helen refuses to return, saying that "my *thumos* even now is confused with sorrows" (3.412).

The sorrow and grief of women become wilder and more insistent as the poem progresses. And although the poet does not use the word "*thumos*" when he is describing these emotions, there is no doubt, given the passages I cited, that these emotional experiences are all associated with it. Early in the poem, Helen feels merely a continual grief over her choices and fate, since the goddess as much as she is responsible for her abandoning her Greek husband for the beautiful Trojan Paris. In book 6, when Hector enters Troy searching first for Paris and then for his wife, Andromache, he finds that she "had taken her place on the tower in lamentation" (6.373). While he tries to comfort her, Hector nevertheless rejects her advice to fight a defensive war rather than seeking individual glory, and their talk only leaves her with her tears. As Andromache returns to her palace, these tears and this sorrow now travel, infusing and inspiriting her handmaidens: "her coming stirred all of them into lamentation" (6.499). Book 22 has a similar pattern, moving from an early individual tearful female supplication to communal grieving led by women of Troy. After he kills Patrocles, and the newly enraged Achilles has reentered the war, Hector faces Achilles' ferocious vengeance by himself. During a lull in their contest, Hector's father and mother implore him to take pity on them, to come inside the city walls rather than to attack Achilles alone. In pleading with his most honored son, Priam describes his many sons who have "gone down to the house of Hades, . . . a sorrow to our hearts [*thumos*], who bore them, myself and their mother" (22.53). Hecuba joins the appeal with "tears in mourning / and laid the fold of her bosom bare and with one hand held out / a breast, and wept her tears for him and called to him in winged words: / Hector, my child, look upon these and obey, and take pity on me" (22.80–83). After Hector returns to battle, is slaughtered, and his body is defiled by Achilles, "his mother tore out her hair and threw the shining veil far from her / and raised a great wail as she looked upon her son; and his father / beloved groaned pitifully, and all his people about him / were taken with wailing and lamentation all through the city" (22.405–9). In yet another scene of communal grief, when Priam returns to Troy with Hector's body, "there was no man left there in all the city / nor woman, but all were held in sorrow passing endurance" (24.707–8).

As is evident from this last passage, crying, lamentation, and what to us late twentieth-century Westerners may appear to be excessive grieving are not limited to women. Men, even stout warriors in the prime of life, do not restrain their tears. After Agamemnon's men take Briseis away, "Achilleus / weeping went and sat in sorrow apart from his companions" (1.348). The leader of the Greek army, Agamemnon himself, is shown standing before an assembly of his soldiers and "shedding tears, like a spring dark-running" (9.14). In fact, the men of the *Iliad*, although able to call upon great reserves of war anger, are hardly immune to debilitating and dispiriting emotions. Just before Agamemnon is shown weeping, the narrator summons the image of emotion as a divine and natural force sweeping through the army: "So the Trojans held their night watches. Meanwhile immortal / Panic, companion of cold Terror, gripped the Achaians / as all their best were stricken with grief that passes endurance" (9.1–3). Men can weep, grieve, and sorrow, but women, in contrast, have few if any socially recognized avenues for expressing anger.

To goddesses Homer attributes a wider range of emotion; sorrow and grief afflict them far less than these do mortal women and anger routinely surges within them. Hera challenges Zeus's decision to hurt the Greeks in revenge for Achilles' dishonor, and later she directly intervenes in the midst of a successful Trojan onslaught, angry at their successes. In these instances her anger is not described in conjunction with a reference to *thumos*, but at other times she surely has a *thumos*: "Now Hera, she of the golden throne . . . her *thumos* was happy" (14.155). Even Aphrodite admits to having a *thumos* when she addresses Hera: "Speak forth whatever is on your mind. My *thumos* is urgent to do it" (14.195). Only Thetis among the goddesses is particularly liable to sorrow: "Hear me, Nereids, my sisters; so you may all know / well all the sorrows that are in my *thumos*" (18.52–53; see also the passages quoted above).

So although the emotional constitution of mortal women may differ from the male warrior's, they have a *thumos*. Men are not immune to sorrow and grief, but the constraint on women's public actions means that as passive observers of male warfare their sorrow and grief will proliferate. In any case, *thumos* is not a thing or quality limited to one sex, or even to human beings. Moreover, while for us, it may not be contradictory to call a woman who is courageous and assertive "manly," in the Homeric case, as should be clear by now, possessing a *thumos* does not make one automatically manly in these senses. Nor does Homer ever imply that women are somehow constitutionally unable to function like a man, and certainly not because they lack *thumos*. A Homeric women or goddess with a *thumos* does not transgress the expected gender code for femininity. Indeed, and this should give pause to anyone considering the history of gender identity, Homer has no sense of a human interior, psychological in our sense, that is fundamentally structured into two dichotomous genders, in other words no femininity or masculinity. And so, even in Homer, the apparent celebrator of aristocratic warrior culture, *thumos* cannot simply be a manly passion.

## Deliberation

Achilles' quarrel with Agamemnon in book 1 confronts us with another thumotic curiosity. Reacting to Agamemnon's threatened seizure of Brisies, Achilles grows angry, almost drawing his sword against the Greek's military leader. He considers checking his *thumos* in order to suppress his anger. Anger surges within his *thumos*, but surprisingly so does some kind of deliberation: "Now as he weighed in *phrenes* and *thumos* these two courses . . ." (1.193). Homer specifies that Achilles deliberates in two parts of his interior, one of which is more normally the site of emotion, something we might suppose is different from deliberation. The problem is twofold: is *thumos* the object or source of decision making and what place do anger and emotion generally have in deliberation, albeit hasty deliberation?

Translators have depicted Achilles' dilemma through significantly different psychological vocabularies, as Alasdair MacIntyre nicely shows.[13] In his sixteenth-century translation, George Chapman presents Achilles' reaction as a conflict between two thoughts in his "discursive part," whereas Alexander Pope in his eighteenth-century version describes a battle between reason and passion. And in another modern translation, by Robert Fitzgerald, Achilles is moved by conflicting passions. These translations all seem to miss that *thumos* is an agent of reflection, a conception of *thumos* that lacks the distinction of emotion and reason employed by later writers.

In another example of decision making, Odysseus, nearly surrounded by Trojans, considers whether to flee with the rest of the Greeks or to maintain his position. The poet describes the Trojans advancing, Greeks fleeing in fear, and then Odysseus's mental process:

> And troubled, *he spoke then to his own great-hearted* thumos:
> "Ah me, what will become of me? It will be a great evil
> If I run, fearing their multitude, yet deadlier if I am caught
> alone; and Kronos's son drove to flight the rest of the Danaans.
> Yet still, *why does the* thumos *within me debate on these things?*
> Since I know that it is cowards who walk out of the fighting,
> but if one is to win honour in battle, he must by all means
> stand his ground strongly, whether he be struck or strike down
>     another."
> While he was *pondering these things in his* phrenes *and* thumos
> the ranks of the Trojans came on against his.
>     (11.401–22; emphasis added)

In the midst of battle Odysseus acknowledges his fear as a solitary soldier standing against a horde of Trojans. Since the poet says that Odysseus speaks to his *thumos*, we can assume the emotion fear is afflicting the *thumos*. His conversation with his *thumos* ends by his applying the principle that warriors stand rather than flee before great danger.

---

13. Alasdair MacIntyre, *Whose Justice? Which Rationality?* (South Bend: University of Notre Dame, 1988), 17.

So readers might easily see this psychological incident as the victory of reason over emotion because Odysseus has successfully quelled his fear. Without emphasizing the suppression of emotion, Bernard Williams argues that Homeric characters act based on reasons.[14] To argue this he trades on how "totally familiar" the characters' thinking is, so discounting the importance of Homer's psychological vocabulary, all those discrete particles or organlike parts of the human. Being cautious, Williams tells us he does not want to enter into the debate about the meaning of these particles, but if he had to say something it would be that no consistent meanings for these parts have been found.[15] Here, unfortunately, he cites David Claus's *Toward the Soul*, which in a mere seven pages concludes that most instances of *thumos* can be translated as "exceedingly" or "very much."[16] So, Williams tells us, to understand Homeric action we should look at the characters' "desires, beliefs, and purposes" rather than to "*thumos, noos*, and so on."[17] This is a strange kind of admiration; in the name of arguing for the superiority of the Homeric and tragic view of the cosmos, he discounts their very words.

Another interpretation questions whether Odysseus reasons at all. In this reading Alasdair MacIntrye suggests that it would be misleading to portray Odysseus as engaging in a "process of reasoning."[18] Odysseus makes no inferences, does not move from premise to conclusion; instead he merely recalls what a good Heroic-age man (an *agathos*) is supposed to do in this situation, including that "it is the part of the *agathos* ... not to allow one's passion-swollen *thumos* to dictate one's actions."[19] Certainly to believe that this interior incident is like other types of "reasoning" would be misleading. MacIntrye describes three alternative types of reasoning, since now he inexplicably claims that he will characterize the "reasoning of agents represented in the Homeric poems."[20] The two non-Homeric types begin either from a premise about what is good for an agent of his or her kind or about what one wants or desires. In contrast, Homeric characters supposedly know what they must do because they so closely identify with their social roles. That is, they reason from what their social roles expect of them to what they must do in their particular

14. Williams, *Shame and Necessity*, 31.
15. Ibid., 27.
16. David B. Claus, *Toward the Soul: An Inquiry into the Meaning of Psuchē Before Plato* (New Haven: Yale University Press, 1981).
17. Williams, *Shame and Necessity*, 33.
18. MacIntyre, *Whose Justice? Which Rationality?*, 16.
19. Ibid., 19.
20. Ibid., 20.

situation. Although this view rejects the idea that reasoning wins over emotion, it still assumes that something wins over emotion.

These interpretations would be right except for one word—*thumos*. Odysseus speaks to his *thumos*; he asks why the *thumos* continues to ponder as the Trojans advance. Both the emotion and the reason seem to reside in the *thumos*. In fact, reason does not win over emotion, emotion is not action diverting or corrupting; rather one package of a reason and an emotion wins over another. On the one hand, Odysseus perceives that he is badly outnumbered; this is a good reason to flee, and fear supports this reason, even depends upon it. On the other hand, he reminds himself of the reason to stay: to win honor as a warrior he must face the danger and he recalls the warrior's characteristic emotion—anger. Without the poet clearly saying that Odysseus *decides* to hold out, it appears as though Odysseus comes to a conclusion or at least possesses the grounds for a decision, based on the emotional imagination. He both reasons and feels himself into staying.[21]

A similar imaginative choice is made by Hector when he chooses to stand before Achilles in book 22. Priam and Hecuba, Hector's parents, try to "move the *thumos* in Hector" by eliciting pity for their terrifying fate if their son should die. Hector listens, and although his battle fury lies in him as venom in a coiled snake, he is moved to emotional confusion. Here Homer again uses the sentence "Deeply troubled he spoke to his own great-hearted *thumos*" to open his account of Hector's interior life. The "speaking" that Hector does means invoking vivid imaginations of alternative scenarios. The first recalls the shame Hector felt when he was reprimanded by a warrior of lesser status and fears this shame would reoccur if he hid within Troy's city gates. In his second vision, Hector dreams he could approach Achilles unarmed with immense reparations for the abduction of Helen. Walking across the field of battle without his

---

21. See additional comments on inner debate in Casswell, *A Study of Thumos in Early Greek Epic*, 45–47. Others who discuss this particular passage include Richard Gaskin, "Do Homeric Heroes Make Real Decisions?," *Classical Quarterly* 40, no. 1 (1990): 1–15; David Gill, "Two Decisions: *Iliad* 11.401–22 and *Agamemnon* 192–230," *Studies Presented to Sterling Dow on His Eightieth Birthday* (Durham: Duke University Press, 1984), 125–34; R. W. Sharples, "'But Why Has My Spirit Spoken with Me Thus?': Homeric Decision-Making," *Greece and Rome* 30, no. 1 (1983): 1–7. The topic of decision making and responsibility has been addressed by A. A. Long, "Morals and Values in Homer," *Journal of Hellenic Studies* 90 (1970): 121–39; K. J. Dover, "The Portrayal of Moral Evaluation in Greek Poetry," *Journal of Hellenic Studies* 103, no. 83 (1983): 35–48; Hugh Lloyd-Jones, *The Justice of Zeus*, 2d ed. (Berkeley and Los Angeles: University of California Press, 1983) in reaction to Snell, *The Discovery of the Mind*; A. W. H. Adkins, *Merit and Responsibility* (New York: Oxford University Press, 1960).

shield, helmet, or spear, offering Achilles Trojan wealth as well as Helen herself, he would approach Achilles "whispering like a young man and a young girl, in the way / a young man and young maiden whisper together" (22.127–28). While in the first scenario he remembers a scene of shame to discourage him from a retreating, in the second he vainly hopes for a reprieve through a scene of apparent longing and infatuation. Hector tells us that he knows he will be rejected, as a young lover must so often fear. Indeed, he fears that he will be slain like a woman, a defenseless creature without weapons to defend her.

At this moment of quiet before the clanging, sputtering rage of the final battle between the two champions, the joy of social life, of love and care lived within the city's enclosure, stands in stark contrast to the theater of war. This contrast has emerged as an important motif found in central passages such as those describing Achilles' new shield and in the conversation between Andromache and Hector atop the walls of Troy. Until book 24, Hector is represented as the warrior able to bridge the divide and best imagine the worth of the social world of cooperation.[22] Hector's journey through Troy in book 6 culminates in the epic's first description of an affectionate relationship between a man and a woman. Hector is the warrior shown surrounded by family and women, so he is the warrior who in book 22 is implored by his father and mother to relinquish the glory of one-on-one combat. He is the warrior who can in wild hope imagine speaking to Achilles with a lover's whisper.

As it turns out, not Hector but his *thumos* speaks and debates, moving through the vivid imaginings of shame, then hope, and finally recovering its focus on fury and anger with the simple words "Better to bring on the fight with him as soon as it may be. / We shall see to which one the Olympian grants the glory" (22.129–30). The *thumos*, then, in these "decision-making" passages, signals that Hector does not give himself reasons for action, but neither does he simply suppress his *thumos* or emotional incursions as such. As MacIntrye recognizes, Hector like other characters knows what to do based on his social role as the leading Trojan warrior, but that role reinstantiates its power to move him through his recalling its emotional paradigm scenario filled with shame and anger. We do not have here a picture of reasoning if this means the exclusive use

22. Marilyn B. Arthur, "The Divided World of *Iliad* 6," in *Reflections of Women in Antiquity,* ed. Helene Foley (New York: Gordon and Breach, 1981); "Early Greece: The Origins of the Western Attitude Towards Women," in *Women in the Ancient World: The Arethusa Papers,* ed. John Peradotto and J. P.Sullivan (Albany: State University of New York Press, 1984).

of reason, but rather a picture of "pondering" [*hormaino*] that unites emotion and reason. So *thumos* appears in this and other similar passages not as a formula or an intensifier, but as a sign of emotional evaluation and choice. *Thumos* is neither superfluous nor inescapably exotic nor unfathomable.

## *Thumos* and Spiritedness

Bruno Snell has called the *thumos* an "organ of (e)motion," a point that is supported by Jan Bremmer and James Redfield.[23] The term suggests three important features of *thumos*. First, as we have seen, it is the place in which most emotions occur. Not just anger, but pain, grief, sorrow, joy, and love are felt in the *thumos*. Second, *thumos* is more an organ than a disposition. It would be inaccurate to say that *thumos is* an organ, since it has an indeterminate status, somewhere between flesh and air, less a piece of the body that could be cut out, more a piece that can dematerialize and rush out of the body during a fainting spell and near death. The association with emotion, as well as its organlike status, account for Redfield's and Lattimore's translation of *thumos* as "heart."

Third, *thumos* is the key source and sometimes, when a god or goddess intervenes, a medium, of human motivation, desire, and movement. It is the source of the impulses themselves that constitute a person's actively being in the world. It combines emotion and action, revealing the way in which emotion is always implicated in action, and even in the activity of thought. Adding the association of motion or action significantly distinguishes this particular conception of emotion from any view of emotions as passive and intrusive on healthy mental life.[24]

Can we still say that there is anything to the identification of spiritedness and *thumos* in Homer? In its most common use, the English word "spirited" means "full of energy, animation, or courage," while in the more restricted sense employed by some political theorists it means a universal psychic disposition, typically expressed as anger against violations of one's honor. On the one hand, *thumos* cannot match either definition,

---

23. Snell, *The Discovery of the Mind*, 9. Jan Bremmer claims that *thumos* is "above all the source of emotions," in *The Early Greek Concept of the Soul* (Princeton: Princeton University Press, 1983). James Redfield writes that it is the seat of the affective life—of passions, wishes, hopes, and inclination," in *Nature and Culture in the Iliad: The Tragedy of Hector* (Chicago: University of Chicago Press, 1975), 173.

24. So MacIntyre is inaccurate when he says, "The passions are on this view causes which by swelling the *thumos* divert someone from doing what he would otherwise do, what it would be appropriate for him to do" (*Whose Justice? Which Rationality?*, 16).

since it harbors emotions other than anger, since it is more an organ than one disposition, since it is key to deliberation. On the other hand, it is not so neutral as Casswell would have it. The emotional style of the characters in the *Iliad* might seem somewhat broad to us in the English-speaking West. Emotions are large, public and, well, spirited—in the sense of energetic or animated. Even though characters are often moved by emotions sent by the gods, there is no sense that humans are passive sufferers of emotional storms or passive funnels for divine emotions. Emotions are actions of the characters within their world, even though these emotions do not necessarily originate from within themselves. Emotions are divine/natural forces and at the same time human forces. In Homer, one might say, the universe and the human being are unified not in *logos*, but in *thumos*.

Moreover, *thumos* is not merely a neutral vessel because it has a characteristic pattern in the *Iliad*. It is the motivation of a warrior. A character will say that he was "driven to fight by my *thumos* which was ready to undertake much with all its boldness" (7.153). Another will ask: "Does the desire in your *thumos* drive you to combat in hope you will be lord of the Trojans ... and of Priam's honour" (20.179–81). Heroes are often called *megathumos* (1.135), for example, the "Son of Tydeus, you with the great *thumos*" (6.145). It stands for the psychic power of a person that, when well expressed, makes him a particularly good warrior, makes him *megathumos*, "great-hearted."

What, then, is responsible for limited understanding of the meaning of *thumos*? Some of the misinterpretation comes from reading backward from Plato to Homer and forwards from Plato to Aristotle. In other words, Plato's definition sets the terms for the discussion. In book 4 of the *Republic*, Plato defines *thumos* along with the other two parts of the soul. This is the definition that is taken to establish the political and moral relevance of *thumos*. In fact, for many readers interested in the ancient Greek philosophers, not least for those who work in the Straussian tradition, Plato sets the terms for the discussion of the meaning of classical philosophy.[25] More important, however, the extant interpretations of *thumos* fail to put the concept into its psychological and historical

25. For example, Bolotin argues that both Plato and Homer understood the "deficiency" of the "life of action" but only Plato explicitly praised the "life of the mind." The contrast between the city or politics and philosophy, equivalent to the contrast between the life of action and the life of the mind, Bolotin derives from Plato, if not Strauss, and reads back into Homer. On my view, using Plato this way leads to some imprecise categories. The life of action only very loosely encompasses both the battle-filled life of the

context.[26] Even Plato, in book 8 of the *Republic*, examines the correspondence between regime and soul. Only by exploring the links between psychology and social-political life will we understand how *thumos* can be a general organ of emotion and yet how Homeric men in the *Iliad* have characteristic emotional temperaments much like spiritedness.

## Psychology and Social-Political Life

Pictures of the psychological interior and its processes vary across history and culture. Where a political psychologist of the late twentieth century may talk of "personality processes and dispositions" composed of object appraisal, mediation of self-other relationships, externalization, and ego defense,[27] and Freud may speak of an unconscious, an id, ego, and superego; Homer describes the human interior with *thumos*, *phrenes*, *noos*, and *psuchē*. Plato and Aristotle have still different versions of the psychological interior. It should go without saying that the language each uses constitutes an interpretation of somatic-psychic life. And each of these interpretations either reflects, opposes, or rearranges social and political phenomena within its historical milieu. None of this suggests that all is constructed, that there is no human nature, or no true picture of human psychology. As I noted in Chapter 1, only recently has substantial new work been done on the relationship of culture and psychology.[28]

---

Iliadic warrior and the life of political action within the culture of the polis. David Bolotin, "The Critique of Homer and the Homeric Heroes in Plato's *Republic*," in *Political Philosophy and the Human Soul*, ed. Michael Palmer and Thomas L. Pangle (Lanham, Md.: Rowman and Littlefield, 1995), 83–93.

26. Of course, Strauss's work castigates historicism both in moral life and in philosophical interpretation; see Leo Strauss, *Natural Right and History* (Chicago: University of Chicago Press, 1953). But the use of historical context in interpretation does not necessarily lead to historicism. I am convinced that a compromise can be reached. In terms of interpretive method, see Peter J. Ahrensdorf, "The Question of Historical Context and the Study of Plato," *Polity* 27 (Fall 1994): 113–35.

27. M. B. Smith, "A Map for the Analysis of Personality and Politics," *Journal of Social Issues* 24, no. 1 (1968): 15–28.

28. Shinobu Kitayama and Hazel Rose Markus, eds., *Emotion and Culture: Empirical Studies of Mutual Influence* (Washington, D.C.: American Psychological Association, 1987); Catherine A. Lutz, *Unnatural Emotions: Everyday Sentiments on a Micronesian Atoll and Their Challenge to Western Theory* (Chicago: University of Chicago Press, 1988); Catherine Lutz and Geoffrey M. White, "The Anthropology of Emotions," *Annual Review of Anthropology* 15 (1986): 405–36; Peter N. Stearns and Carol Z. Stearns, "Emotionology: Clarifying the History of Emotions and Emotional Standards," *American Historical Review* 90 (1985): 813–36; Carol Z. Stearns and Peter N. Stearns, eds., *Emotion and Social Change: Toward a New Psychohistory* (New York: Holmes and Meier, 1988).

While recognizing the biological components of psychological phenomena such as emotion, those scholars involved in this work warn against assuming the existence of universal basic emotions identifiable through behavior. Instead, through anthropological research, they have explored the existence of culturally specific emotions and attitudes to emotion in general.

Taking this perspective, I can consider some ways in which the social and political life of the Homeric heroic class, imaginatively reconstructed by a poet, might have structured the somatic-psychic life. Of course, this is a huge question of which at least three aspects are relevant. I could address why the interior is divided into a multiplicity of small parts with no obvious unity; why most emotions occur in a movable, breathlike substance/part called the *thumos*; or why some emotions are more important than others in the repertoire of the Homeric warrior. Here I will consider only the last with some suggestions about the second.

The political form of the heroic class was a mix between a simple monarchy and a small aristocracy.[29] Each major warrior ruled over his own small area—Agamemnon over Mycenae, Menelaus over Sparta, Achilles over Phithia, Odysseus over Ithaca. To preserve their rule they depended on personal might, a loyal entourage, prestige, and booty gathered in warfare and raiding. Without a bureaucracy and a docile aristocratic class, their rule was extremely vulnerable. As Finley notes, while Nestor and Menelaus managed an easy reassertion of power upon their homecoming, Agamemnon was murdered by his wife and a rival aristocrat, and Odysseus had to eliminate 108 claimants to his position. The very instability of kingly rule, then, required a peculiar force of character amenable to emphatic display, with kings alternately using threats, feasting, or gift giving to maintain sway over other aristocrats. Warfare permitted public display of one's potential threat to friends, while enacting the real threat

---

In the ancient Greek context, Jean-Pierre Vernant advocates and practices historical psychology, arguing, for example, that the Greeks lacked the modern conception of will. He has not to my knowledge addressed concepts of emotion directly. See Jean-Pierre Vernant and Pierre Vidal-Naquet, *Myth and Tragedy in Ancient Greece*, trans. Janet Lloyd (New York: Zone Books, 1990); Jean-Pierre Vernant, *Mortals and Immortals: Collected Essays*, ed. Froma I. Zeitlin (Princeton: Princeton University Press, 1991); Jean-Pierre Vernant, ed., *The Greeks*, trans. Charles Lambert and Teresa Lavender Fagan (Chicago: University of Chicago Press, 1995).

29. Oswyn Murray, *Early Greece* (Atlantic Highlands, N.J.: Humanities Press, 1980); C. G. Thomas, "The Roots of Homeric Kingship," *Historia* 15 (1966): 387–400; William Merritt Sale, "The Government of Troy: Politics in the *Iliad*," *Greek, Roman, and Byzantine Studies* 35 (Spring 1994): 5–102.

to adversaries. Anger is the fulcrum of both this kind of personalized kingship and individualized warfare; anger is essential to the political order. Therefore, it is hardly surprising that the emotional constitution of the hero is centered on anger, and that the *Iliad* is the story of a great anger.

The heroic way of life—its values, ideals, and sentiments—again suggests that anger is invaluable. In Lutz's approach, "particular moral ideas take what force they have from the commitment people learn to feel to them. The notion that violence is bad would be an empty norm were it not that people on Ifaluk in fact feel intense horror or panic when the prospect of aggression arises."[30] Here Lutz suggests that emotions, especially ones of pleasure and pain, reinforce communal norms. But an even more complex relationship between emotion and morality is apparent from Justin Oakley's neo-Aristotelian analysis of why emotions are morally valuable.[31] Emotions contribute to our achieving certain goods—insight, good judgment, understanding, strength of will, love and friendship, self-worth. All these make sense within the Aristotelian scheme. But the heroic ethic differs from both the Ifaluk system of value and Aristotle's. The heroic ethic is composed of four elements: honor, glory, shame, and the maxim to help your friends and harm your enemies.[32] Striving for honor, for example, requires continual monitoring of one's reputation, revenging insults, preserving appearances. So a person striving for honor is particularly sensitive to slights, making for an irascible temperament. In the *Iliad*, even though some anger-motivated actions are censured (Agamemnon's seizure of Briseis and Achilles' mutilation of Hector's corpse, for example), anger in general is expected. So it is accurate to say: "The Homeric poems are about great individuals whose standing and power are threatened; their reaction is, and is expected to be, violent."[33]

In Homeric characters, then, certain emotions predominate, and other emotions remain undeveloped. Anger can be read as central to *thumos*, since anger is central to the story of the *Iliad* and to the life of the Homeric nobleman. As A. W. H. Adkins writes, the poems are written from the point of view of the *agathos*, a man who is commended for excellence in

---

30. Lutz, *Unnatural Emotions*, 213.

31. Justin Oakley, *Morality and the Emotions* (New York: Routledge, 1992).

32. Adkins, *Merit and Responsibility*; Mary Whitlock Blundell, *Helping Friends and Harming Enemies: A Study in Sophocles and Greek Ethics* (Cambridge: Cambridge University Press, 1990); Dover, "The Portrayal of Moral Evaluation," 35–48; M. I. Finley, *The World of Odysseus* (New York: Penguin, 1979); Long, "Morals and Values," 121–39; Redfield, *Nature and Culture*.

33. C. J. Rowe, "The Nature of Homeric Morality," in *Approaches to Homer*, ed. Carl A. Rublino and Cynthia W. Shelmerdine (Austin: University of Texas Press, 1983), 248–75.

war and in defense of his household, a man who is also necessarily high born and prosperous.[34] The defense and appropriation of honor, which includes and indeed is signified by material goods, is the principal motivation of the *agathos*. Justice and injustice indicate only getting and losing honor, so when anger is associated with injustice, it is anger at the loss of honor. According to mythology, the Trojan War itself was sparked by the abduction of Helen, a portion of Menelaus's honor, and the quarrel on the Greek side begins with the threatened seizure of Briseis. The most emotional event for the Homeric aristocratic man is the loss of honor, because the accumulation of honor is the center of life. Central to his emotional repertoire and central to his *thumos*, flooding the hero at such a loss, is anger. Added to the pervasive concern for honor are the physical requirements of intense hand to hand combat. For such intimate warfare, the only route to male honor, Homeric warriors require the frenzy of rage and anger. Anger is the announced subject of the poem and it is the predominant emotion even outside of the quarrel between Agamemnon and Achilles. Homeric warriors are trained for anger by both a social and a political structure that values honor and glory above all else and that uses warfare as a means for acquiring such honor and glory. How appropriate that we readers have hardly noticed the love, the pity, the fear, the sorrow within *thumos*. Achilles himself hardly noticed this until his meeting with Priam, a meeting that completes the Homeric story of Achilles and of warrior anger.

## The Story of Achilles

Granting to Adkins that the *Iliad* portrays men with such qualities, we might still ask whether it is simply a straightforward adulation of such men and their particular spiritedness. If we look at the poem as a whole and interpret it as a critique of the heroic ethic, we find that this critique centers on a crucial change in the *thumos* of Achilles.[35] The movement of

34. A. W. H. Adkins, *Moral Values and Political Behaviour in Ancient Greece* (New York: Norton, 1972).

35. Not surprisingly, debate surrounds the question of the poem's political or social intent or result. Ian Morris argues that eighth-century Greek aristocracy's need for propaganda accounts for the first transcription of the oral poem. See "The Use and Abuse of Homer," *Classical Antiquity* 5, no. 1 (1986): 124. King and Schein both suggest that Homer ultimately takes a critical stance toward the heroic ethos. See Katherine Callen King, *Achilles: Paradigms of the War Hero from Homer to the Middle Ages* (Berkeley and Los Angeles: University of California Press, 1987); Seth L. Schein, *The Mortal Hero: An Introduction to Homer's Iliad* (Berkeley and Los Angeles: University of California Press, 1984), 1, 153. Gutzwiller and Michelini propose how a literary work that embodies a way

the psyche of the central character of the *Iliad* reveals both the inherent pugnacity of *thumos* and its potential as a reservoir for other emotions, in Achilles' case for grief and sympathy. Achilles is of course the man of the great, lionlike *thumos*. Through *thumos* he shows the potential both for the destruction of civilization and for the constitution of kinship between strangers. The destructive, savage force appears in Achilles' rage for revenge, in his attempt to mutilate the body of Hector, in his sacrifice of twelve Trojan sons at the funeral pyre of Patrocles, and perhaps in his unceasing lamentations. With this savagery is allied divinity; Achilles kills Hector with the help of the goddess Athena. His actions become inhuman, both subhuman and superhuman.

And yet the *Iliad* ends with a return to the human in a reconciliation of Priam and Achilles. In the poem, set in the midst of relentless war, the aged ruler of the Greeks' enemies and the "best of the Achaeans" reach a temporary alliance. With his frenzy of revenge spent, but with its sputtering continuing even after Patrocles' funeral, Achilles is impelled to achieve reconciliation. Priam arrives with a ransom for the body of his son; he has come by nightfall through the enemy camp, protected by Hermes. As Hermes leaves him inside the fortification, he urges Priam to "move the spirit [*thumos*] within him [Achilles]" (24.467). Achilles receives Priam with wonder and, hearing his supplication, is stirred to grieve for his own father whose "single all-untimely" son he is (24.540). They remember together, they weep together, Achilles feels pity and interprets their common humanity in shared sorrow (24.525–33), shared partly because Achilles is the cause of both Priam's and Peleus's grief. In a brief end to their sorrows, they eat, and they sleep in the same house. To bring them to the meal Achilles tells how Niobe, after the killing of her fourteen sons and daughters by Apollo and Artemis, "remembered to eat when she was worn out with weeping" (24.613). Since the reason for the slaughter of Niobe's children was her honoring herself above Leto, the mother of Apollo and Artemis, Achilles may be suggesting that they should not honor themselves above the gods by forgetting the potential sorrow of the human lot, by believing themselves invulnerable. By eating they acknowledge the ability of humans to live on despite misfortune

---

of life can harbor a "hidden code, operating parallel with, and in opposition to, the major one. The 'weaker' virtues are required to resolve the intolerable paradoxes of the heroic view, yet they remain a kind of negative element in the system." See Kathryn J. Gutzwiller and Ann Norris Michelini, "Women and Other Strangers: Feminist Perspectives in Classical Literature," in *(En)gendering Knowledge*, ed. Joan E. Hartman and Ellen Messer-Davidow (Nashville: University of Tennessee Press, 1991), 70.

through alleviating their sorrow. By sleeping they establish trust—
neither will be killed in his bed. We might say they have even set up a
temporary household or established ties of ritualized friendship.[36]
Achilles agrees to put off an attack until Priam has given Hector an adequate funeral. No more fighting is described in the *Iliad* and the poem
ends with the mourning and cremation of Hector. Thus two men,
although they return to their opposing sides, seem to have bridged an
insurmountable gap, and at least Achilles will no longer be waging the
same war he had begun. Achilles of the great anger-filled *thumos* has
come around to a *thumos* moved by pity, sympathy, and mercy by a route
that is the *Iliad* itself.

Critics have given renewed attention to book 24's extraordinary reconciliation. Kevin Crotty emphasizes the role of pity (*eleos*) and supplication, suggesting the possibility of a new social order outside of warrior
society.[37] Katherine King argues that instead of the old reward of *kleos*
after death and *time* in life for martial excellence, Homer acts as critic of
heroic society, offering a new criterion of human worth, "transcendent
personal sympathy," and a new highest human excellence, communion
with the enemy in recognition of common human sorrow.[38] Graham
Zanker portrays Achilles as the founder of a new mode of cooperation
grounded in magnanimity.[39]

Others may acknowledge the central place of pity in book 24, but see
the ending of the epic as pointing not to Achilles' transcendence of, but his
reconciliation to, the heroic community. Arlene Saxonhouse starts with a
definition of *thumos* as the "spirited sense of what is right, of what brings
honor and glory," a sense that "defends and preserves . . . [political] rules
of order." She finds that Achilles' disaffection with the rules governing
the distribution of military spoils is resolved through his acceptance of
the limits of justice and therefore the limits to anger and grief. His *thumos* is moderated in his discovery of limits and he reenters the "community of mortals."[40] By using *thumos* and anger interchangeably (in one

---

36. On ritualized friendship or *xenia*, see Gabriel Herman, *Ritualized Friendship and
the Greek City* (Cambridge: Cambridge University Press, 1987).

37. Kevin Crotty, *The Poetics of Supplication: Homer's* Iliad *and* Odyssey (Ithaca: Cornell University Press, 1994).

38. King, *Achilles*, 45, 221.

39. Graham Zanker, *The Heart of Achilles: Characterization and Personal Ethics in the*
Iliad (Ann Arbor: University of Michigan Press, 1994).

40. Arlene W. Saxonhouse, "Thymos, Justice, and Moderation of Anger in the Story of
Achilles," in *Understanding the Political Spirit*, ed. Catherine Zuckert (New Haven: Yale
University Press, 1988), 30, 43–44.

instance his *thumos* is moderated [40], in another it is his anger that is moderated [44]), Saxonhouse fails to consider how the political impulse, the creation and defense of rules or order, can be based on pity as much as on anger and desire for honor.

Unlike Saxonhouse, but like Crotty, King, and Zanker, I argue that Achilles surmounts the heroic way of life and its accompanying emotional orientation. At first, Achilles' anger is in keeping with the heroic system. The balance of honors is disturbed, Achilles loses his proper compensation. But the dispute cannot be settled in terms of the system itself. Achilles is left to wonder about the greatest compensation: glory, or *kleos*. His allegiance turns more domestic—to his companion Patrocles, and to Briseis. Yet his sole concentration on his own circle becomes even more dangerous—his anger becomes absurdly large, leading him to battle a river and to desecrate Hector's body. Only slowly does another emotion lead to a reinterpretation of cosmology. Pity expressed toward an other, an enemy, accompanied by the domestic practices of eating and sleeping reorients Achilles' *thumos*.

Achilles breaks out of the confines of the socially structured and dramatized emotions of his time. A new incipient order arises through the experience of pity and shared sorrow. Achilles does not simply return to the human community he has known, but he points beyond the heroic order as a signpost, and oracle, of what is to come. In the world of the warriors, pity was underutilized, even uncoded. Although pity and sorrow could be found in the sphere of women's lives,[41] it was unrecognized by men until Achilles expresses pity for and shares sorrow with a non-Greek, a stranger. The polis was to come and did come.[42] Pity and sorrow point the way to the polis and the civic institution of tragedy.

So is *thumos* manliness? Is this a desire for recognition? Is this love of one's own? At least in the *Iliad*, *thumos* is none of these. Pity and

41. Arthur, "The Divided World of *Iliad* 6," 34; Crotty, *The Poetics of Supplication*, 46, 55.

42. Others have pointed to intimations of polis values in the epic's conclusion. Seth Schein writes that "the laments and burial of Hector ... constitute a triumph ... of the civilized values of Troy: though defeated and destroyed militarily, they have the last word poetically.... In this way the *Iliad* concludes by pointing beyond conventional heroic values toward and ethic of humaneness and compassion. For Homer's audience, such an ethic must have strongly affirmed the values of the newly emerging city-state. While the juxtaposition of the values of warrior-heroism and humane compassion probably was conventional in the poetic tradition, Homer developed this juxtaposition into a fundamental thematic contrast sharpened and clarified through his portrayal of Hector and the Trojans" (*The Mortal Hero*, 186, 187). Scully also argues for the relevance of the polis to the story as a whole. See his *Homer and the Sacred City* (Ithaca: Cornell University Press, 1991).

domesticity balance manliness expressed as an overweening, lionlike, full-throttle anger in the *thumos*. *Thumos* is not one drive, although it can become ossified into one emotional tendency within certain structures such as a political community divided into small, equally powerful monarchies whose rulers' maintenance of power depends on their share of glory (heroic reputation) and honor (material goods). If this ethos is breached through an irreconcilable argument, the emotional orientation may be altered. In the case of Achilles, the orientation is alerted toward pity and domesticity.

# Platonic *Thumos*

From the Homeric epics to the Platonic dialogues, Greek conceptions of psychological life undergo remarkable changes. While in the late eighth-century *Iliad, thumos* was the most prominent among a variety of psychic elements, in Plato's fourth-century *Republic*, *thumos* is downgraded and narrowed to one of three parts optimally ruled by reason, or *logos,* in a unified soul, or *psuchē*. And while *thumos* is slowly diminished, both reason and soul rise in stature until the rule of reason in the soul constitutes for Plato the best life, the life of the philosopher. The history of the newly favored psychological elements is fascinating in its own right and a brief sketch should help to situate Platonic *thumos*.

In Homer, *psuchē* named an airy substance that upon a warrior's death flees out of his body alighting in Hades, where it endures a pitiful twilight existence. In no sense does it refer to the mental or spiritual interior as a whole, nor does it appear in passages describing a living person. Two centuries later, in Ionia of the fifth century, there is evidence of a new understanding of *psuchē*, not as the shadowy representative of the dead person, but rather as an active element in a living person.[43] Later, religious ferment and the Greek encounter with shamanistic cultures introduced a conception of the soul radically divorced from and oppressed by the body. In the Orphic maxim, the body is the tomb of the soul.

As the conception of the soul was changing, *logos* and the diverse practices of reason were displacing mythic and religious explanations. Indeed the "Greek miracle" has often been identified as the emergence of

---

43. Dodds, *The Greeks and the Irrational* (1951; reprinted Berkeley and Los Angeles: University of California Press, 1968), 120ff. and Snell, *The Discovery of the Mind*.

reason in accounts of the natural world (Thales), in stories of human affairs (Thucydides), in evaluations of moral and political life (Socrates). Rational argumentation, first emerging in the midst of the civil disruptions and political revolutions of the archaic era, nurtured philosophic argumentation itself.[44]

The two concurrent expansions of *psuchē* and *logos* merge in the Socratic teaching best exemplified in Plato's early dialogue, the *Phaedo*. In Plato's account of the last conversation between Socrates and his followers, just as Socrates is about to die on the orders of the Athenian court, the unperturbed philosopher describes body and soul as two radically separate substances, although the soul lives in the mortal body. In the soul, he places reason and in the body, the passions and desires. Only philosophy can free a person from the tyranny of the body, allowing the soul to "attain to the divine nature" (82c). For this reason, true philosophers "abstain from all bodily desires and withstand them and do not yield to them" (82c). While the word *thumos* does not appear in the *Phaedo*, it is implicitly included among the passions in an example from the *Odyssey*. This quotation attesting to Odysseus's reason reprimanding his *thumos* Plato later uses in the *Republic* to illustrate a point about *thumos*. *Thumos*, then, can be considered just one more of the disparaged bodily passions.

## Manly *Thumos*

The *Phaedo*'s portrayal of the best life as a preparation for death is so austere and unrelenting that, read in succession, the *Republic* is a surprising relief. Here Plato splits the soul into the reasoning, the desiring, and the spirited, or thumotic, parts. From the Socratic unitary, homogenous soul now emerges as the Platonic tripartite soul; emotions and appetites once attributed to the body are now acknowledged as part of the soul. When trying to define Platonic *thumos*, most commentators describe it as the spirit or the spirited part and note its primary attachment to anger.[45]

---

44. Jean-Pierre Vernant, *The Origins of Greek Thought* (Ithaca: Cornell University Press, 1982).

45. Julia Annas, *An Introduction to Plato's* Republic (Oxford: Clarendon Press, 1981); George Klosko, *The Development of Plato's* Politics (New York, Methuen 1986); Ernst Barker, *The Political Thought of Plato and Aristotle* (New York: Dover, 1959); Eric Voeglin, *Order and History, Plato and Aristotle*, vol. 3 (Louisiana State University Press, 1957); C. D. C. Reeve, *Philosopher Kings: The Argument of Plato's Republic* (Princeton: Princeton University Press, 1988); Thomas Pangle, "The Political Psychology of Religion in Plato's Laws," *American Political Science Review*, 70, no. 4 (1976): 1059–77.

Unlike the group of commentators I discussed in Chapter 1, some even beckon to the Homeric inheritance by describing it as the "emotional part," but by doing so they miss the crucial fact about Plato's *thumos*—he leaves most emotions out.[46] One might argue that in describing anger as the characteristic emotion of the thumotic part, Plato is merely illustrating with one or a few examples the kind of mental phenomena found in the thumotic part.[47] But this position would neglect that the *thumos* represents not just a part of the soul, but also a particular human character devoted to the pursuit of angry deeds, and that the *Republic* is not merely abstract speculation on the nature of the soul, but a narrative of a conversation and of the building of a human society. Certainly Plato might have included other emotions in the thumotic part, but his story gains its character partly from his pointedly excluding some emotions and ignoring other emotions.

Here I must make some preliminary qualifications. First, the *Republic* certainly contains the most detailed treatment of *thumos* and the most influential version of Plato's political philosophy, yet in later dialogues such as *Symposium, Laws*, and *Phaedrus*, Plato significantly changes his views on the nature of the soul and the effect of emotions. Writing a comprehensive account of Plato's treatment of *thumos* and the emotions is beyond the scope of this book. I mean to use Plato as a point of contrast with Aristotle. Yet, for all that, I still believe my reading of the *Republic* is a just one, eliciting significant connections between a narrow emotional repertoire and disagreeable politics. So, although I shall refer to some extent to these later developments, I will concentrate my attention on the *Republic*. Second, it would clumsy and naive to distill a theory of emotion or of *thumos* from the *Republic* or even from a set of Platonic dialogues. Such a topic is obviously not Plato's first concern; even the images of the psyche that appear in different forms in various dialogues are designed to elucidate questions of moral life first and politics second. In general,

---

46. Terence Irwin, *Plato's Moral Theory* (Oxford: Clarendon Press, 1977), 193–95; Martha Nussbaum, *The Fragility of Goodness: Luck and Ethics in Greek Tragedy and Philosophy* (New York: Cambridge University Press, 1986), 134, 141; G. M. A. Grube idiosyncratically describes the soul as divided between reason, feelings, and passions in *Plato's Thought* (1935; repr. Boston: Beacon Press, 1958), 131. "The literal meaning is anger," he writes; and then in explanation: "Fear, indignation and the like belong to this part of the soul. I have therefore called it feelings, which in that sense are quite distant from passion, as when we talk of saving a person's feelings (134 n. 2).

47. Terence Irwin takes this position, citing N. R. Murphy. See Irwin's *Plato's Ethics* (Oxford: Oxford University Press, 1995), 216; and N. R. Murphy, *The Interpretation of Plato's Republic* (Oxford: Oxford University Press, 1951), 29f.

I would argue that even in the dialogues where emotions, specifically eros and mania, lead to true knowledge and wisdom, the passions stirred by political affairs are to be avoided, and the life of philosophy divorced from the tumult and myopia of politics remains the ideal.

With these qualifications understood, my approach will be, first, simply to itemize the various qualities of *thumos* as though we could extract one sense from the text, but afterward I will address the question of the political effects of this *thumos* by considering the dialogic elements of the *Republic*.[48] Four qualities are essential to understanding Platonic *thumos* as portrayed in the *Republic*—its association with war, its characteristic expression as anger, its ennobling tie to courage and justice, and its manliness.

On the trail of the elusive meaning and worth of justice, Socrates and his interlocutors turn to political philosophy, to imagining what a just city might look like. One of the principal interlocutors, Glaucon, rejects the first city for its extreme austerity, accepts the second city, a luxurious one filled with proliferating needs, including the demand for new lands, which opens the gates to war. War over new lands to provide the luxuries of spices, silks, and delicacies means the city will need soldiers. And good soldiers, Socrates says, must be spirited, or thumotic (*thumoeides*). Socially and politically speaking, it is our attachment to our desires that leads to violent war that in turn requires cultivating spirited soldiers. War provides the context for introducing *thumos*, and war remains crucial as metaphor and scene for thumotic phenomena. In Book 8, Socrates describes the second best city, the timocracy, ruled by "spirited and simpler men . . . naturally more directed to war than to peace . . . holding the wiles and stratagems of war in honor . . . spending all [their] time making war" (547e). The people who rule recommend themselves based not on their abilities as speakers but on their love of physical training and hunting, on their "abilities and exploits in warfare and warlike activities" (549a). When Socrates returns to evaluating which life is most just, he explicitly endows the thumotic part of the soul with the military aims of honor and victory: "Don't we of course say that the spirited part is always wholly set on mastery, victory and good reputation" (581a)?

---

48. For a discussion of methodology, see the essays in Charles Griswold, ed. *Platonic Writings, Platonic Readings* (New York: Routledge, 1988). For examples of this approach, see Peter Euben's "Plato's *Republic*: The Justice of Tragedy," in *The Tragedy of Political Theory: The Road Not Taken* (Princeton: Princeton University Press, 1990), and John Evan Seery, "Politics as Ironic Community: On the Themes of Descent and Return in Plato's *Republic*," *Political Theory* 16, no. 2 (1988): 229–56.

War accounts for the next key quality of *thumos*—its attachment to anger. While in the *Iliad* anger continually fills especially the male human characters' *thumoi*, it was not the case that the human *thumos* as such is angry. Even in Plato *thumos* is not simply equivalent to anger. Nevertheless, *thumos* could be accurately described as the angry part of the soul. In justifying the existence of *thumos* as distinct from both reason and bodily desires, Socrates introduces the "spirited part by which we get angry" (439e) and later too he calls *thumos* the "part with which [a person] gets angry" (580d). To illustrate the world of *thumos*, Socrates tells the odd story of Leontius who indulged his strong desire to gaze at freshly executed corpses, yet angrily chastised himself for his intemperance. Here anger "makes war against the appetites" (440a). In all humans, "when appetite forces someone contrary to rational calculation, he reproaches himself and gets angry with that in him that's doing the forcing" (440b). Plato never writes of *thumos* as the part by which we feel love or grief or joy. Even in the Leontius example, where shame seems to play a part, it is the angry concomitant of shame that identifies *thumos*.

A third feature of *thumos* is its intimations of virtue or morality. Anger at its most developed depends on a belief that an injustice has been committed against oneself. Angry people show great attention to getting their due. If a person believes that he is the victim of injustice, his *thumos* will be "boiling and angry, fighting for what he believes to be just" (440c). Similarly, the virtue courage is its special expertise: "And it is because of the spirited part, I suppose, that we call a single individual courageous, namely, when it preserves through pains and pleasures the declarations of reason about what is to be feared and what isn't" (442b–c). In fact, this part of the soul harks back to the way of life associated with Homeric society—the warrior ethic focused on honor and fame. When Plato is assigning desires to each part of the soul, he describes the thumotic part as "always wholly set on mastery, victory, and good reputation" (581a), so that it can be in general called "victory-loving and honor-loving" (581b). A person dominated by this part of the soul is contemptuous both of material or monetary desires and of intellectual pursuits, dismissing learning as "smoke and nonsense" (581d). As a kind of shorthand, Plato continues to talk about such a person as an honor-lover (581d–c). Even if dominated by the thumotic part, then, a person has a natural grasp of elementary justice and of honor's superiority in comparison with vulgarity of the bodily pleasure.

Finally, through courage, *thumos* is itself identified as a constituent of the gender phenomenon manliness. The Greek word for courage is actually *andreia,* derived from *andros,* "man," instead of from *anthropos,* "human being." Therefore, some commentators have taken *thumos* itself for a kind of manliness. For J. C. B. Gosling, the "spirited element is being treated as a tendency to be attracted to certain ideals of manhood."[49] This is best shown by Plato's account of the decline of a son living in a philosophic regime into a man dominated by his *thumos* (549c–550b). His mother complaining that his father is unmanly, the servants urging him to revenge wrongs done his father, the young man is driven to becoming a real man, something the regime ruled by philosophers had in some measure discouraged. I say "in some measure" because commentators disagree on the gender consequences of Platonic philosophy.[50] To judge Plato's treatment of gender issues, I think we should compare him to Homer. The life for women in the society Homer portrays was certainly harsh in its rape, enslavement, and the various forms of coerced sexual service of women. But scholars have noted the relative lack of misogyny in the poems and the generally kinder tone of the relations between men and women. Plato, on the contrary, proposes a radical, and for some commentators,[51] feminist, plan for establishing a ruling class whose male and female members are entirely equal in political and social affairs, yet at the same time, the *Republic* is punctuated by disparaging remarks about the abilities and character of women. From my reading of Homeric *thumos*, it appears that although in the epic men might disdain occupying the position of women in war, manliness has not yet been theorized as part of an emotional repertoire requiring disciplinary inculcation. While in the *Iliad thumos* is simply not equivalent to manliness; in the *Republic* it is. Plato, therefore, invents manliness as a psychological, not merely a material, practice. Of course, it should be remembered that Plato also provides a decisive challenge to fifth- and fourth-century Greek conceptions of manliness. No longer may the man devoted to fame, honor, and victory in agonistic public contests remain the paragon of mortal life. The new model, the philosopher attuned to the abstract forms, fearing political entanglements, clearly does not represent the fifth- or fourth-century Greek ideal of manhood. Nevertheless, Plato psychological innovations conspire with his criticism of contemporary manliness, understood by

49. J. C. B. Gosling, *Plato* (London: Routledge and Regan Paul, 1973), 43.

50. For these debates, see the good collection of articles in Nancy Tuana, ed., *Feminist Interpretations of Plato* (University Park: Pennsylvania State University Press, 1994) and Salkever, *Finding the Mean*, chapter 5.

51. See, for example, Gregory Vlastos, "Was Plato a Feminist?" in Tuana, *Feminist Interpretations of Plato.*

Greeks themselves as a matter of practice, by Plato as a matter of the soul, to deprive his political theorizing of an adequate account of political emotion.

## The Story of the Guardians

Any reading that merely extracts quotations and links them together as I have done is inadequate to understanding Platonic *thumos*. We have to understand something about the overall effect of the *Republic*, a whole out of which we have as yet extracted only some parts. Just as to understand Homeric *thumos* I had to account for its role in the story of Achilles, here I have to understand Platonic *thumos* through the story of the philosopher.

Alasdair MacIntyre has argued that in certain essentials Periclean Athens was still Homeric, that in its injunction to its citizens to be best and preeminent among others, in its belief that excellence and rewards always appear together, in its pursuit of wealth and power for the sake of honor and glory and in striving for freedom from the dictates of others, Athens and Homeric Greece were twins.[52] Plato was anxious about this conglomerate morality, which depended on unexamined traditions and conventional beliefs founded on a highly appealing mythic and narrative bedrock.[53] He was, moreover, anxious about the men who possessed political power in this world, those conceiving themselves in the mold of Agamemnon and Achilles, and about the men who threatened to possess this power, those like Cephalus and their tyrants. If the men of old had been identified with *thumos* and the new men with desire, then he would have to show the proper relation of these two impulses, to organize the soul and the polis at the same time. Thus Plato couched his critique of traditional morality and theology in a critique of Homer and his poetic descendants. And part of Plato's critique of the poets' influence was a critique of both who should rule and the place of the emotions and *thumos* in the soul. In the *Republic* Plato's criticism of poetry, and thereby of traditional morality, appears within his plan for the education of the thumotic men, the guardians of the ideal city, being at the same time the beginning of the education of the just soul.[54]

---

52. MacIntyre, *Whose Justice? Which Rationality?*, 48–50.

53. E. R. Dodds, in *The Greeks and the Irrational,* writes about an "inherited conglomerate" that was the fund of knowledge about the soul in Greece.

54. *The* Republic *of Plato*, trans. Allan Bloom (New York: Basic Books, 1968). Subsequent references to this translation will appear in parentheses. For the Greek I have consulted *Platonis Opera*, 5 vols., ed. John Burnet (Oxford: Clarendon Press, 1900–1907).

At the same time, Plato is concerned primarily not with the morality of the many, but with the way of life chosen by the elite. Three ways of life were possible for Plato, two—the life of desire and the life of honor—were readily available, while the third, the life of philosophy, was vigorously contested in Greek culture. Tempting in its insouciance and unconventionality to young men, but feared by the elders who executed Socrates, the practice of philosophy was still mysterious. And so in the *Republic* Plato undertakes above all to depict that way of life with new clarity. But of course there are three levels to the book: the definition of justice and the arguments for the contention that the just life and the philosophic life is best and happiest; the narrative of a city's founding, construction, and decline; and the story of the interlocutors as depicted by Plato, beginning from the meeting on the road from Piraeus to Athens, ending with the telling of the myth of Er. Given this structure, Plato's intention is one of the most obscure in political philosophy, hence the radically different interpretations of the *Republic*. Is this portrayal of a long pre-dinner conversation, for example, the first utopia, the greatest antidote to political idealism, or an artful construction of ironies, images, metaphors and puzzles seducing readers into practicing political philosophy on their own? This last approach probably can deal best with divergent elements of Plato's treatment of emotion. John Seery argues that Plato's use of imitative poetry, of myths, allegories, images and metaphors while criticizing imitative poetry and the non-rational appeal of such devices points to distinctive intent. Rather than teaching us to imitate his utopia or to give up on dreams of justice, Plato means to make us devotees of irony and questioning itself.[55] Similarly, J. Peter Euben contends that in the *Republic* Plato portrays two cities—one composed of the interlocutors, the other of best regime—and two modes of philosophy, Socrates' and Plato's—but withholds unconditional approval of either city or either practice of philosophy.[56] Instead he calls attention to a tragic choice between two modes and so the *Republic* is the last Greek tragedy.[57] As such it elicits our grief and a sense of loss, and so finally "passional knowledge."[58] In concluding in this way, Euben explicitly argues against Martha Nussbaum's characterization of the *Republic* as "anti-tragic" theater in which the style of

---

55. Seery, "Politics as Ironic Community."

56. J. Peter Euben, *The Tragedy of Political Theory: The Road Not Taken* (Princeton: Princeton University Press, 1990), 265–56.

57. Ibid., 269.

58. Ibid., 268.

dialogue may elicit intellectual curiosity from its readers, but which abjures emotional engagement.[59] For Nussbaum the *Republic* is single-mindedly devoted to convincing us that only philosophers, perfected in their intellects, divorced from the appetites and emotions, can serve as the standard for judging what is worthwhile in human life. Euben then sees the dialogue as emotionally evocative, while Nussbaum portrays it as emotionally numbing.

A good deal of evidence suggests a Plato hostile to the emotional yet there are glimmers of another view and the *Symposium*, but particularly the *Phaedrus,* show Plato steadily contemplating the role of emotive experience particularly eros and madness. In the *Republic* the story of the *kallipolis*, or beautiful city, is mostly the story of the education of the guardians. But their training to quell their appetites and their anger so as to better reach knowledge of forms, is offset by the humor, the anger, and the grief that some see as integral to the third level of this artful construction. If Plato's final intent was to make the reader ask questions, with me he has succeeded. It was the oddly narrow portrayal of the middle part of the soul that led me to ask: what is *thumos* really? So while I will say that the story of the guardians both shrinks and expands the meaning of *thumos* from its Homeric understanding, in a way that is detrimental to understanding political life, and particularly to women, in the end Plato opens up a discussion rather than closing one down.

At the level of the story of the construction of the best city, Plato has Socrates propose an alliance between thumotic and philosophic people in which the thumotic will recognize the superiority of the philosophic life and aid the philosophers in constraining the appetites. But in the plan for establishing the best city, this redirection of the thumotic calls for meticulous training and education to align reason and recalcitrant spirit. Beginning in early childhood, this training modeled on musical harmonization includes instruction in music and poetry, but also necessitates the creation of a new paradigm moral character through a detailed critique of Greek poetry, whose heroes transmit moral lessons. Both Homer and the impassioned oral performance of his poems are subjected to intense moral criticism.

The just person "harmonizes the three parts of himself like three limiting notes in a musical scale—high, low, middle" (443d). The musical metaphor is actually quite literal. In its early stages, a good education requires both physical exercise and music joined with poetry. Gymnastics

59. See Interlude 1 and chapter 5 of *The Fragility of Goodness.*

arouses the *thumos*, which the guardians will certainly still need. Music and poetry soften and cultivate the *thumos*, apparently not by acting directly on it but by arousing the philosophic part of one's nature.

This kind of training is required since, to be acceptable to polis life, the guardians must be "gentle to their own and cruel to enemies" (375c). In other words, *thumos,* by itself is incompatible with political life. It has no conception of any other person as anything but an enemy; no common ties are available to restrain it. The psychic quality that might integrate thumotic people into political life, gentleness, is explained by means of two analogies—the "noble dog" and philosophy. A dog's habit of greeting warmly those it knows and of growling at strangers shows us, according to Socrates, that *thumos* is compatible with gentleness. This added feature of the dog is called "truly philosophic"; gentleness arises from philosophy: "[A] human being too, if he is going to be gentle to his own and those known to him, must by nature be a philosopher and a lover of learning" (375b–c). Although *thumos* may be useful for fearsome soldiers, and soldiers are useful for securing political communities from outside enemies, it is philosophy, or at least something resembling philosophy, that can tame guardians for community life.

Knowing only this passage, one would expect Plato to develop the political role of gentleness into a full, philosophically psychological account of political life. Far from it; his critique of poetry challenges sympathetic emotions as dangerous for the just man. Gentleness cannot, then, be an emotion at all; that it arises from philosophy and not from the *thumos* already reveals its status as a nonemotion. Plato's discussion of poetry, replete as it is with descriptions of the emotional reactions of audience and actors or readers, manages to separate the question of emotion from the question of the *thumos*. It manages to tie *thumos* to one emotion only, anger, and thus to obscure the role of other human emotions.[60] The wild,

---

60. This point is noticed by A. W. Price in *Mental Conflict* (New York: Routledge, 1995), 68–70. One reason, he writes, for the *Republic's* narrow *thumos* is that Plato's purpose is political and metaphysical and not psychological—a point that would discourage someone from exploring the political ramifications. Here I want to understand how Plato's truly innovative psychology influences his politics. On the other hand, some may be dissuaded from connecting the psychology and the politics based on the view that Plato has "no logical or psychological arguments" for distinguishing *thumos* as a unique part of the soul, as Tony Penner contends in "Thought and Desire in Plato," in *Plato: A Collection of Critical Essays*, ed. Gregory Vlastos (Notre Dame: University of Notre Dame Press, 1978). Here I am not concerned with the cogency of Plato's arguments for the partitive soul, as many philosophical commentators are, but rather with the effects of what does not fit so well into the parts.

antipolitical *thumos* can only be tamed, according to Plato, by gentleness-inducing philosophy, by a rule from without, rather than by emotional resources from within.

Because the mere character endowments of the guardians cannot guarantee that they will act in the best interests of the city, Socrates, in book 3, argues that the city should provide a reformed education beginning with the tales heard in early childhood, those that "Hesiod and Homer told us, and the other poets too." Unfortunately, these tales mistakenly represent gods and humans: "They surely composed false tales for human beings and used to tell them and still do tell them" (377d). Just as the resemblance to the subject in a painting can be faulty, the poets have been mistaken in their representations of gods and heroes. Here the central concern for Plato is that gods should not be shown doing unjust and evil things so that only true justice can be said to rule the universe, but this stricture is directly tied to taming the *thumos*, that is, it is directly tied to the issue of anger. The first demand is that the gods must not be shown warring, battling, or scheming against each other, for this representation of strife would indulge the *thumos,* promoting irascibility in the guardians. Rather, they must learn that "no citizen was ever angry with another and that to be so is not holy" (378c). Here, clearly, anger appears as the dominant and, insofar as we know, the only emotion in the *thumos*, and as a thing easily exacerbated by tales of gods or men in conflict.

Socrates also demands that poets refrain from showing gods dispensing evil, changing form, or lying; Hades must not be described as the lamentable place of shades that appears in the *Iliad* and *Odyssey*. In addition to their being an attempt to clear the ground of the unjust deeds of divinities in preparation for the image of the good, these reforms are meant to plant courage in the guardians. Courage, in fact, emerges as the one virtue of the *thumos* (381a,e). In addition, endurance may be thought of as a kind of courage and it too is a product of a well-functioning *thumos*. Socrates approvingly cites an incident involving Odysseus (*Ody.* 20.17–18) as an example of *thumos* enduring (390d and 441b). Yet if we look at this section of the epic to see what Odysseus is spiritedly enduring, we find that he has just seen a group of his servant women slipping away to see their lovers, the suitors who by day are normally occupied with the insistent attempts to seduce Penelope. Odysseus's anger rises presumably at their disloyalty, but his reason reproaches his *thumos* to put off revenge until a more favorable moment. In the incident, *thumos* does not appear particularly exemplary; its endurance is simply the patience of a harsh and vengeful anger, more frightening for its cunning patience. Moreover, the endurance springs from the counsel of reason, not directly from the *thumos* itself. It is as though Plato tried hard to find one acceptable lesson from the two epics, and could remember only the one that cast such an appalling light on the work of *thumos*.

Other reforms of traditional poetry about gods and heroes are meant to restrain the appetites of the guardians. Moderation, or ruling the "pleasures of drink, sex, and eating" (389e), will be propagated by expunging passages such as "heavy with wine, with eyes of a dog and heart of a deer."[61] At the start of book 3, Socrates tells us that these expurgations of poetry will lead the guardians to honor gods and ancestors as well as not to "take lightly their friendship with each other" (386a). This explanation suggests, like the canine simile, that the problem of positive emotions cannot be avoided in political questions. Yet only this minimum will suggest itself to the scrupulous reader, since not very much results from this hint about the role of friendship. The only significant discussion of friendship appears in book 5, where it turns out that more than just cultural lessons and character endowments are needed to create a guardian soul. Only the elimination of private property and private families will eliminate faction and produce a "community of pleasure and griefs" (462b, 464d). Only ignorance about one's parentage will prevent fellow guardians from regarding one another as outsiders (462c). Instead, upon meeting, each will believe the other to be kin (463c). This is apparently what the few early references to friendship mean; friendship is established based on a lack of knowledge about the guardians' own children. We may suppose that this friendship enriches and is part of the purpose of their way of life. Socrates, after all, spends most of his time in animated discourse among friends, although not necessarily philosophic friends. But when we look at the best city itself, rather than at the setting of the conversation that constitutes the *Republic*, we get a picture of friendship only as the maintenance of alliance between the thumotic and the philosophic class. The decay of the best city begins from irregular intercourse allowed by mistakes in administrative calculations governing who may be sexually engaged.

Instead of an examination of either gentleness or friendship, Plato censures the imitative experience of emotion. After the critique of the description of the gods, heroes, and Hades, the difference between narrative and imitation in poetry is introduced. Socrates decries imitation of

---

61. This quotation from the *Iliad* 1.225 appears in *Republic* 389e.

bad men, but also anyone in psychic states other than the calm of steady reason. Neither slaves, nor cowards, nor drunks, nor madmen, nor blacksmiths nor rowers at work, nor animals nor rivers nor seas nor thunder should be imitated (396a–b). As little imitation as possible is appropriate for the good person, and only imitation of the steady and the prudent person unaffected by "diseases, loves, drink, or some other misfortune" (396d). The longest description of what the good person should not imitate is of a woman: "[E]ither a young woman or an older one, or one who's abusing her husband, or one who's striving with gods and boasting because she supposes herself to be happy, or one who's caught in the grip of misfortune, mourning, and wailing. And we'll be far from needing one who's sick, or in love or in labor" (395d–e).

As in the rest of the passage, it is not readily apparent how guardians would be harmed by imitating such women. Some of the actions include arrogance beyond one's status, others suggest extremes of emotion, pain, and pleasure. But the first line suggests imitation of any woman is deleterious. Generally, Plato wants imitation of a "decent," not a "slavish or shameful" man, but what makes a "decent" man? We will not know precisely what is meant by decent or why a woman cannot be imitated until he develops a fuller description of the soul and of the just person—until, that is, he returns to the question of poetry in book 10.

Reacting to this concerted attack on traditional poetry and to Socrates' severe restriction of the guardians' property and wealth, Adeimantus complains that Socrates has deprived the guardians of happiness. In response, Socrates tells him that happiness is for the whole of the city, not for individual members, but his response includes at the same time a deepened analysis of *thumos*, housed in a detailed description of a tripartite soul. This structural "psychology" should be understood as an image or myth, much like the image of the divided line, the noble lie of the three metallic classes, the myth of the cave, and others. This metaphorical understanding of psyche is the only way to speak of it. Although those active in modern experimental psychology and brain research have worked toward the scientific truth of the psyche (not the soul), the philosophic understanding of psyches and souls are more likely to reveal the self-creating nature of human understanding.

Unlike Homer's quasi-physical organ located in the midriff, entirely separate from *psuchē*, Platonic *thumos* is one of three parts comprising the soul. To define these parts, Socrates first distinguishes reason from appetite, the part that reasons from the part that desires. Since humans often desire something but try to curb that desire, there must exist at least two parts of the soul. With the desiring or appetitive part, the soul hungers, loves, thirsts, and is agitated by other desires. With the reasoning part the soul sometimes turns away from its desires. To establish that the soul has a third part Socrates recalls a psychological phenomenon with which Glaucon appears familiar, but that he equates with the desiring part of the soul. To dissuade Glaucon, Socrates first tells the brief story of Leontius, who surrendered to his desire to look at corpses yet berated himself in anger for his indulgence (439e). Such anger indicates that there must be an emotional (angry) part of the soul acting against desires in alliance with reason. This angry part is *thumoeides*, or the spirited part of the soul. Reason is distinct from desire because it often opposes desire; anger occurs when desires overcome reason. In the same way, Socrates may be hoping that the guardians will come to the aid of philosophers in the event of a coup by the money-loving class or will act as a threat to prevent such a coup.

In his second argument for why the spirited part of the soul differs from the desiring part, Socrates intends to make the guardians believe that they have as part of their endowment an intuition into justice. When a person perpetrates an injustice, he tells us, the person is less angry at the punishment he or she must suffer. When victims of injustice have spirited parts that "boil and become harsh and form an alliance with what is just" (440c), the perpetrator of injustice is less angry at the punishment he or she must suffer. The implicit point is that since the desires are the core of corruption, they never side with justice. If anger sides with justice, it must be distinct from desire.

Whereas in book 2, *thumos* appeared to be antipolitical, in these two arguments it acquires a semblance of principles. Socrates flatters thumotic men such as Glaucon and Adeimantus into an alliance with philosophers. But if thumotic men are roused when desires overcome reason—in the Leontius story, for example—what are they to do when reason is preeminent? It appears there is not much for them to do except to refrain from war making and anger, and allow reason to do its work. The obedience and secondary role that this view of thumotic people implies is reinforced by the reappearance of the dog analogy, whose meaning Socrates finally states bluntly: "[W]e put the auxiliaries in our city like dogs obedient to the rulers, who are like shepherds of a city" (440d). The spirited part, like the dog, chases straying sheep and then stays calmly on watch.

As I noted earlier, J. C. B. Gosling interprets Plato's *thumos* as an ideal of manliness whose purpose is to guard against the indulgence of lower desires for comfort or for money.[62] It is, however, a manliness slightly improved through education in literature and the arts. The improvement means that these men are more law-abiding. Plato's treatment of *thumos* does point to such an emphasis on the standard of manliness not only as a guard against the low desires but also as a guard against "womanliness." Gosling is blind to the problem with claiming that manliness for Plato is an "integral part of a human personality,"[63] so that the urgency to repress womanliness is unsaid and unseen.

If manliness is courage and disciplined behavior including self-control and law-abidingness, what womanliness is can be seen from Plato's final discussion of poetry in book 10, especially in the third and "greatest accusation against imitation" (605c): "When even the best of us hear Homer or any of the other tragic poets imitating one of the heroes in mourning and making an extended speech with lamentation, or if you like, singing and beating his breast, you know that we enjoy it and that we give ourselves over to following the imitation. ... But when personal sorrow comes to one of us, you are aware that, on the contrary, we pride ourselves if we are able to keep quiet and bear up, taking this to be the part of a man and what we then praised to be that of a woman" (605c–e).

Why should Plato's moral and theological claim that no good man can be unhappy, that there is no unmerited suffering, be tied to a suppression of emotion and to an equation of womanliness with emotion? The only way that this moral and theological claim is workable is to reduce one's genuine unhappiness at the events that make one potentially unhappy. Emotion, then, is revealed as the world's access to us and as our connection to the world. Through emotions we are tied to the lives and actions and feeling of others; by allowing ourselves to feel emotion we allow the fortunes or misfortunes of the world to affect us.[64] The association of woman and emotion has a long tradition, one of whose points of origin is in this text. By looking at this connection we can see what social and political effect the suppression of emotion has. In one sense, women were and are more tied to emotion insofar as they have responsibility for basic connections and life events—for the family, for birth, and for nursing the ill and old, for death. These very things Plato minimizes in the lives of the guardians; all guardians, male and female, must be manly. The provision of care or welfare becomes peripheral or auxiliary to politics.

---

62. Gosling, *Plato*, 41–51.
63. Ibid., 50.
64. On issues of fortune, ethics, and emotion, see Nussbaum, *Fragility of Goodness*.

The absence of awareness of emotional ties to the world leads finally to a concern for the individual soul above all else in the Platonic political philosophy—so much so that we cannot say whether a just man will have any concern for political life. This ultimate unconcern for the political is revealed in the elegiac ending to book 9 of the *Republic*. Glaucon asks whether the just person will be "willing to mind the political things" (592a). Socrates replies: "Yes, by the dog, he will in his own city, very much so. However, perhaps he won't in his fatherland unless some divine chance coincidentally comes to pass." Glaucon clarifies the import of this: "You mean he will in the city whose foundation we have now gone through, the one that has its place in speeches, since I don't suppose it exists anywhere on earth." Then Socrates concludes, "But in heaven, perhaps, a pattern is laid up for the man who wants to see and found a city within himself on the basis of what he sees. It doesn't make any difference whether it is or will be somewhere. For he would mind the things of this city alone, and of no other" (592a–b).

The most obvious challenge to emotion-hostile view of Plato is his treatment of eros or sexual love. In the *Republic*, eros is one the most persistent themes, from Cephalus's confession that he is free of its domination, to the portrayal of the tyrant as enslaved to his own eros. Yet Plato does not identify eros as an emotion or *pathos*, but rather as an element of the lower third part of the soul—the appetitive (439d). In general, along with other low desires there seems to be a disparagement of eros. And yet eros, particularly homosexual eros, provides a model of the pursuit of knowledge by the philosopher, a model that becomes much more prominent in the *Symposium* and the *Phaedrus*. We might wonder then why both the best and the worst of human souls are related so centrally to eros, and whether eros, ostensibly an appetite, must qualify what Plato has to say about emotion.

The schooling for philosophers of course consists of mathematics, geometry, astronomy, and dialectic, all meant to raise the soul from the world of becoming to that of eternal being, from the affective images of this world to the rational world of the forms. Freedom from this world should be the purpose not only of education but also of daily habits. To ensure that the philosopher's sleep remains free from vice-filled dreams, Plato recommends the following regimen:

> First, he rouses his rational part and feasts it on fair arguments and considerations, coming to an understanding with himself; second, he feeds the desiring part in such a way that it is neither

in want nor surfeited—in order that it will rest and not disturb
the best part by its joy or its pain, but rather leave that best
part alone pure and by itself . . . and third, he soothes the spirited
part in the same way and does not fall asleep with his spirit
aroused because it has indulged itself in anger against someone. When the man has silenced these two latter forms and the
set the third—the one in which prudent thinking comes to be
—in motion, and only then takes his rest, you know that in such
a state he most lays hold of the truth and at this time the sights
that are hostile to law show up least in his dreams. (571d–572a)

Thus the rational part best ensures virtue when the other two parts of
the soul are silenced. In fact, Plato calls eros a tyrant (573b) and erotic
desire the "most distant" from philosophy and argument (587b). The
tyrant, whose soul is the vice-ridden mirror image of the just philosophic
soul, has been implanted with the "drone" of eros.

Yet, in overt contradiction, Plato describes the philosopher's quest for
knowledge in this heated way: "[I]t is the nature of the real lover of learning to strive for what *is*; and he does not tarry by each of the many things
opined to *be* but goes forward and does not lose the keenness of his passionate love nor cease from it before he grasps the nature itself of each
thing which is . . . And once near it and coupled with what really is, having
begotten intelligence and truth, he knows and lives truly, is nourished
and so ceases from his labor pains, but not before" (490a–b).

Yet in the end I don't think we need to square his contradictory treatment of eros. We know there is more to explore in later books. But the
treatment opens onto new territory. By inventing the tripartite description, Plato creates an apparent order out of disorder in the soul, but then
he disrupts the system by introducing desires for each part of the soul, so
that desires spill over their apparent lower tier home and by analogizing
philosophy on eros. At one level Plato does provide memorable characters
and narrative situations, on the other hand he invents a whole area of
philosophical investigation—political psychology—and so prompts us
to question. Indeed, it is the oddity of Plato's characterization of *thumos*
or the thumotic part in particular that prompts the specific research for
this book.

The great Socratic/Platonic innovation in Greek culture was the advice to
care for the soul, to doctor of the soul, to harmonize it, to make it just by
altering its desires. But this aim to displace the desires for money, power,

and honor with the desire for true knowledge was at the same time to be a source of political participation. In the *Gorgias* Socrates claims that he practices the true art of politics or true statesmanship; in the *Symposium* Socrates is portrayed both as given to bouts of sudden contemplative states and to endless conversations with fellow citizens. We end with an ambivalence or an impasse between the philosophical and the political, between the advocacy for the life without *eris* or strife and the discovery that such a life depends on political community.

Plato's initial discussion of *thumos* depicts thumotic people as savage and antipolitical, as well as antiphilosophical. Such people can understand others only as enemies. They cannot desist from imposing themselves on and over others. Both politics and philosophy, however, require yielding to the equal claims of at least some others. In argumentation and philosophical discussion as in politics, we must consider the claims of others. Plato planned to bring thumotic men into the community by plying them with compliments that they really had intuitions into justice, and were capable of resisting vulgar desires, but more importantly by a poetic reeducation. This reeducation would at the same time reduce the influence of disturbing emotions and concentrate the *thumos* on its one activity, feeling anger against the desires. Plato hardly mentions the possibility of emotions other than anger in the *thumos*. In concentrating on the bad effects of poetry he implicitly accepts the connection of poetry, *thumos*, and other emotions. Nevertheless, Plato's corrections of poetry serve to expunge sympathetic emotion. Apparently, there is no good model of emotional response other than that of the thumotic person in civil defense and war. Poetry cannot educate the emotions; on the contrary, it fuels a rage of indiscriminate desires and emotions.

Returning once again to my emotion terminology, I can summarize some of the differences between Homer and Plato. In the *Republic*, Plato gives us the one important *emotion paradigm scenario*—of anger—and a desire paradigm scenario—of eros or sexual love. Although eros is primarily an appetite for Plato, we might read it as partly an emotion. Since *thumos* is restricted almost exclusively to anger, the thumotic man or the warrior-guardian becomes the character in the paradigm scenario of anger. The philosopher-guardian in his or her search for knowledge of the good vies with the tyrant sunk into the slavery of desire as the exemplary character in the scenario of eros. The *emotional repertoire* of the good person ought to be oriented around these two emotions, but includes the subsidiary emotion of shame, whose work is to instigate anger at the desires. Other emotions especially grief and pity are to be avoided as much as possible. Friendship and fellow-feeling are only briefly mentioned in book 5. The *governing emotion scenario*, the key representation of what it means to experience emotion, is defined outside of *thumos*. Sitting in the middle of the soul between reason and appetites, *thumos* appears to be the seat of the emotions, but in fact no longer functions as the *governing paradigm scenario of emotion* generally, but of anger only. As we have seen in the later books, Plato portrays the experience of emotion as disturbance particularly associated with women.

Finally, although in book 8 Plato connects regimes to the typical psychological make-up of the ruling elites, he emphasizes the changes in desire rather than in the emotions. The best regime, ruled by philosophers and their desire for wisdom, declines into the timocracy ruled by the desire for honor, and then into oligarchy ruled by the desire for wealth. Desires, not emotive relations, are crucial. Certainly, Plato has nothing near a theory of political emotion, but he could, without too much distortion, be said to identify the direction in which speculation on politics and emotion must begin. T. M. Robinson writes that the political analogy of the state and the soul "seems to account for the birth of the notion of the 'spirited element.'"[65] While this comment is meant to depreciate the independence of the *Republic*'s psychology, it also inadvertently suggests the core of Plato's originality. By raising the stature of *thumos*, whatever its new obscurities, Plato opens the question of politics and emotion. If, for the sake of argument, we could identify a *governing scenario of political emotion* it would be that of the philosopher-ruler, since in effect only the rulers participate in "politics" as understood in the *Republic*.

Platonic *thumos* on this account remains innovative in its integration into a unified soul and in its tie to politics. Plato assimilates the Homeric hero to the *kallipolis*, not losing the appeal this hero has for Glaucon and Adeimantus, to show them that such opposites can truly be reconciled. In so doing he fixes a character that was arguably not even in the *Iliad* itself. Furthermore, in this fixing he confines *thumos* to anger without the variety of possible emotional expressions that still appeared in the *Iliad*. Plato initiates the question of the relationship between emotion and politics, even if the question is posed more broadly and answered quite differently by Aristotle.

---

65. Robinson, *Plato's Psychology*, 45.

# 3

# Varieties of Aristotelian *Thumos*

> Emotions are considered no less a part of human beings than reasoning is.
>
> —Aristotle, *Nicomachean Ethics*

Traditionally, Aristotle has been seen as a rationalist, albeit of the classical, not modern, variety. This view is not without merit or evidence. Near the beginning of the *Ethics*, Aristotle warns that the young are ill suited for this discussion of how to live one's life because they are typically driven by emotion (*NE* 1095a5). At the start of the *Rhetoric*, he notes that previous writers of rhetoric handbooks have neglected argumentation, teaching instead mere appeals to emotion (*Rhet.* 1354a15–17). Sometimes Aristotle employs an uncomplimentary distinction between living according to reason and living according to emotion (*NE* 1169a5). Moreover, he is known to have famously said that what distinguishes humans from animals and plants is *logos*, speech or reason, so that our characteristic work is the "activity of the soul that expresses reason ... or obeys reason" (*NE* 1098a8). Yet hidden within the proponent of reason has always been the friend of emotion.

The theme of emotion threads its way through most of the crucial elements of Aristotelian moral and political philosophy. Being ethically good means practicing virtues that are dispositions not only to act but to feel in certain ways. So practicing the virtue of gentleness does not require suppressing anger, but rather supports feeling anger for the right reason, in the right manner, at the right time. Insofar as the purpose of politics is to live well—that is, to practice the virtues—and the aim of the politician is to make citizens good, political persuasion should appeal to both reason and emotion. So even though Aristotle criticizes the appeal to emotion, he does not reject *all* such appeals, but instead carefully examines publicly relevant emotions in book 2 of the *Rhetoric*. Perhaps his most distinctive difference from Plato, displayed in the *Poetics*, is his appreciation of how tragedy educates the emotions. The *katharsis* of pity and fear amounts not to their negation, as had long been thought, but to their cultivation.

Aristotle's specifically political psychology shows its origins in the Platonic discovery of political psychology itself. Near the conclusion of the *Republic*, the reader is taken on a tour of regimes descending from the perfection of the best regime. The transformations of timocratization, democratization, and tyrannization are due to decline of the hegemony of reason in the souls of the ruling class's members, who appear to set the temperament for the whole community. In timocracy, *thumos* dominates the soul, while in democracy and tyranny appetites progressively gain more freedom. In the *Republic*, then, we are treated to the first presentation of the interplay between psychology and political regimes in a philosopher for whom the true art of politics is the care of the soul.

Rather than remaining Plato's disciple in his work on political psychology, Aristotle moves beyond Plato. In his analysis of regimes, rather than focusing on the ruling class he devotes more attention to both the interplay of classes in the city and the nature of citizenship as such. As for the individual soul affected by the regime, the description of ethical action delineates a life possible for anyone brought up in a fine regime, not just the arduous and limited life of a philosopher. His treatment of *thumos* and emotion, like his treatment of class and political change, reveal a political philosophy useful both for political analysis and for normative theorizing.

A survey of the *Rhetoric, De Anima, Eudemian* and *Nicomachean Ethics,* and *Politics* reveals that Aristotle uses *thumos* in three different ways: as one word for the emotion anger; as the psychic drive of the traditional, aggressive, impetuous character; and as a name for one of the soul's capacities, the capacity to feel emotions in general. Since the first two uses correspond most closely with Plato's usage, these have been mistaken as Aristotle's only meanings of *thumos*. But I shall argue that it is the third use that, by partially returning to the Homeric sense, moves beyond the Platonic to a new account of the role of emotion in political life.

## *Thumos* as Anger

Aristotle's simplest use of *thumos* designates the name for one emotion or *pathos*, anger, without any immediate interpretation of anger's causes or consequences and without any association with a way of life. Looking at this usage shows that translators and commentators are sometimes right when they understand *thumos* as anger. In addition, it displays some important traits of Aristotelian emotion in general. This simple use most obviously occurs in several short lists of emotions employed as examples of *pathē*. Alongside *thumos*, one list includes gentleness, fear, pity, joy, love, hate (*DA* 403a16–17); another fear, shame, appetite (*EE* 1220b11–12).[1] Thus *thumos* can initially be understood as just one among a variety of *pathē*. Although *pathos* is often translated as "emotion," it means more than what we today understand to be emotion; it signifies any feeling that affects one for good or ill. The difference between emotion and other *pathē* can be understood from *epithumia*, the only nonemotional example of a *pathos* that Aristotle provides. *Epithumia* are desires for food, drink, or sexual pleasure. Emotions are also partly desires, but less for any particular objects than for more-complex social situations. At the moment I would like to leave the explication of the nature of these desires for the end of the chapter. It is clear that *thumos* occurs in passages that discuss the desire not for an object but for these complex situations. So although *thumos* might be understood as a *pathos*, it is a *pathos* in a different sense from that of desires of the body.

*Thumos* is not the only word for anger; *orgē* appears frequently as an example of the same emotion. In the *Rhetoric*, *pathē* generally are "all those affections which cause men to change their opinion in regard to their judgements, and are accompanied by pleasure and pain; such are anger [*orgē*], pity, fear" (*Rhet.* 1378a21–22).[2] The first of the emotions

---

1. *De Anima* and *Eudemian Ethics* in *The Complete Works of Aristotle: The Revised Oxford Translation*, ed. Jonathan Barnes (Princeton: Princeton University Press, 1984). For the Greek I have consulted *De Anima*, ed. David Ross (Oxford: Oxford University Press, 1956), and *Eudemian Ethics*, trans. H. Rackham (Cambridge, Mass.: Loeb Classical Library, 1935).

2. *Rhetoric* in *The Collected Works of Aristotle*; the Greek text in *The "Art" of Rhetoric*, trans. John Henry Freese (Cambridge, Mass.: Loeb Classical Library, 1926).

Aristotle analyzes is anger, but, despite his earlier announcement that he would deal with *thumos* when he turned to emotions (*Rhet.* 1373b35–36), he uses *orgē* rather than *thumos* (*Rhet.* 1373b35–36). In this, the most sustained description of anger in the Aristotelian corpus, he begins the discussion with *orgē*, but also feels free occasionally to use *thumos*. Yet, although *orgē*, like *thumos*, sometimes appears as an example of a *pathos*, the two words never occur together in such lists, indicating that the words are synonyms.

*Thumos* is again treated as one *pathos* in the *Nicomachean Ethics's* discussion of responsibility: "When the injury is inflicted in full knowledge but without previous deliberation, it is an unjust act, for example, any act due to anger [*thumos*] or to any other unavoidable or natural emotion to which human beings are subject" (*NE* 1135b20–25).[3] Such acts, done out of *thumos,* are less blameworthy than identical acts on the basis of a decision or *prohairesis.*[4] To choose to injure someone is deliberately to desire injustice, and so to be unjust and wicked. To injure someone out of anger signals one has a propensity for injustice, but does not actually amount to being unjust. Emotions are voluntary, but they lack the searching reflection implied by decision (*NE* 1111a24–b4).

More extended discussions of the *pathos* anger appear in the treatment of the virtue of gentleness, and later of moral weakness or incontinence. The discussion of gentleness (*praotēs*), the virtue in relation to anger, is more cursory in the *Eudemian Ethics* than in the *Nicomachean,* and the *EE* version differs from the later *NE* in one more important respect. In the *Eudemian Ethics, thumos* is used for anger: "For we see that the gentle is concerned with the pain that arises from anger [*thumos*], being characterized by a certain attitude to this" (*EE* 1231b6–7). The *NE* passage begins differently and uses *orgē* for anger: "Gentleness is the mean in feelings of anger [*orgē*]" (*NE* 1125b27). When *thumos* is used in the *NE* passage, it describes the long-simmering anger that sullen people repress until they relieve themselves with revenge.

On the other hand, in the *NE* 7 discussion of moral weakness, *thumos,*

---

3. *Nicomachean Ethics*, trans. Martin Ostwald (New York: Macmillan, 1962); the Greek text in *Nicomachean Ethics*, trans. H. Rackham (Cambridge, Mass.: Loeb Classical Library, 1939). Although Terence Irwin's translation of the *Ethics* is more consistent in its rendering of key terms, it is also less fluid. Therefore, I have opted to rely on Ostwald, but to indicate the Greek as necessary.

4. Several translations have been advanced for this difficult Greek term. "Choice," formerly the common rendering, has yielded to "deliberated or deliberate choice," and "decision," which I use as the most economical. See Irwin's glossary in his translation of the *Nicomachean Ethics* (Indianapolis: Hackett, 1985).

not *orgē*, is used and *thumos* quite clearly designates anger. Aristotle speaks at some length about the many ways in which a person can know that some action is unethical or detrimental to flourishing, but still do it. This yielding to one's desires or pleasures, desires that one nevertheless knows to be wrong, or at least exercised in the wrong manner (*NE* 1148a10), he calls moral weakness. A person may give in to inappropriate desires for certain foods or drinks, or for honor and wealth, and even for love of one's children, although succumbing to bodily desires is moral weakness proper. Giving in to a desire for goods such as money, honor, and to emotions like love and anger is a special case of moral weakness.

In section 6 where he details moral weakness in anger, Aristotle chiefly wants to show why this second type of moral weakness is less blameworthy than moral weakness in bodily desires. For understanding emotion, the first reason for this superiority is the most interesting and also indicates that by *thumos* he means one *pathos*. "[*Thumos*] seems to listen to reason but hear wrong, like hasty servants, who run off before they have heard everything their master tells them, and fail to do what they were ordered.... In the same way, the heat and swiftness of its nature makes anger hear but not listen to an order, before rushing off to take revenge. For reason and imagination indicate an insult or slight has been received, and anger ... simply flares up at once" (*NE* 1149a26–34). That Aristotle refers to a situation involving an insult, the reactive desire to fight, the taking of revenge, proves he is speaking about anger, for anger as described in the *Rhetoric* contains insult and revenge as definitive elements (*Rhet.* 1378a31–33). But anger is not the only emotion in which a person can be morally weak. Love also can be felt in excess and lead to inappropriate actions. Both emotions sometimes hear reason but do not listen. People morally weak in certain emotions are partially rational and partially arational in terms of that emotion. They have the correct perceptual belief that they have been wronged or that another person is lovable, but they fail to consider (or fail to have learned) whether this person, in this circumstance, requires their anger or love in this manner, to this degree.

Thus *thumos* often means anger, one *pathos* or one mental/bodily event that affects a person, differing from bodily desires in its object, voluntary but not chosen, in moral weakness only partially harmonized with reason. Yet ultimately anger is not simply anger. Although anger may have a similar structure, different people get angry at different things and different cultures will tend to promote anger at some things and not others. For the Greeks, *thumos* inevitably harked back to the epic tradition and the life of the angry warrior. So *thumos* as anger cannot fail to be enmeshed in cultural interpretations of emotion and sometimes to mean a full disposition of character as in Aristotle's second usage of *thumos*.

## *Thumos* as Spiritedness

This second manner in which Aristotle uses *thumos* and its derivative adjectives is most akin to the Platonic association of *thumos* with anger and aggression and to the way in which the Homeric warrior frequently but not, as we saw, exclusively uses his *thumos*. In this conception, *thumos* is more like a universal drive toward the particular goods of honor and freedom from tyranny, and with specific social consequences of both a continuity and tension between the early aristocratic and later polis way of life. I shall call this conception spiritedness or the martial *thumos*.

As I noted in the previous chapter, Plato's version of martial *thumos* is governed by anger. A similar idea appears in the *Rhetoric* where *thumos* is understood as a certain kind of ruling anger, not simply as a synonym for *orgē* or anger, but as an interpretation of anger. Take Aristotle's two references to the same Homeric description of anger as "far sweeter than dripping honey" (*Rhet.* 1370b11; 1378b4–5). This line appears in Achilles' conversation with his mother, Thetis, in which he decides to return to battle in order to avenge Patrocles. It is Aristotle who claims that this is a description of *thumos*, whereas Homer makes reference to a *cholos*, meaning gall or bitter anger. The anger to which he refers is the one at the violation of his honor by Agamemnon, not the anger used in the fury of battle. So one anger suppresses another until the death of his companion, Patrocles.

Martial anger typically leads to acts of revenge or retribution, leaving its mark on Aristotle's conception of anger in general: "*Thumos* and *orgē* are the causes of acts of revenge" (*Rhet.* 1369b10–11). Using *orgē* for anger in book 2's excursus on emotions, he defines it as composed of a desire (*orexis*) for revenge (*timorias*) accompanied by a feeling of pain due to a slight or insult (*Rhet.* 1378a32). In the same paragraph is the second mention of the Homeric passage about the pleasure of anger. Earlier, he had mentioned revenge or the prospect of it as one kind of pleasure (*Rhet.* 1370b30–32).

Typically, *thumos* is found in the characters of young, impetuous men. Such men are "passionate [*thumikoi*], hot-tempered, and carried away by impulse and unable to control their passion [*thumos*]" (*Rhet.* 1389a9–10), as well as ambitious for honor, but especially for victory. This picture of the young is in contrast to the surprisingly irreverent picture of the old. In Aristotle's view, the old are hesitant, malicious, calculating in love and hate and in *thumos* they are feeble (*Rhet.* 1390a10–11). But the character of the middle-aged man is a mean between the characters of the young and old. "[I]n regard to passion [*thumos*] and desire [*epithumia*] ... their self-control is combined with courage, their courage with self-control" (*Rhet.* 1390b1–2).

In the *Politics, thumos* occurs in seven passages, the longest of which I will treat in detail in the following chapter. In five of the remaining passages *thumos* refers to the martial *thumos* in its polis guise. Here recall the problem of assimilating the Homeric warrior ideal into the city-state. Such a warrior, devoted to the pursuit of honor and glory in one-on-one combat, and to the founding of a family line, was ill adapted to the compromise and cooperation necessary for polis life. Even so the Greek polis was expert at channeling aristocratic competition into the pursuit of ruling, of athletic contest, and of military victory in the name of the city. Athens, in Thucydides' eyes, transformed the individual pursuit of martial heroism into the collective pursuit of glory. Spiritedness aptly names the psychological propensity needed for success in the period of both Homer's *Iliad* and the city-state.

This kind of spiritedness is what Aristotle has in mind when he counsels that the *Republic* was mistaken to require the same people to rule always, since the spirited (*thumoeides*) and warlike (*polemikois*) men are likely to claim their own turn at ruling (*Pol.* 1264b8–9). He similarly warns that insolent tyrants will stir up the *thumoi* (pl.) of their subjects (*Pol.* 1312b29), causing their own downfall. A statesman should be concerned about the presence of *thumos* even in agricultural laborers; in the ideal system such workers should be slaves, drawn from different tribes, and lacking a spirited character. Their lack of spiritedness, meaning the lack of a strong desire for escape from slavery and tyranny, will ensure their obedience.

The presence of *thumos* is both advantageous and perilous not only in the ruled but also in rulers. On this account, *thumos* suggests both a desire for independence and self-government and the desire to become a tyrant oneself: "One who asks law to rule, therefore, is held to be asking god and intellect [*nous*] alone to rule, while one who asks man adds the beast. Appetite [*epithumia*] is a thing of this sort; and spiritedness [*thumos*] perverts rulers and the best men. Hence law is intellect without desire [*orexis*]" (*Pol.* 1287a28–32). This passage suggests to Carnes Lord that spiritedness is a thing that must be tamed.

The most prominent appearance of the martial *thumos* is in Aristotle's discussion of qualities mistaken for the virtue of courage (*andreia*). There, using several quotations from the *Iliad*, he portrays *thumos* as a fit of temper, as in a wounded animal, which attacks all the more ferociously. But neither pain nor anger is the right motivation for the excellence of courage. Instead, since nobility is the end of virtue, courageous acts must be done for the sake of being a noble person who performs noble acts. Such a purpose and the activity of deciding when added to *thumos* make courage.

A decision is the conclusion of a deliberation (*NE* 1113a10) concerned with means in each circumstance to reach a person's end or *telos*. Choosing with reference to an end means choosing with reference to a certain way of life, the political or philosophical, for example. This is crucial for seeing how Aristotle in the *Ethics* is working on the received notion of *thumos*. He first acknowledges the prevalence of its presence in the Greek cultural bible, the *Iliad*, and the widespread interpretation of it as the psychic quality indispensable for martial excellence. His criticism is not only that it is ungoverned by reason, but more specifically that it is ungoverned by a sense of a noble way of life: "[D]eath and wounds will be painful for a courageous man and he will suffer them unwillingly, but he will endure them because it is noble to do so or base to do otherwise" (*NE* 1117b7–9). There is good indication that in seventh- and sixth-century Greece the expression of anger and martial aggression was governed by a sense of a way of life whose exemplar was the *agathos*, or good man, as A. W. H. Adkins has described it.[5] Aristotle's claim that *thumos* was not governed by a sense of a way of life reveals that the Homeric warrior way of life differs from Aristotle's preferred way of life precisely on the role of the emotions, or on how they are integrated into the soul.

We can see how Aristotle's views make sense by looking at Homeric psychic management. In the *Iliad*, a character sometimes speaks to his *thumos* as though speaking to another person. While speaking, a character can beat down the anger or other emotion in his or her *thumos* but he or she does not yet understand how emotional habits might be changed uncoercively. The way of life of the *agathos* was imperfectly related to psychic habits, so that it could not be an adequate source of educating the emotions. The imperfect relation was due mainly to the autonomy of various psychic/organic parts inside the Homeric person. Aristotle recognizes that emotions are no less a part of our humanness than reason, a

5. See Chapter 2, page 40 above.

part of a unified core and not a part necessarily at odds with some other part of us. He is still saddled with many of the old associations with *thumos*, but in the midst of the conventional, he begins to construct the tools for an alternative view of *thumos* and of the education of the emotions.[6]

So *thumos* appears as both a synonym for the *pathos* anger and as a name for the characteristic feature of a particularly young man devoted to the acquisition of glory through martial combat. The two uses are easily connected since combat would seem to require a steady dose of anger. Putting the two uses together provides us with a picture of a man prone to anger at insults to his honor, where honor signifies public recognition, material rewards, and independence or self-reliance. Commentators, as I mentioned in the Introduction, see this *thumos* as a universal drive or at least as a tendency in the better examples of human beings. So much so, that Francis Fukuyama, adopting these commentators' interpretations, argues that were liberal democracy to become the universal form of government, the boredom of its peace and order would drive certain men to desire and provoke war.[7] This contention is drawn from the view that three things motivate humans in politics—reason, material desire, and *thumos* understood as a desire for recognition. But are these really all that motivates humans? Can Aristotle be used to support the case for only three motivations? I think not. Aristotle offers a compelling alternative derived from an innovative third use of *thumos*.

## *Thumos* in a Transformed Soul

Aristotle's third and most innovative use of *thumos* is best understood through his reimagination of the *psuchē,* or soul. The first time Aristotle comments on the *psuchē* in the *Nicomachean Ethics* he is considering the question of a distinctive human *ergon*, characteristic work or function (*NE* 1097b21ff.). Such a function must be based on a distinctive aspect of the human soul, one that plant and animal souls do not share. The work or function of metabolism is common to humans, animals, and plants;

---

6. See Gerald Mara, "The Near Made Far Away: The Role of Cultural Criticism in Arisototle's Political Theory," *Political Theory* 23 (1995): 280–303.

7. Francis Fukuyama, *The End of History and the Last Man* (New York: Free Press, 1992), 330. He consoles us with the idea that certain other pursuits such as capitalist entrepenuership and running for and serving in political office offer a semblance of thumotic activity.

sense perception can be found in both animals and humans. But the activity of the rational element is uniquely human. It is true that both the metabolic and the perceiving part of the human soul are subject to ethical influence.[8] But Aristotelian practical philosophy elaborates the work of the soul's rational element.

This rational element itself he is willing to divide into two parts: one part obeys reason and the other "possesses and conceives reason" (*NE* 1098a4). A little later, he repeats this formulation: "If it is correct to say that the appetitive part, too, has reason, it follows that the rational element of the soul has two subdivisions: the one possesses reason in the strict sense, contained within itself, and the other possesses reason in the sense that it listens to reason as one would listen to a father" (*NE* 1103a1–4). Stated somewhat differently, the second part "complies with reason and accepts its leadership; it possesses reason in the way we say it is reasonable to accept the advice of a father and of friends" (*NE* 1102b31–33). So the "rational principle," or *logos,* should be conceived in two ways, as reason in the strict sense and as desires and emotions functioning with reason. Taking what is rational in this liberal manner allows us to better understand Aristotle's formulation of the proper function of the human as "activity of the soul in conformity with a rational principle or at least not without it" (*NE* 1098a7). The proper function of the human being is not pure reason, but a variety of soul activities infused with, "in conformity with," and "at least not without" reason, the exact relationship waiting to be worked out.

Yet Aristotle will often write as though the soul contains two separate parts—the *logon,* rational, and the *alogon,* arational (*NE* 1102a28, 1139a4; *Pol.* 1333a17, 1334b18–19). In fact, the bipartition of the soul is considered to be Aristotle's innovation.[9] Are the *logon* and *alogon* both part of one rational element? Or are there actually four parts, the nutritive, the desirative, the calculative, and the scientific, as it appears from *NE* 1144a9? The bipartite formulation is most likely a rhetorical device. It comes, after all, from the less technical discussions, or the exoteric

    8. Sibyl Schwarzenbach, in "A Political Reading of the Reproductive Soul in Aristotle," *History of Philosophy Quarterly* 9, no. 3 (1992), argues that Aristotle really believed that the *threpikon* had its own specifically human excellences, despite his assertion in *NE* 1.13 that this part has "no natural share in human excellence or virtue." (See also *NE* 1144a9–10: "the nutritive does not have a virtue . . . since it does not play any decision to act or not to act.")
    9. W. W. Fortenbaugh, *Aristotle on Emotion* (London: Duckworth, 1975), 31; P. A. Vander Waerdt, "The Peripatetic Interpretation of Plato's Tripartite Psychology," *Greek, Roman, and Byzantine Studies* 26 (Autumn 1985): 283–302.

writings (*NE* 1102a26), designed to provide some cursory knowledge of soul. The statesman and the student of politics (*to politikos*) must study the soul only in so much detail as he needs for his aim to make the citizens good and law-abiding (*NE* 1102a17–26). But since the state of goodness is a certain kind of goodness, one that Aristotle has argued is the "activity of the soul in conformity with perfect virtue" (*NE* 1102a5), the activities of the soul and how they may accord with virtue must be studied. It is to highlight the most important aspects of the soul for the purposes of good citizenship that Aristotle employs the rhetorical division of *logon* and *alogon*.

For an idea of the relation of the two he gives us a proposition as a question: "Whether these two elements are separate, like the parts of the body or any other divisible thing, or whether they are only logically separable though in reality indivisible, as convex and concave are in the circumference of a circle, is irrelevant for our present purposes" (*NE* 1102a29–32).

The indivisibility of the circle metaphor returns when he describes the rational element with two parts, one having reason, the other obeying reason. So the use of the *logon-alogon* division simplifies appreciation of the working of the soul for students of politics, especially in its correspondence to the three ways of life—of pleasure, of politics, and of philosophy —he wants his readers to consider and weigh. A life devoted to pleasure exercises only the lowest parts of the *alogon*, while a life devoted to philosophy uses only the *logon*. But the political life appears as the harmonizer of the *logon* and the *alogon*. But just as these three ways of life become entangled in the best way of life,[10] so in the most complete characterization of the structure of the soul, *alogon* and *logon* will have a close intimacy.

Despite Aristotle's warning about too much detail in the study of psychology for politics, for philosophy it is necessary to explore how he consistently offers a practical philosophy that depends on a close relation between the rational and arational. But before proceeding with the *Nicomachean Ethics* and the *Politics*, we may profit from a look at the *De Anima*, which offers a more detailed discussion of the structure of the soul. There Aristotle becomes more guarded about using the terminology

---

10. I am obviously on the side of the inclusivists, that is those who believe that pleasure, moral virtue, political participation on at least a moderate level, and contemplation all go into making up the best life. For a review of the issue see J. L. Ackrill, "Aristotle on *Eudaimonia*," in *Essays on Aristotle's Ethics*, ed. Amelie Oksenberg Rorty (Berkeley and Los Angeles: University of California Press, 1980); Aristide Tessitore, *Reading Aristotle's Ethics: Virtue, Rhetoric, and Political Philosophy* (Albany: State University of New York Press, 1996).

of parts and divisions and so leads us to a better understanding of the relation of the two parts of the rational element, of the interplay of reason, desire, and emotion.

The soul encompasses a great variety of activities. To understand them we must divide them, yet the division, according to Aristotle, necessarily distorts. "For in a sense there is an infinity of parts: it is not enough to distinguish, with some thinkers, the calculative, the passionate [*thumikon*], and the appetitive [*epithumikon*], or with others the rational and the irrational; for if we take the dividing lines followed by these thinkers we shall find parts far more distinctly separated from one another than these, namely those we have just mentioned: the nutritive, . . . the sensitive, . . . the imaginative and lastly the desirative [*oretikon*]" (*DA* 432a24–27).[11] Notice that the tripartite division he mentions at the start of the passage is Plato's, while the second is his in the *Ethics*. The parts in either the tripartite or the bipartite are less different from one another than from nutritive, sensitive, imaginative, and desirative parts. Neither tripartism nor bipartism satisfies as an accurate account of the soul; they fail particularly on the question of what moves the soul.

For Plato, each part has its own desire, while for Aristotle the partitive idea of the soul breaks down on the question of desire. It is especially absurd to break up desirative activity since it tends to appear throughout the soul (*DA* 432b5). "Those who distinguish parts in the soul . . . find themselves with a large number of parts, a nutritive, a sensitive, an intellective, a deliberative, and now an desirative; for these are more different from one another than [from] the faculties of desire and passion" (*DA* 433b1–4). Using only the terminology of "parts" does not enable us to account for the interaction of these supposedly separate parts; it misses the fluidity of the soul's operations depending on some unified movement.

Instead of "part" (*meros*), Aristotle favors "faculty" or "capacity" (*dunamis*) as the word to describe the various operations of the soul. Instead of accepting the clearly separate activity of soul-parts, he portrays desire as the unifying element responsible for all movement, both action and thought. Capacities are themselves secondary sources of movement in something other than itself or in itself "qua other" (*Meta.* 1019a15–1020a5). Among the capacities in the human soul are metabolism or the nutritive, sensory, locomotive, imaginative or perceptual, rational, and the desirative. The emphasis on capacity instead of parts reveals how

11. Translations are from *The Complete Works of Aristotle,* except for two words: *epithumikon* is rendered as "appetitive," while *oretikon* is rendered as "desirative." The reverse is true in the Oxford translation.

Aristotle is interested not in the architectonic stasis of the soul, but in the interaction and reciprocal influences of the various potential movements grouped into the various capacities.[12]

Such interaction is evident in the universal role of the capacity of desire. "Orexis," or desire, is probably a word coined by Aristotle to answer the question of how a human soul moves the human person.[13] Because desire is the originator of all movement, even thought or *dianoia* requires desire in the form of *boulēsis* (*DA* 433a21–24). Along with intellect, *orexis* generally must be present along with intellect for *praxis* or action to occur.[14]

For understanding the topic of *thumos*, our interest is piqued when we learn that there are three species of *orexis* (desire)—*epithumia* (appetite), *thumos*, *boulēsis* (wish). This use of *thumos*, as a subcapacity of desire governing a particular class of desires, is found in the *De Anima* at 414a1–2, 432a24–25, 432b5–6, 4334–35),[15] as well in *De Motu* at 700b22–23, the *Eudemian Ethics* at 1223a26–27 and 1225b25, and in the *Nicomachean Ethics* at 1111b11–13. Martha Nussbaum has proposed that the three forms of desire should be distinguished according to their objects: wish is a desire for the good or the end (*Rhet.* 1369b2–3; *NE* 111b26, 1113a5, b3) whereas *epithumia* is a desire for the pleasant. What object of desire may be assigned to *thumos*, however, she cannot say. Revenge or harming one's enemies seems to be the one candidate, yet it surely has the fault of overspecificity and narrowness. Nussbaum concludes that "Aristotle nowhere gives a sufficiently clear analysis of the objects of *thumos*, of its relation to reason and to pleasure, and of its various types and manifestations."[16] A more politically relevant possibility garnered from Aristotle's passage on *thumos* at *NE* 1327b is that *thumos* expresses the desire to be self-determining and free, to rule oneself as a

12. For a useful comparison of the modern, post-Cartesian concept of mind with the Aristotelian *psuchē*, or soul, highlighting the capacities, see K. V. Wilkes, "*Psuchē* versus the Mind," in *Essays on Aristotle's* De Anima, ed. Martha C. Nussbaum and Amelie Oxenberg Rorty (New York: Oxford University Press, 1992).

13. Martha C. Nussbaum, *The Fragility of Goodness: Luck and Ethics in Ancient Greek Philosophy* (New York: Cambridge University Press, 1986), 273.

14. See A. W. H. Adkins, *From the Many to the One* (Ithaca: Cornell University Press, 1970), 189ff; Jonathan Lear, *Aristotle: The Desire to Understand* (New York: Cambridge University Press, 1988), 141–51; and Nussbaum, *The Fragility of Goodness*, 273–80, 283–89, on the issue of desire in Aristotle's psychology.

15. As Jonathan Lear points out, the Oxford J. A. Smith translation incorrectly uses "appetite" for both *epithumia* and *orexis* (see *Aristotle*, 142 n. 110, and 143 n. 113).

16. Martha C. Nussbaum, *Aristotle's* De Motu Animalium: *Text with Translation, Commentary, and Interpretive Essays* (Princeton: Princeton University Press, 1978), 206.

free person and not as a slave. But this desire, although probably a part
of *thumos,* is unlikely to articulate adequately the striving of many other
emotions potentially gathered within this capacity. Even if Aristotle does
not provide the analysis, his enduring concern for issues related to emotion and friendship in political regimes allows a reading that draws
together suggestive aspects of issues related to *thumos* to clarify *thumos.*

To understand the meaning of any part of the soul, we must know its
*ergon,* its function, and then its *aretē,* its excellence. This is the sort of
analysis he proposes, for example, to delineate the scientific and the calculative rational capacities. After taking up this division between these
two capacities in *NE* 6.1, he suggests that "we must now take up the
question which is the best characteristic of each element, since that constitutes the excellence or virtue of each. But the virtue of a thing is relative to its function" (*NE* 1139a15–17). *Thumos* needs the same analysis,
but Aristotle himself did not provide it.

In fact, the moral virtues are the excellences of the *oretikon* or the
desiring aspect of the soul. Thus to look for the function and excellence of
*thumos* we should look at his extended treatment of all the excellences or
virtues of the *oretikon.* Because this capacity has three parts—the appetite, *thumos,* and wish—it is necessary to ask next which virtues correspond to which of these three parts. Self-control is clearly a virtue of
the capacity of appetite, for it involves desires for the pleasures of touch
and taste (*NE* 1118a26), although the pleasures of massages and warm
baths are excluded (*NE* 1118b7). Virtues for *thumos* and wish are more
difficult to find. Since wish is a desire for a good generally speaking, no
virtue seems to belong uniquely to this desire. In any case, "the activities
in which virtues find their expression deal with means." Thus, strictly
speaking, it should be said that the moral virtues deal directly with two
parts of the *oretikon* and indirectly with the third, *boulēsis.* As I have
mentioned, *boulēsis,* or wish, is a desire for the good, some examples of
which are immortality (*NE* 1111b23), health, happiness (*NE* 1111b27), or
generally "things which cannot be obtained through our own agency" (*NE*
1111b24). Wish concerns desiring an end, while decision concerns acting
to secure the means to that end (*NE* 1111b27–29). No particular action
and no particular virtue, then, can be said to secure the end, it only
secures the means.

This leaves us with the rest of the virtues and *thumos.* We have already
seen how the virtue of courage relates to *thumos,* but particularly to
the emotion of fear. But Aristotle never says that courage is a virtue *of
thumos,* only that many people think possessing *thumos* is the same as

courage. Gentleness, too, is a candidate for being a virtue of *thumos*, in the way that temperance is certainly a virtue of appetite, yet it is such a virtue only if *thumos* is narrowly interpreted as anger or as a synonym for *orgē*. Aristotle clearly had a tendency to understand *thumos* in this way. Yet if we accepted this narrow interpretation, the emotions involved in the rest of the virtues—magnificence, generosity, high-mindedness, proper level of ambition, friendliness, truthfulness, wittiness, modesty— would be psychically homeless.

Before Aristotle discusses particular virtues, he defines virtue generally. There are three states in the soul: emotions (*pathē*), capacities (*dumaneis*), and characteristic attitudes (*hexeis*) (*NE* 1105b20). Virtues turn out to be characteristic attitudes or "the conditions either good or bad, in which we are in relation to the emotions, for example, our condition in relation to anger [*orgē*] is bad, if our anger is too violent or not violent enough" (*NE* 1105b26–29). In contrast, capacity is "that by virtue of which we are said to be affected by these emotions, for example, the capacity which enables us to feel anger, pain, or pity" (*NE* 1105b23 –25). Although we already know that the capacities he means are those grouped together as the general capacity *oretikon*, it is worth explaining why other capacities are not referred to here. This passage cannot refer to the capacities of sensation, locomotion, perception, or metabolism, because the capacity to feel emotion cannot be reduced to some more simple, physical feeling or physical process. It is true that for Aristotle emotion and most mental processes are partly physical; nevertheless, just as a house should be described both as an organization of stones, bricks, or timber, and as a structure whose purpose is shelter against harsh weather (*DA* 403b5–10), an emotion has both a material and a formal explanation. Although emotions may involve thought, in the sense of a background belief or judgment, emotional capacity is not thought or reason itself. And since we know that appetite is the capacity involved with the virtue of self-control or temperance, *thumos* must be the capacity that enables us to feel anger, pain, pity, as well as the rest of the emotions.

Can we answer Nussbaum's challenge and find a common object for the desiring capacity of *thumos*, that is, is there anything similar that all emotions desire? In the *Rhetoric*, Aristotle describes each emotion according to six indicators: what thought or belief is involved, whether pleasure or pain accompanies it, what the desire is, in what frame of mind a person will likely feel it, toward which people we are likely to feel it, and finally, on what grounds we are likely to feel it. Benevolence (*charis*), for example, is a desire to care for those in need; friendliness is "wishing for him what you believe to be good things, not for your own sake but for his, and being inclined ... to bring these things about (*Rhet.* 1380b38–1381a1). Indignation, or "pain caused by the sight of unde-served good fortune," by implication is a desire for the deserving to get good things and the undeserving to lose them. The rest of the emotions discussed—anger, calmness, enmity, fear, shame, envy, emulation, like benevolence, friendliness, and indignation—are desires for a certain state of social relations, a desire, for example, for social inclusion, for social belonging, for social recognition but not in the narrow sense of status.

This same sense of social engagement as emotion's aim appears in Catherine Lutz's study of emotional life on Ifaluk island.[17] As I have noted, in her view, emotions are best understood through "scenes," simi-lar to de Sousa's paradigm scenarios, which are prototypical examples of when and how the emotions should be felt. These will usually be social scenes in which the respective emotions "create"[18] social relationships between individual people and between people and groups. Yet emotions are also "about"[19] social relationships and the "outcome" of social rela-tions.[20] Thus, social relations are present before, during, and after an emotion. Before an emotion, social relations give us rules, scenes, or sce-narios for emotion. During an emotion, we feel indignant with, or feel benevolence for, other people; we fear, in Aristotle's world, for example, a sudden change in socially recognized goods. After an emotion (or after the start of an emotion), we put ourselves in some particular relationship to actions of others.

While Lutz's analysis derives from the recent drive for a revisionist view of emotion in the late twentieth century, one that in her case mis-takenly contains the idea of a monolithic "Western" view of emotion, the kernel of such a view is evident in Aristotle's treatment of emotion in both the *Ethics* and the *Rhetoric*. I noted that for Aristotle the best way to understand a capacity of the soul was to examine its characteristic work or function and then its excellence. The work of *thumos* is in its desire, expressed through any number of emotions, for a good social relation-ship. More generally, it carries within itself a sense of community, of how one is to live with others, but worked out over time piece by piece in

---

17. Catherine Lutz, *Unnatural Emotions: Everyday Sentiments on a Micronesian Atoll and Their Challenge to Western Theory* (Chicago: University of Chicago Press, 1988), 209.

18. Ibid., 211.

19. Ibid., 216.

20. Ibid., 209.

reaction to others' actions and lives. Emotions encapsulate our sociality; even when we want to disengage from others, to become solitary, we always move in relation to others. Although Aristotle takes *logos* (reason, speech, argument) as the unique capacity of human beings that enables them to be *political* animals, we must keep in mind that speech is often emotional—in fact, emotion is necessary to successful rhetoric—and that reason ultimately articulates what is hidden in judgments inherent in emotions. Thus *logos* requires that the capacity of *thumos* be already present for political community. We will see this more clearly in Chapter 4's discussion of the *Politics*.

So within a degree of continuity with Plato there is in Aristotle not exactly a break but a new channel escaping from the main stream. The identification of *thumos* as a capacity places it into the more complex soul that Aristotle imagined. Whereas in Homer the parts of the mental life are still inchoate and unclearly related, and in the *Republic* the soul had a simple tripartite structure, for Aristotle the distinction between the rational and the nonrational part is merely heuristic. He prefers to comprehend the soul as possessing multiple capacities, including sensation, locomotion, desire, and imagination, rather than parts. Defining *thumos*, then, cannot be done without reference to Aristotle's psychology, for this psychology suggests that Aristotle was working toward a comprehensive understanding of emotion. In the *Rhetoric* he first mentions *thumos* as one of seven causes of human action, the other six being chance, nature, compulsion, habit, reason, and appetite. Thus *thumos* is elevated above other emotions or *pathē* to a role in human action commensurate with such things as chance and nature.

# 4

# Emotion and Aristotelian Politics

Emotions come off badly in the first book of the *Politics*. In the book's most famous passage, *logos* (reason or speech) destines human for political community, making human political animals; children, women in general, and the portion of men and women who are natural slaves are inferior owing to the varying deficiencies of their reasoning capacities. Whereas in a healthy soul "intellect [*nous*] rules desire [*orexis*]," these three categories of people incline toward the other animals that obey their emotion (*pathē*) rather than their reason (*Pol.* 1254b5; 1260a9–13; 1254b24).[1] Desires and emotions, then, must be ruled by the higher faculty of reason or intellect. The reign of reason is supported by apparently transparent passages in the *Ethics*: human *ergon* is "the activity of the soul in conformity with reason or at least not without it" (*NE* 1098a6–7). Reading the *Politics,* one can easily believe that the *oikos,* or household,

1. All translations are from *Politics*, trans. Carnes Lord (Chicago: University of Chicago Press, 1984). For the Greek, see *Politics*, trans. H. Rackham (Cambridge, Mass.: Loeb Classical Library, 1944).

the realm of women and slaves, is dominated by emotion, hierarchy, and the needs of the body, whereas the public is dominated by reason, equality, and the needs of the intellect.[2] Apparently, male citizens and statesmen should diminish the sway of emotion as much as possible.

In spite of this appearance, desires, appetites, and emotions are not merely suppressed and then philosophically disregarded in Aristotle's political handbook. He uses emotion in multiple ways to correct Plato's *Republic*, to elaborate the benefits of the regime called polity, to define the character of the best regime, to understand the impact of political speech, to judge the possibilities of political cooperation. These passages should be read against the background of the virtue theory where emotions are central, against the background of the historical shifts in *thumos*, and, finally, against the background of his place as the originator of the cognitive theory of emotion. Recall that in the previous chapter the most innovative use of *thumos* was as a name for the capacity to feel emotion, one of the three types of desire. From Homer *thumos* retains a sense of being the seat or house of a variety of emotions. But whereas in the *Iliad* it was a quasi-material substance, in Aristotle's theory of the soul *thumos* is one of the capacities or powers of our mental (albeit biological) life. From Plato, it retains the sense of being managed by *logos,* or reason, if functioning well, something missing from Homeric psychology. But whereas in the *Republic* it included only a few emotions, here it encompasses a full spectrum. In the *Topics*, for example, Aristotle speaks of *thumos* as the seat of anger as well as of hatred and fear, while in the *Politics thumos* potentially contains affection or friendship. This understanding of a unified capacity of emotion, subject to configuration or shaping, gives greater prominence and order to his scattered comments on emotion in political life.

In the preceding chapter, I described three ways in which *thumos* is used in Aristotle's work, concluding that its use as the name for the capacity to feel emotion would best help us to understand the depth of Aristotle's attention to emotion, especially political emotion. Here I explore Aristotle's both diagnostic and normative understanding of political conflict, cooperation, and institutions through the lens of emotion. In

2. As many have argued. See for example, Susan Okin, *Women in Western Political Thought* (Princeton: Princeton University Press, 1981) and Wendy Brown, *Manhood and Politics: A Feminist Reading in Political Theory* (Totowa, N.J.: Rowman and Littlefield, 1988). Page Dubois also contends that Aristotle, along with Plato, infuse Greek thinking with hierarchy, create the "chain of being" which arranges all creatures on one scale from inferior to superior, and prepare the way for the demise of the city-states and the arrival of empire. See *Centaurs and Amazons* (Ann Arbor: University of Michigan Press, 1982).

the first part of the chapter I look at Aristotle's claims about the characteristic emotional problems of real and imagined regimes; in the second part I begin my discussion of his recommendations for the best configuration of political emotion, a topic continued into the following chapter's interpretation of the *Poetics*. As it turns out, emotion is a crucial unit of political analysis.

## *Thumos* and Political Diagnosis

In the *Politics,* the first time Aristotle employs an analytic concept of emotion, he is critiquing Plato's elimination of the private family and private property among the *Republic*'s guardians. When Aristotle examines the *Republic* in book 2 while evaluating real and imaginary regimes, he first questions the extent to which citizens should share in the regime. In the *Republic*, the ruling classes seem to share everything; instead of there being private families, the guardians consider everyone else in their own generation as sisters or brothers, in the generation above them as mothers or fathers, and the generation below them as daughters or sons. This arrangement dismays Aristotle for a number of reasons, but especially because he believes that Socrates as portrayed misunderstands the nature of human affection. According to Aristotle, we care for things and love them (*kedo* and *philein*) best when we own them individually and when these things are *agapetos* or lovable (*Pol.* 1262b22–23). Whereas Socrates believed that when we combine our property, we can harmonize our affections, Aristotle believes that multiplication of owners divides the affection.

In the case of property, Aristotle advises us to consider two points. First, partnerships, although desirable, are emotionally thorny: "In general, to live together and be partners in any human matter is difficult ... this is clear in the partnerships of fellow travelers, most of whom are always quarreling as a result of friction with one another over everyday and small matters" (*Pol.* 1263a15–18). Aristotle endorses balancing a city's needs both for partnership and for a reduction in possible disputes. His recommendation is for private ownership with common use (*Pol.* 1263b38).

Second, both pleasure and virtue, and thereby, one could say, our good emotional repertoires, are threatened with communal ownership. Private property does not immediately lead to selfishness; a great deal of pleasure seems to come from simply having it, but only an overweening greed or affection for oneself constitutes selfishness. In fact, the virtue of liberality or generosity (*eleutheriotēs*) depends on having something of worth to give away: "It is a very pleasant thing to help or do favors for friends, guests, club mates; and this requires that possessions be private" (*Pol.* 1263b5–6).

T. H. Irwin has written that the need for private initiative and individual freedom that Aristotle requires for true generosity does not necessarily demand a system of private property and so, as a result, Aristotle's argument against Plato fails.[3] In addition, Irwin suggests that this failure imperils even deontological justifications for private property because they must ultimately depend on an argument that individual freedom requires private property. What is important to note is that unlike later arguments for private property, Aristotle's argument relies on claims about emotion, since emotion is part of the virtue of liberality or generosity just as it is for all virtues. This element, the entanglement of virtue and emotion, distinguishes his approach from both deontological and utilitarian arguments. Locke, for example, famously argues that ownership in one's body demands ownership of the material mixed with one's labor. Attention to elements of ethical motivation are absent from Locke's argument except as consequences of this institution. Private property results in animosity between humans, animosity that then demands the formation of a civil government. In contrast, Aristotle's argument depends on the concept of an optimal emotional makeup, itself based on an optimal ethical character. The notorious difficulty of Locke's idea of ownership in our bodies as a premise for his argument, and, in utilitarian accounts, the ambiguity of the measurement of pleasure point to the superiority of Aristotle's argument. Although I agree with Irwin that it is not conclusive, it provides a better sense of what is at stake in arguments about property. Even deontological ones must depend on a view of human psychology, its preferred passions and dispositions.

So a system of communally held property fails to incorporate an adequate conception of how institutions influence human affection. The same is true for a social system in which two ruling classes are arranged as one communal family. In the *Republic* guardians and philosophers regard as their children everyone a generation below them and do not practice monogamy—women and children are "held in common," as Plato

3. T. H. Irwin, "Aristotle's Defense of Private Property," in *A Companion to Aristotle's Politics*, ed. David Keyt and Fred D. Miller Jr. (Cambridge: Blackwell, 1991), 200–25.

writes. Troubled by these familial arrangements, Aristotle maintains that any city necessarily consists of a multitude of dissimilar persons, so in encouraging the ruling classes to unify in their interests and affections Plato's plan would imperil the diversity needed for any city. More important, even if we agreed that unity was more crucial than diversity, his arrangement will fail to achieve their stated goal. As in the argument about property, Aristotle contends that people will care most for what is their own and where common possessions are concerned they will, in contemporary parlance, "free ride" on the labor of others. Instead, Aristotle recommends that families be private, or more precisely that the existing familial structure in which one person is related to others in many different ways—as son, cousin, husband, clansmen—spreads the feelings of affection more widely than the *Republic*'s pseudo-family. By themselves these passages sound quite conventional, stodgily so in contrast to the radicalism of Plato's best city, but assessed alongside Aristotle's continuing attention to the emotional possibilities and effects of institutional arrangements and to the central worth of a variety of friendship relations, they offer a suggestive method for political analysis.

One of the most striking examples of such analysis is Aristotle's discussion of the polity or the regime best for most people. "Speaking simply," a polity is "a mixture of oligarchy and democracy" (*Pol.* 1294a37–39). So to construct a polity one mixes a variety of typically oligarchic practices, such as fining the wealthy for not attending the legislative assemblies or using elections to choose government officeholders, with democratic practices, such as paying the poor for attending the same assembly or choosing officeholders by lot. A polity is a sort of median not only in its political arrangements but also in its socioeconomic structure; it is composed of a numerically dominant middle class, but one that is middling not only in incomes but also in honor, beauty, and strength (*Pol.* 1295b).

Knowing these features of polity may not explain why Aristotle recommends this regime so highly. What is so distinguished about middling people, with middling beauty and wealth, with a mixture of political institutions? Here, in response, the apparently rationalist Aristotle appears: "For it [the middle class] is readiest to obey reason, while for one who is overly handsome, overly strong, overly well born, or overly wealthy—or the reverse of these things, overly indigent, overly weak, or very lacking in honor—it is difficult to follow reason" (*Pol.* 1295b5–9). So he contrasts polity with its middling or middle-class population to a regime sharply divided between rich and poor. In such a regime of inequality, then, the population will be less likely to obey reason. Yet the phrase "obey reason" is deceptive. Disregarding reason turns out to be more than simply a lack of reasoning but instead a presence of certain unfortunate emotions, specifically the emotions of arrogance, malice, envy, and contempt. A reader might believe that Aristotle is counseling emotional quietude or freedom from these distasteful emotions. Instead, he recommends changing institutions, in this case flattening the economic stratification of one's society, creating a middle class. As rulers we should not say to our citizens: release your covetousness, renounce your contempt, just say no to class struggle. Instead, rulers or founders must either begin with favorable social and economic structures or help create them. More significantly, the goal of our institutional work is not simply to eliminate these emotions, but to allow others to emerge with greater force. The consequences of large economic stratifications are not only arrogance, malice, envy, and contempt, but also the lack of affection. Of the polity divided into extremes of wealth, he writes: "Nothing is further from affection and from a political partnership" (*Pol.* 1295b24). If we found a regime with a population dominated by a middle class, or if we created one, then affection, or *philia,* would flourish, enabling the citizenry to live more virtuous lives. Thus Aristotle does not hope merely to replace disagreeable emotions with rational behavior, but to stimulate citizens to feel more affection, and only then to become more reasonable with the aid of this emotion.

Such emotional concerns of Aristotle's analysis could be fruitfully added to Bernard Yack's recent discussion of the mixed regime.[4] In fact, this addition is indispensable to understanding Aristotle's particular superiority over many other modes of political analysis and to his relevance for our most important contemporary concerns, qualities that Yack himself appreciates. In his *Problems of a Political Animal*, Yack portrays Aristotle's various mixed regimes including the polity as attempts to thwart the disruption caused by domestic factional conflict. Aristotle's recommended reforms can diminish tensions by "broadening the conceptions of justice" through mixing the qualifications for political office. Once claims to equality, as well as claims of wealth, birth, and virtue are admitted, citizens will become habituated to this variety, will be less likely to take these claims as unjust, and therefore less likely to engage in civil conflict. Yet the proposal to mix qualifications for political office does

---

4. Bernard Yack, *Problems of a Political Animal: Community, Justice and Conflict in Aristotelian Political Thought* (Berkeley and Los Angeles: University of California Press, 1993), chap. 7.

not exhaust Aristotle's recommendations for how to create mixed regimes like the polity, nor does it capture just how a person broadens his or her conception of justice. The sense of book 4, chapter 11, indicates that Aristotle also recommends reducing the numbers of rich and poor by increasing the numbers of the middle class. Only this middling amount of wealth conduces to the optimal political and social emotions. In addition, the mixing of criteria for political participation probably works, although Aristotle is not explicit here, by more than mere habituation to ideas of justice. The acceptance of a moral idea requires both our rational and our emotional faculties. Ultimately, then, Aristotle intends to encourage citizens to accept the relevant standards of justice rationally, but also to feel attached to them and to enter into the emotions that necessarily accompany each standard.

Finally, Aristotle analyzes emotional causes and consequences in his discussion of revolutions and factional conflict. I do not mean to suggest in any way that Aristotle employs individualistic psychological explanations for political strife, no universal irrational human penchant for power accounts for all manner of revolutions and conflicts. Rather each case will present a complex mix of material, economic, social, philosophical, and emotional causes. Still, any political analyst ought to consider the general causes and a typology of regime changes, which later can be applied to particular cases. In fact, *phronēsis,* or practical wisdom, the development of which in the Athenian statesmen Aristotle hoped to encourage by lecturing on political issues, entails a sensitive application of abstract, generalizing theory to concrete practice.

In general, people revolt or precipitate conflict because they feel and believe that they are being treated unjustly (*Pol.* 1301a27–b4). Revolutions are good subjects especially for the study of the emotion narratives underlying judgments of injustice in their interaction with material causes. Regimes have an economic character that influences people's sense of injustice and their disposition for emotion. We already saw how in a polity, with its large middle class, people are less likely to feel either contempt or envy, and as a result affection predominates among citizens. The regime's governmental institutional structure reinforces what economics enables by satisfying oligarchs with practices such as fining the rich for not attending the assembly and placating democrats by offering pay for attendance.

The harmony of polity is precisely missing in democracies where narratives of envy are especially prone to exploitation. Demagogues may, for example, escalate the poor's envy of the propertied in order to prey on the wealthy. If the wealthy then rebel against the threat from the poor, they may transform democracy into oligarchy. At other times these demagogues or popular leaders, when attacking the wealthy, will gain extraordinary trust and the affection from the people, and if they also have military renown and already possess a powerful office and in addition if the population is generally preoccupied with agricultural labor, they might transform the regime into a tyranny. So, oligarchies may in some cases be traced to the escalation of class envy, tyrannies to the exaggerated trust and affection of the democratic masses.

## Unmanly Aristocracy

Aristotle, then, finds attention to emotion an inescapable part of political analysis. As I have shown in the case of his critique of Plato's *Republic*, in his recommendations for forming a polity, and in discussions of revolution, he returns to the emotional dynamic of the conflicts, and to underlying ideas of preferable emotional dispositions. The same attention to emotional dynamics should be seen to underlie Aristotle's portrait of the best regime, or at least the regime that displays some though not all of Aristotle's ideals. It is in his discussion of the character of this regime's citizens that he uses *thumos* in a way that suggests both the second and the third of the three major uses of *thumos* I described in Chapter 3. That single page, brief as it is, should kindle the reader's interest in the many other ways in which emotions appear in Aristotle's ethics and politics. This passage in book 7 of the *Politics* more than any other suggests that *thumos* is the key to unlocking Aristotle's teaching on political emotion.

After considerable time spent assessing present and past regimes and the "best possible" regime or the one suited to most cities, Aristotle in book 7 turns to the best regime, his apparently ideal regime. He starts in a way that is opposite to Plato's in the *Republic*. Rather than sketching the best (just) regime in order to define the best (just) person, he consistently asks first what is the best person and only then asks what is the best regime. This allows him to appreciate the diversity of human lives and human goods, without aiming for an artificial abstract unity. To know the best regime, one must know the most choice-worthy way of life both for an individual and for the city as a whole. Aristotle's discussion proceeds in this order because for him a regime itself is a way of life and is ultimately based on and adapted to the perpetuation of the particular ways of life of its citizens. What Aristotle concludes about the way of life for the city and the individual will help us to make sense of his treatment of *thumos* in book 7.

He considers first whether the best life is the same for the city and for the individual. The initial answer is that the life accompanied by virtue is the best and that this is true for both the city and the single person. Addressing more specifically what a life accompanied by virtue would be like, he writes that it must either manifest some kind of external activity or some kind of internal activity. For a single person a life of external activity means the life of a citizen, of participation in political affairs, while for a city it means a life of imperial domination. On the other hand, internally focused life, for the person, would be divorced from external affairs and devoted to study, but for the city the internal life is harder to characterize.

It surely means renouncing imperial domination, but what does it mean positively? The city's internal activity "can come about on the basis of [a city's parts]: there are many sorts of partnership [*koinonia*] that belong to the parts [*meros*] of the city in relation to one another" (*Pol.* 1325b25–27). Later he will speak of the city's "parts" as being those sections of the city that engage in one of the six needed tasks of the city: food supply, manufacture, defense, wealth, religious administration, and judgment concerning the advantageous and just things. Internal activity resides in the practice of partnership, of what is in common in the polis, the political partnership: "[A] perception of good and bad and just and unjust and other things [of this sort]; and a partnership in these things is what make a household and a city." (*Pol.* 1253a17–18). Political partnership thus shares with the household partnership either a consensus or a common concern about what is good and bad and what is just and unjust. But the political partnership will also have something distinctive to it. So, since justice and judgment of good and bad lives apply to the household, and we know a certain appropriate emotion is required for the household, then we must know what emotion is appropriate to political life.

Because the person without a city has a "desire for war, as if he were an isolated piece in a game of chess" (*Pol.* 1253a7), then the person who has a city must desire affection and active benevolence, but in this case for relative strangers. How can I say that affection and active benevolence and not peace are the opposite of war? The reason is the emergence of a reconceived *thumos* in book 7:

> It is evident ... that those who are to be readily guided to virtue
> by the legislator should be both endowed with thought and spir-
> ited [*thumos*] in their nature. For as to what some assert should
> be present in guardians, to be affectionate toward familiar per-
> sons but savage toward those who are unknown, it is spirited-
> ness that creates affectionateness; for this is the capacity of soul
> by which we feel affection. An indication of this is that spirited-
> ness is more aroused against intimates and friends than against
> unknown persons when it considers itself slighted. Hence
> Archilochus, when complaining of his friends, appropriately
> addressed his spiritedness: "Yes, it is among friends you are
> choked with rage." Both the element of ruling and the element of
> freedom stem from this capacity for everyone: spiritedness is a
> thing expert at ruling and indomitable. But it is not right to say
> that they are harsh toward those who are unknown. One ought
> not to be this sort toward anyone, nor are magnanimous persons
> savage in their nature, except toward those behaving unjustly.
> Moreover, it is reasonable that this should happen. For when it is
> among those they suppose should be under obligation to return a
> benefaction, in addition to the injury they consider themselves
> deprived of this as well. Thus it has been said: "harsh are the
> wars of brothers," and "those who have loved extravagantly will
> hate extravagantly too." (*Pol.* 1327b36–1328a15)

There are four aspects to to what amounts to a criticism of Platonic
*thumos*. First, whereas Plato relies on an analogy to animals, Aristotle
employs human examples. For Plato it is a problem to show how the spirited person could be gentle to his or her fellow citizens (375b), and he can
solve the problem only by pointing to an apparent canine fact: dogs are
both fierce to enemies or strangers and kind to friends. This analogy
accomplishes less than might be hoped in elucidating human moral psychology, as this excursion into city-building was meant to do. The assertion that this spiritedness makes dogs philosophical animals simply adds
to the inhumanness of the puzzle. Aristotle, on the other hand, immediately recalls for the reader certain regularities of *human* action and feeling. When slighted, we are more likely to become angered with friends
than with strangers. This may be because of our affection for them,
because with friends we may more easily display our emotion. Or, since
we know our friends better than strangers, since we are intimate with
our friends, a slight carries greater weight and can less easily be excused
as due to causes extraneous to our character.

Second, where Plato speaks of enemies, Aristotle speaks of strangers. Plato first characterizes the guardians' nature as "gentle to their own and cruel to enemies" (375c), and although later he uses the category of the stranger or the unknown, they are understood as enemies, so that the guardians, like dogs, are said to be the opposite of gentle to those who are unfamiliar. For Plato, because cities inevitably encroach on the land of neighbors and incite war (373d–e), neighbors appear primarily as enemies. Aristotle never mentions enemies, but simply those who are unknown. In the following chapter I argue that Aristotle's views of strangers can be understood more fully through the *Poetics* and its preference for two plays in which strangers figure centrally.

Third, Aristotle claims that harshness is always inappropriate. Of the Platonic thumotic person he writes that "it is not right to say that they are harsh toward those who are unknown. One ought not to be of this sort toward anyone" (*Pol.* 1328a7–10). In another of Aristotle's allusions to Plato's discussion of guardians, moral weakness in regard to *thumos* is like "dogs, which bark as soon as there is a knock without waiting to see if the visitor is a friend" (*NE* 1149a26–29). Such dogs are harsh toward those who are unknown; better dogs would bark only if an injustice were being committed, if, for example, a visitor did not knock, but forced his or her way through the door.

Fourth, Aristotle contends that *thumos* is not primarily the seat of anger but the seat of affection. The passage ties *thumos* to affection by calling *thumos* a capacity: "[T]his is the *capacity* [*dunamis*] of soul by which we feel affection. . . . Both the element of ruling and the element of freedom stem from this *capacity* for everyone: spiritedness is a thing expert at ruling and indomitable. But it is not right to say that they are harsh toward those who are unknown" (emphasis added). The argument of the whole passage ties spiritedness as primarily and fundamentally, but not only, affection to a generous view of the other, not as an enemy but as a potentially related stranger. The tenor of the entire passage encourages us to see *thumos* as, first, a seat of affection and only second, and derivatively, of anger.

By suggesting this progression—from affection to anger—Aristotle transvaluates *thumos* from its Homeric and Platonic uses. Homer, as I have shown, understands *thumos* to contain a variety of emotions. These, however, are often subject to intervention by gods and are molded by the traditional social roles within an aristocratic, warrior society. Only with the revolution in thought, the turn to political and moral philosophy, do the emotions become a problem and the possibility of tutelage emerge. Plato, while he borrows the language of *eros* to describe philosophy, does not yet theorize the ability to organize the emotional capacity in general. With Aristotle's final word on the best regime, *thumos* in its most complex sense loses its meaning of one emotion or of one drive or instinct, becoming instead the soul's capacity for emotion, one that like other capacities can be educated or organized to respond in habitual ways. The reorganization or reconfiguration that Aristotle proposes is around friendship, with anger appearing only after clear injustice. This is at least what can be inferred from this passage. In the following chapter, we shall see how this preliminary characterization must be refined.

The most straightforward way to expand our understanding of Aristotle's connection of *thumos* and friendship would be to set before us everything he has to say about political or civic friendship and to see particularly if he mentions *thumos*. Here, however, Aristotle disappoints us, for he spends only limited time discussing political friendship and never mentions *thumos* in the chapters devoted to friendship in the *Nicomachean Ethics*. Until recently, the secondary scholarship mirrored Aristotle's volubility on friendship in general in contrast to his reticence on political friendship in particular. Partly as a result of the dissatisfaction with the Kantian hegemony in moral theory the topic of friendship has attracted significant interest in philosophy.[5] Yet in the recent group of new works on Aristotle's political theory, only a few have anything to say about political friendship.[6] This is surprising because the topic is so prominent in the *Nicomachean Ethics*, which introduces itself as a study in political science. Moreover, Aristotle's view that the practice of virtue toward others is the most important part of virtue introduces his lengthy treatment

5. Some examples are: John M. Cooper, "Aristotle on the Forms of Friendship," in *Reason and Emotion* (Princeton: Princeton University Press, 1999), 312–35; David K. O'Connor, "Two Ideals of Friendship," *History of Philosophy Quarterly* 7, no. 2 (1990): 109–22; Dennis McKerlie, "Friendship, Self-Love, and Concern for Others," *Ancient Philosophy* 11, no. 1 (1991): 85–101; Paula Reiner, "Aristotle on Personality and Some Implications for Friendship," *Ancient Philosophy* 11, no. 1 (1991): 67–84; Donald N. Schroeder, "Aristotle on the Good of Virtue Friendship," *History of Policital Thought* 13, no. 2 (1992): 203–18; Michael Pakaluk, "Friendship and the Comparison of Goods," *Phronesis* 37, no. 1 (1992): 111–30; Anne Marie Dziob, "Aristotelian Friendship: Self-Love and Moral Rivalry," *Review of Metaphysics* 46 (1993): 781–801.
6. A chapter on political friendship appears in Yack, *Problems of a Political Animal.* Judith A. Swanson in her book *The Public and Private in Aristotle's Political Philosophy* (Ithaca: Cornell University Press, 1992) devotes part of a chapter to political friendship. Other recent books include that do not include discussions of friendship are David Keyt and Fred D. Miller Jr., eds., *Companion to Aristotle's Politics*; Carnes Lord and David K. O'Connor, eds., *Essays on the Foundations of Aristotelian Political Science* (Berkeley and Los Angeles: University of California Press, 1991); Mary Nichols, *Citizens and Statesmen: A Study of Aristotle's Politics* (Savage, Md: Rowman and Littlefield, 1992).

of justice and friendship. Not only is the practice of justice and friendship the better part of individual virtue, but it is also the better part of what a political community does. A regime may provide security and order for commercial exchange, or even provide for basic needs, but only in its encouragement of just and friendly dispositions and acts does the political community become a true polis.

Not only do these points give impetus to a thorough consideration of political friendship, but other points suggest political friendship and *thumos* ought to be discussed together: the close connection of the *logon* and *alogon* treated in Chapter 3, his cognitive view of emotion, the prominence of the book 7 view of *thumos*, the claim that the hardest but best part of virtue is the virtue practiced toward others. Putting all these reasons together allows a better understanding of Aristotle's intention, for he truly uses *thumos* in a new way that elucidates the rest of his thought. It also allows me to read out of Aristotle a more consistent application of political emotion than he himself had. To concentrate on the ways in which Aristotle uses *thumos* as the name for the locus of emotional capacity allows us to see emotions as falling into patterns subject to education and emendation. The gathering together of the rather dispersed group of emotions in Homer and in Plato lets us see emotions as explicable and beneficial, as part of the normal functioning of the human psyche.

When political or civic friendship is discussed in the secondary literature, the chief concern is usually to determine whether it is a form of advantage, pleasure, or virtue friendship. Having determined what category it fits in, no further discussion seems necessary. Considerable dispute, however, swirls about which category of friendship political friendship fits. The major rift is between those who believe that political friendship can be only a utility or advantage friendship and those who believe that at least in some political regimes citizens are virtue friends.[7] A good number of interpreters believe that Aristotle differs significantly from modern contract theory in arguing that citizens must be bound by something stronger and more concerned for a good outside of oneself than self-interest. It seems to me that Aristotle's injunction that in the best

---

7. Those who argue the first position include: Yack, *Problems of a Political Animal*; John M. Cooper, "Political Animals and Civic Friendship," in *Friendship: A Philosophical Reader*, ed. Neera Kapur Badhwar (Ithaca: Cornell University Press, 1993), 303–26; Richard Mulgan, *Aristotle's Political Theory* (Oxford: Oxford University Press, 1977). Those of the second persuasion are: A. W. Price, *Love and Friendship in Plato and Aristotle* (Oxford: Clarendon Press, 1989); Paul Schollmeier, *Other Selves: Aristotle on Personal and Political Friendship* (Albany: State University of New York Press, 1994); Sibyl Schwarzenbach, "On Civic Friendship," *Ethics* 107, no. 1 (1996): 97–128.

regime citizens need a good *thumos* suggests something beyond self-interest. Now on the traditional reading, this means a concern for honor which, although in good measure also self-interested, supersedes a vulgar concern for self-preservation or material comfort and accedes to community standards for success. But as I have noted, in the *Politics* 7 passage Aristotle presses *thumos* even beyond these confines.

In a book written to criticize communitarian appropriations of Aristotle that assume community is the answer to political conflict, Bernard Yack argues resolutely that for Aristotle, political friendship is a form of "shared advantage friendship. As such it is one of the two inferior forms of friendship that fall short of the best form of friendship: the friendship shared by virtuous individuals."[8] In fact, Yack goes even further to deflate communitarian illusions; political friendship is "best practiced when it eliminates any element of the so-called ethical advantage friendship."[9] ("Ethical advantage friendship" is his term for what in Aristotelian scholarship is normally known as "virtue friendship.") His views recall that of R. G. Mulgan who also considered political friendship, in his words, a utility friendship.

The evidence marshaled by Yack and Mulgan is quite similar and equally unconvincing. Both cite a passage from the *Eudemian Ethics* in which Aristotle seems to explicitly define political friendship as advantage friendship: "Civic friendship has been established mainly in accordance with utility" (*NE* 1163b34, *EE* 1242a5–10).[10] Yack believes Aristotle is making a similar point in the NE when he writes: "Men combine with an eye to some advantage or to provide some of the necessities of life, and we think of the political community as having initially come together and as enduring to secure the advantage [of its members]" (*NE* 1160a10–13). Mulgan quotes Aristotle's observation that "In a friendship between fellow citizens, for example, a shoemaker receives an equivalent recompense in exchange for his shoes, and the same is true of a weaver and of the other craftsmen" (*NE* 1163b33). Somehow for Yack these passages by themselves settle the case, and so he writes, "Given these explicit definitions of political friendship, we must abandon the view that for Aristotle

---

8. Yack, *Problems of a Political Animal*, 110. Susan Bickford, while acknowledging that Aristotle thought that a friendship composed of both advantage and virtue was one way in which a political community could be bonded, argues that "attention" may likewise bond a community in the face pervasive enmity. See "Beyond Friendship: Aristotle on Conflict, Deliberation, and Attention," *Journal of Politics* 58 (1996): 398–421.

9. Yack, *Problems of a Political Animal*, 117.

10. Richard Mulgan, *Aristotle's Political Theory*, 204.

'the properly human friendship—the one that constitutes the political bond—is specified as being based on virtue.'"[11]

Despite the appearance of conclusiveness, not one of these passages or even the cumulative force of the passages that Yack or Mulgan cite can settle the issue. First, using the *Eudemian Ethics* as though it is synchronous with the *Nicomachean* is troubling; the strongest case should allow for the possibility that Aristotle changed his views and so rely primarily on the *Nicomachean Ethics*. But both Yack's and Mulgan's most decisive quotations are from the *Eudemian*.

The other passages admit other interpretations. Take, for example, the 1160b passage. Aristotle qualifies what he has written in lines 10–13 by proposing a distinction between short-term and long-term utility or advantage: "the political community does not aim at the advantage of the moment, but at what is advantageous for the whole of life. Thus all associations seem to be parts of the political community, but the kind of friendship prevalent in each will be determined by the kind of association it is" (*NE* 1160b28–30). A reader other than Yack might be tempted to conclude that long-term advantage, or "what is advantageous for the whole of life," is the practice of virtue and a comprehensive set of external goods. Virtue friendship, of course, provides advantages and pleasures, but more serious advantages and superior pleasures to that provided by those two lesser friendships. There is, admittedly, enough ambiguity in Aristotle's direct statements about political friendship in the *Nicomachean Ethics* to support either the view that political friendship is based on virtue or the view that it is based on utility.

Isolated statements cannot count as evidence without an explanation of how Aristotle's position on any one point fits into his overall argument. Yack has given most attention to the issue of friendship and so I will concentrate on his views. If we ask why Yack believes it significant to show that Aristotle's political friendship is not virtue friendship, and how this view fits in the context of the rest of the political philosophy, we find two main issues. First, Yack believes that the city is a means to flourishing rather than a constituent part of flourishing. This contention founders on too little attention paid to Aristotle's most important discussion of the purpose of a true polis. In book 3 of the *Politics* Aristotle rejects protection against injustice and economic prosperity as the highest purposes of a genuine polis. The city, for Aristotle comes into being not only for living but for the living together and for living well. It cannot be a simple

11. Yack, *Problems of a Political Animal*, 111.

military alliance, or union for exchange and protection against injustice to oneself. Yack's contention that the city is essentially instrumental neglects the nobility of other directed actions and their occurrence in the political sphere. The work of the legislator, like the general aim of politics, is "make citizens and good and disposed to perform noble actions" (*NE* 1099b30–32). We need a polis, we need political and public action, because it is in these spheres, as well as in the household and in personal friendships, where we can act for the good of others.

Second, Yack believes that Aristotle intends to show the dangers of too much political intimacy. Aristotle's criticism of how Plato consolidates the sentiments of the *Republic*'s two ruling classes is apparently a warning against confounding virtue and political friendship. But this interpretation caricatures Aristotle's view of even personal virtue friendship, since friends will not necessarily have the same emotions, but will share their joys and sorrows. Here, the modern disbelief that emotion serves good public purposes may deflect both Yack and Mulgan from imagining how political life could incorporate friends devoted to each other's good characters. While in Aristotle's schema, virtue friendships are probably not more "emotional" than advantage and pleasure friendships, nevertheless we now associate intimate friendships with greater emotionality. So Yack and Mulgan may be relying on these modern presumptions to misread Aristotle.

Yet emotion is circumscribed even by a feminist author who believes that not only is political friendship a version of character or virtue friendship, but also that Aristotle's account of *philia* usefully combines with women's traditional care work to inspire a transformed contemporary politics. Sybil Schwarzenbach writes that the "mutual concern of fellow citizens for one another's good character is what Aristotle means by 'politikē philia' [political friendship]." But political friendship differs from personal friendship in that the first lacks "intimate knowledge and a close emotional bond." In fact, both the emotive dispassion of liking and the activity associated with friendship "works *via* the political process, the constitution and the public standards of acceptable civic behavior."[12] In the contemporary context of pluralism in moral beliefs, the chief concern of citizens will be less for one another's moral character than for their political character, and respect for rights will be a crucial way in which political friendship is expressed. So, the chief emotion between citizens will be the weak sounding "concern." This apparent diminishment of emotion is somewhat redressed by comments on how the emotional

---

12. Sibyl Schwarzenbach, "On Civic Friendship," 105, 108.

elements in practical deliberation distinguishes Aristotle from modern theories and on her parting account of one institutional change which could help educate citizens' emotions.

But if as in my account of Aristotle citizens have to possess a good *thumos*, they must be capable of, at least, appropriate anger and affection, but also fear and, as we shall see in the next chapter, pity. It seems to me that Aristotle believes that citizens must actually feel these emotions, rather than that acceding to constitutional norms of political justice and rights could take the place of individual feeling. If Schwarzenbach means something like that these institutions help structure emotions, than I would agree. But then we would be talking about more than "concern." Although it is true that political friendship, like the virtue friendship on which it is based, does not involve an affection for the particular person that is one's fellow citizen (*NE* 1126b24), the object of the emotion is simply wider, less tied to my personal friend or enemy, more to the other conceived as a citizen or stranger. On Schwarzenbach's main account it appears as though citizens will have not have to do much of anything except to accede to certain norms. What this neglects is active involvement in institutions and practices which shape emotions. Again her comments on changing the military in regimes that have compulsory military service into civic service organizations goes some way to describing what citizens might actually do in order to cultivate friendship. Here it crucial to see that Aristotle furnishes us with the opportunity to examine our own practices and speculate about new ones with a view to how they habituate a variety of emotions more robust than concern. Stepping slightly outside his institutional framework, we might also speculate about how social movements are particularly fruitful because they galvanize and script the emotions more forthrightly than "normal" politics.

Not all studies of Aristotle's politics, even book-length studies, address his views on friendship, although they recognize it as an important element of political practice. Two liberal interpretations of Aristotle that are otherwise provocative readings only glance at Aristotelian friendship. Both interpretations also bypass the extensive political implications of Aristotle's valuation of emotion. In her *Citizens and Statesman,* a work that aims for a median between aristocratic and democratic interpretations of Aristotle, Mary Nichols mentions that the statesmen's "special concern" is to promote friendship among citizens through common meals and through their sharing the use of their private property.[13] Stephen Salkever's *Finding the Mean* charts an Aristotelian approach to

---

13. Nichols, *Citizens and Statesmen,* 67, 131.

modern liberal democracy superior to individualist and republican (or communitarian) accounts, an approach that centers on "questions of how various public policies affect the development of democratic virtues and vices."[14] In this context, friendship should not be construed on republican terms as either "essentially" a political relationship or in its best form as political.[15] Now these two claims would certainly be a curious Aristotelian position—that the best friendships are political or that friendship itself is essentially political. These positions are certainly republican distortions of Aristotle (also, we might add, masculinist republican distortions). And yet neither of these positions could necessarily represent the view that some political friendships are a type of virtue friendship. Salkever does not, as far as I can tell, directly argue against the view that political friendship might be virtue friendship; rather, his ultimate placing of Aristotle with two other theoretical alternatives implies such a position. Instead, Salkever argues that Aristotle essentially agrees with liberalism on the greater value of private life and private friendship over political life and political friendships. Thus the point of Aristotle's discussion on friendship encourages Greeks to turn from an overemphasis on the pursuit of glory and honor in war and politics to domestic pleasure, including the life of philosophy lived among friends.

Salkever's analysis is immensely subtle and fruitful. Take, for example, how he articulates Aristotle's connection of happiness and politics:

> [F]ully human happiness requires that we regard politics as less crucial (in one sense) to our well-being than our relationships with close friends. It is at this point, I think, that the agreement between Aristotle and modern liberal politics (although not modern liberal theory, which has nothing to say about friendship) becomes strongest: anyone who takes politics too seriously will, like those who take commerce too seriously, overlook the central importance for human developments of relationships that are neither political nor commercial (although they may be familial).[16]

Notice two distinctions—the first between liberal politics and liberal political theory, the second between a liberalism that supports commercial life and one that nurtures private or domestic life. In other words,

14. Stephen G. Salkever, *Finding the Mean: Theory and Practice in Aristotelian Political Philosophy* (Princeton: Princeton University Press, 1990), 8.

15. Ibid., 242.

16. Ibid., 243.

liberal political theory fails to adequately understand liberal political practice, and Aristotle is better suited for this understanding, at least at the present time. This judgment is, in fact, Salkever's last sentence in his book. Immanent in the life of those who live in a liberal polity, or in liberal politics, if we could understand it properly, is an account of the liberal good life, and of "communities of practice" that better support liberal life. In effect, Aristotelian philosophy is better placed than the traditional liberal theories for a serious understanding of the requirements of life in a liberal polity.[17]

Sometimes resistance to the view that any political relationship could incorporate virtue friendship suggests a particularly late modern cynicism and incredulity at the possibility of good emotional political dispositions. These fears are reminiscent of a fear of the blurring of the private and the public, the affective world of the family and women and the world of power, gain, and men, of emotion and reason. We still tend to hope that rational prudence and interest can more reliably motivate a just and livable politics. This is not to say that there is no good reason to fear romanticizing and sentimentalizing Aristotle and community along with him, regarding conflict as a certain evil. At the same time, we cannot escape Aristotle's challenge: how can we construct a political regime whose purpose is not just to provide the means to good lives, but actually makes humans good and disposed to perform noble action? Let me emphasize the noble. Noble action is virtuous action, for virtues motivate us through a sense of the noble. While we can imagine doing noble acts in private family life, in our businesses and occupations, in private philosophical gathering, we cannot escape the political for the very reason that conflict and public debate about the good is an inescapable feature of human life.

Given, then, that political friendship can in some regimes become virtue friendship, what can we learn from an examination of friendship about properly constituted political emotion, the properly constituted *thumos*? Work such as Yack's that focus on the question of what type of friendship political friendship is deters us from speaking directly about what political friendship actually is, what parts of the soul are involved, what dispositions should be cultivated, what activity should result. Of course, the question of the motivation behind political friendship and the character of the goods shared, two features used for categorizing this friendship into one of three forms, is relevant to these questions, but

17. Ibid., 9.

these questions do not exhaust what we need to know about political friendship.

Aristotle introduces the topic of political friendship in his general discussion of friendship in book 8 of the *Ethics*. All friendship is accorded high praise, and in its various guises it is the most essential external good. It provides us the opportunity to practice good works, aids us in time of misfortune, enhances our ability to think and act, and finally, even above justice itself, holds states together. This task of holding together (*sunechein*) a political community is what must be explained, and in some ways is the chief topic of all of Aristotle's political writings. Language, common advantage, agreement on the good life or on the just are all necessary for the polis, but alone they are insufficient. Unlike agreement on the good life, which is an aspect of reasoned knowledge, friendship describes both the attitude and the activity of a political community.

In the same passage Aristotle also tells us political friendship is concord (*NE* 1155a23–24), which in contemporary Greek usage meant being of one mind, or agreeing. At first, concord does not appear to have much to do with emotion; it consists in an agreement on important governmental issues. Aristotle gives three examples of what citizens might agree upon—a military alliance should be concluded with the Spartans, political offices should be elective, Pittacus should rule (*NE* 1167a31–32). So, bringing the issues up to date, the election of a president or the passage of a treaty displays concord among citizens. For us, however, to call the election of one person to office or the passage of a treaty with a foreign nation an instance of friendship would appear quaint. We would hardly admit to feeling much as citizens, at least in comparison to our personal lives, so that calling the result of an often extremely conflictual process something like friendship is to appear sentimental. But Aristotle, expanding on his understanding of the common Greek usage, tells us that concord is not just a comity of decisions, it exists more importantly in the realm of action. Good citizens are better than bad citizens at achieving concord because they are ready to heed the common interest and to practice public service. So concord is not just agreement on public decisions, but the readiness and actual performance of actions to create and execute those decisions.

The stress on activity reappears if we ask how *thumos* oriented around friendship produces movement of a person's psyche and of a person's choices in the world. Ruling and freedom, as Aristotle has told us, stem from *thumos* viewed as the capacity to feel affection. Friendship, like ruling, is a reciprocated *hexis* (characteristic attitude) and an *energia* (activity) concerned with the good of another (*NE* 8.5). The characteristic attitude is a disposal to feel affection for a person. As a disposition, friendship has both a spontaneous and a habitual element. We feel affection but we also develop a debt of affection. One cannot be friends for a day, since in friendship there is a promise of continuing to feel affection in the future. More than a feeling, friendship is also an activity. Actively assisting someone to reach the good is one of the things that distinguishes friendship from goodwill (*NE* 1167a9–10). Broadly construed, the chief activity is wishing and acting for the other's good. This friendship requires living together, because "[n]othing characterizes friends as much as living in each other's company" (*NE* 1157b18–20). Such activity presupposes that friends share pleasure and joy in one another's company.

The major part of this activity is benefaction, acting on the wish for a friend's good. A friend is greatly concerned with what is owed to one's friend (*NE* 8.13, 8.14, 9.1). Friendship is the opportunity for the exercise of benevolence, for being a benefactor. A part of the character of the good man is the actual performance of beneficent acts: "A man of high moral standards will need people to whom he can do good" (*NE* 1169b13–14). The benefits provided by friendship may be merely pleasure or usefulness, but "perfect" friendships include learning to be good by observation of the other. Pleasure, usefulness, and virtue define three types of friendship and what is exchanged in these friendships. But Aristotle mentions more particularly honor and profit, the first appropriate for a superior partner, the second for a needy partner (*NE* 1163b2–4). A difference between the partners requires a difference of amount and kind of benefit, so Aristotle provides a variety of guidelines for what benefits and how much of each are due to people according to their superiority in virtue.

Like a friend, a person who rules or is ruled has a *hexis* (characteristic attitude) and an *energeia* (activity) concerned with the good of another. Like a friend, a ruler or citizen must necessarily be interested in benefaction. Just as friends wish for one another's good, a ruler wishes for the good of the ruled, and the ruled wish, not so much for the good of the ruler, as for the good of the community. In addition, since citizenship is defined by participation in ruling and in being ruled interchangeably, we might say the character of citizenship is the mutual concern for one another's good. At the most elementary level the typology of regimes requires this concern, for "when the one or the few or the many rule with a view to the common advantage, these regimes are necessarily correct"

(*Pol.* 3.7.1279a28–29). The notion of common advantage is constitutive not only for a correct regime but also for citizenship: "For either it must be denied that persons sharing [in the regime] are citizens, or they must participate in its advantage" (*Pol.* 3.7 1279a31–33). That is, a citizen is one who shares in the common advantage (as well as in ruling, which is surely part of the common advantage). The common good or advantage requires the beneficence of the ruler. A polis is in fact defined as the community that aims at the most supreme good—*eudaimonia*, happiness or the flourishing of the human, "what is advantageous for the whole of life" (*NE* 1160a28). This means that the ruler is ultimately concerned with the good of the ruled. The polis and the ruler have large responsibilities because a good polis is "that arrangement according to which anyone whatsoever might do best and live a flourishing life" (*Pol.* 1324a23–25) and what makes a good ruler is overseeing "how a city, a family of human beings, and every other sort of partnership will share in the good life and in the happiness that is possible for them" (*Pol.* 1325a8–10).

One view of how the political arrangement and the ruler produce happiness has been developed by Martha Nussbaum: "The aim of political planning is the distribution to the city's individual people of the conditions in which a good human life can be chosen and lived. This distributive task aims at producing capabilities. That is, it aims not simply at the allotment of commodities, but at making people able to function in certain human ways."[18] Although Nussbaum calls this a conception of "political distribution," it is essentially the same as distributive justice. By "producing capabilities" Nussbaum means that the legislators will be concerned to create or nurture institutions that produce two sorts of capabilities: internal capabilities of intellect, character, and body that are principally developed by families and public education, and external capabilities encouraged by conditions such as close ties to family and friends and sufficient nourishment, or facilitated by the elimination of obstacles such as repetitive, menial labor. Through the political system, the legislators are entrusted to "train I-capabilities in the young, to maintain those in the adult, and simultaneously to create and preserve

---

18. Martha Nussbaum, "Nature, Function, and Capability: Aristotle on Political Distribution," *Oxford Studies in Ancient Philosophy*, suppl. vol. (1988): 145–83, 155. Nussbaum developes this framework further and later applies of this notion of capability to the issues of national development in Nussbaum and Amartya Sen, eds., *The Quality of Life* (New York: Oxford University Press, 1992), and Nussbaum and Jonathan Glover, eds., *Women, Culture, and Development: A Study of Human Capabilities* (New York: Oxford University Press, 1995).

the E-circumstances in which those developed capabilities can become active."[19]

Is there justification for this stress on developing capabilities in the discussion of friendship? Do friends strive to develop the capabilities of friends? As soon as he introduces the topic of friendship, Aristotle writes that friends provide the opportunity for good works and enhance one another's ability to think and act. Two examples that he uses here are those of developing internal and external capabilities respectively: helping the young avoid error and giving older people care "to supplement the failing powers of action which infirmity brings in its train" (*NE* 1155a13). Later on he will stress the need for friends to live together in order to share each other's thoughts and words because only by living together can "the perception of a friend's existence be activated" (*NE* 1171b35). Lovers rely on seeing each other, while friends need to share a common activity, such as are hunting, playing dice, or doing philosophy, pastimes that express what they value most in life. Since friends develop one another's capabilities, it would not be odd to say that rulers also develop capabilities.

Orienting citizens and rulers around developing capabilities is connected to an elimination or alteration of the desire for domination over other peoples and nations. The intensity of domestic concerns works to correct impulses of human beings to dominate and oppress others. The connection between the two first shows up when Aristotle's characterization of the polis as directed to discovering how all can share in the good life concludes a discussion of the militaristic polis. *Thumos* had been needed in the Platonic regime initially to gain land from neighbors; it had been an imperialistic regime. In three separate passages, two in the discussion of the best regime, Aristotle criticizes the common adulation of Sparta, and through it the equation of politics with domination.

The most extended treatment of militarism appears in book 7, chapter 2, where he at the same time considers the question of whether happiness is the same for the individual and for the city. Some people believe, according to Aristotle, that the best life for a man (*aner*) is the active and political way of life. But here he does not consider the active, political life per se, but rather the political life seen in the imperialist mode, as the rule of a master over neighboring territories. He mentions Spartans, Cretans, Scythians, Persians, Thracians, and Celts as governed by laws dedicated to educating the citizenry for warfare. Domestic politics in this

---

19. Nussbaum, "Nature, Function, and Capability," 164.

imperialist mode becomes the legislative training for war. Military service becomes the noblest act of citizens, who thereby lead their polis into the honor of mastery. In this state citizens have regard for fellow citizens insofar as they contribute to this end of the state and have little regard for strangers.

Aristotle remarks on the oddness of supposing that the task of the political expert is domination. Since the legislator is concerned with law, his concern cannot be to compel neighbors to submit to rule. Second, mastery should not be exerted over anything whatsoever but only over what should be mastered. Third, an isolated city living alone without any neighbors but with fine laws is certainly conceivable. More important for his argument is the restatement of his view that the proper task of the legislator is "to see how a city, a family of human beings, and every other sort of partnership will share in the good life and in the happiness that is possible for them" (*Pol.* 1325a.8–10). The activity of politics should shun domination and turn to promoting the good life.[20]

Thus the *energeia* or activity of politics, as in friendship, must be benefaction, not domination or mastery. Far from requiring domination, politics calls for awareness of how to bind together different others. Unlike a tyrant, a citizen-ruler must know how to promote deep thought, trust, and capacity for activity (*Pol.* 1313b1). In addition, having the capacity for *philia* is a requirement for the good functioning of a polis. Aristotle's comment "When people are friends, they have no need for justice, but when they are just, they need friendship in addition" is true perhaps for the reason that there can be justice between strangers, but to be fellow citizens there must be friendship in addition.

Like friendship, which requires living together, *thumos* in citizen-rulers requires an institutional base. Friendship is always related to institutional arrangements.[21] For example, when discussing the purpose of the polis, Aristotle tells us that affection is the decision of living together. The binding or togetherness is accomplished by intermarriage,

---

20. What this view might imply for what we think of as "welfare" is subject to dispute. See Martha Nussbaum, "Aristotelian Social Democracy," in *Liberalism and the Good*, ed., R. Bruce Douglass, Gerald M. Mara and Henry Richardson (New York: Routledge, 1990), and Judith Swanson, "Aristotle on Liberality: Its Relation to Justice and Its Public and Private Practice," *Polity* 27, no. 1 (1994): 3–23.

21. Salkever, in *Finding the Mean*, recognizes but does not tackle this issue: "What is required ... is some way of evaluating economic and political institutions at least partially in terms of the extent to which they make genuine friendships possible," 244. It would make a difference whether by "genuine friendships" he meant personal or political ones. I would argue that institutions support or subvert both types.

clans, festivals, and pastimes. Although merely living together is not the point of the polis, it provides the occasion for noble actions (*Pol.* 1280b34–43). Again, in a discussion of tyranny, we are shown what a good regime should encourage by what a tyrant suppresses. The tyrant aims at three things: the suppression of all deep thought, the creation of distrust, and the elimination of capacity for activity. This mention of capacity (*dunamis*) recalls both the understanding of *thumos* as the capacity for friendship and Nussbaum's stress on capabilities as the point of political distribution. The tyrant's aims show the extent to which trust, action, and thought are connected in politics. In a healthy regime, all of these seem to be encouraged by common messes, clubs, education, and particularly leisured discussions (*Pol.* 1313b1).

Having looked at the various manifestations of Aristotle's concern for emotional aspects of political life, I think it is now easier to see how a concept of political emotion is an indispensable part of his appraisal of regimes. A regime is a complex and multifaceted creature for Aristotle. Sometimes he means by the word simply what pertains to government, to the institutions of assembly, to judicial courts or administrative office, or to the practices of lot or election, for example. At other times he speaks of regimes as a way of life, as a sharing of political aims, of economic structure and typical occupations, of educational aims and of cultural production, and—least noted—of typical patterns of political emotion or the habitual affective relations among citizens, and between citizens and foreigners. His manual for political statesmen and citizens ranges widely over the choices any founder or ruler must make. Regimes could be organized to share the aims of economic prosperity or simply the prevention of injustice and foreign intervention, but Aristotle recommends the goal of living well or virtuously. Regimes could be deeply divided between rich and poor, dominated by a middle class, or ruled by a moderately wealthy aristocracy. The population could be devoted to farming, to trade, when freed from economic necessity depending on the labor of slaves, to leisure. A regimes could allow each family to educate its children privately or, as Aristotle advises for the regime "one would pray for," it should provide a public, common education teaching not professional vocations but how to be at leisure, how to practice the lifelong study of music. Cultural productions such as tragedy might portray bad men rising, but it ought to portray only good characters declining due to a *hamartia,* or mistake, possibly connected to their character. Some of these elements of regimes have been adequately addressed in the secondary literature. Of the various facets, the issue of political emotion has been least conceptualized and analyzed. Without consideration of the habitual emotions that animate a population and that its institutions and practices encourage, the analysis or a regime is seriously incomplete.

One way to understand this short history of *thumos*, which I have traced through Homer, Plato, and now Aristotle, is to use the narratological approach to emotion seen in Catherine Lutz but also in Ronald de Sousa's concept of paradigm scenarios (see my discussion in Chapters 1 and 2).[22] In effect, the *Iliad* contains many of the most important paradigm scenarios for ancient Greek culture. It is easy to see that the chief subject of these scenarios was anger so that the *thumos* as the inner life of the hero could be easily mistaken for anger itself. Plato concentrates on a scenario with this character because the threat in politics that he perceived came from those who were often unreservedly attached to this scenario of honor and outrage. Aristotle sees the threat more as an absence or too restricted an application of some emotions such as friendship, rather than as a presence of too much undisciplined anger. He aims to expand the emotional repertoire and revise governing scenarios by emphasizing the integrative emotions any polis needs to achieve the good life. Virtues are guides or channels for action involving both right feeling and right doing. While guided by a conception of the best life for humans, the virtues will in turn reinforce this conception. What they turn out to reinforce in the best case is a regime devoted as much as possible to the welfare, education, and conditions of the good life, dependent on the regular beneficent actions of individual citizens.

In some ways comparing Plato and Aristotle is a mistaken enterprise. Reading Plato as though he offers a simplistic blueprint for a utopia, rather than reading him with his irony, dialogue, mythology, and depth-probing questioning intact, is the problem. What we cannot ignore, no matter how we choose to read him now, are the associations and resonances he set in motion, those presently inscribed in our intellectual tradition. For Plato sympathetic emotion is harmful and the philosopher hardly returns to the cave for benevolent reasons. If the state of the soul, especially one devoted to the rule of reason, is the one and only care, then politics will suffer. Any politics might suffer, but especially a politics in which welfare and care are central. In Aristotle we have an intimation of a connection between just how emotional habits are organized and what

---

22. Ronald de Sousa, *The Rationality of Emotion* (Cambridge: MIT Press, 1987); Catherine Lutz, *Unnatural Emotions* (Chicago: University of Chicago Press, 1998).

citizens will think they are to do and expect in political communities. This is, as yet, a vague formulation that I will continue to refine, first with an examination of the *Poetics* in the following chapter. It is precisely in his consideration of dramatic situations, or tragedy, that Aristotle seeks to reconfigure the *thumos*, to give it a new characteristic attitude to accompany the new activity of benefaction.

# 5

# Tragedy and the Configuration of Political Emotion

And surely we would also give its protectors, those who aren't poets but lovers of poetry, occasion to speak an argument without meter on its behalf.

—Plato, *Republic*

In Chapter 3 I argued that Aristotle employed at least three different senses of *thumos*, as a particular emotion, equivalent to *orgē,* or anger, to characterize a brash aggressive man, and as a capacity of the soul among other general capacities. Furthermore, I maintained that we have to take seriously how different Aristotle's conception of emotion is from Plato's and from much of the rest of the Greek tradition. I emphasized his innovative use of *thumos* as a general capacity for emotion and I focused especially on how he speaks of *thumos* as a capacity in book 7 of the *Politics*. In that passage political *thumos* is connected both to an activity and to an emotional disposition. Although the division between activity and disposition is artificial because one supports the other, in the preceding chapter I set out to explain the activity of the good citizen's *thumos*. But the activity discussed was the public one supported by this *thumos*, not the activity of the soul itself. In this chapter I delineate more overtly the political *thumos* as a name for the characteristic emotional response of citizens for one another, one that is inculcated by laws, by the way of life of the regime, and by the regime's cultural production.

To find the emotional disposition of the citizen's *thumos*, I interpret one clue located in the book 7 passage—Aristotle's admonition that citizens should not be cruel to those who are unknown or strangers. One of the ways to understand how citizens regard one another is to see how they regard strangers. The way this is put implies that citizen and stranger are mutually exclusive categories, but a citizen can be a stranger to another citizen, while a noncitizen, an immigrant or resident alien, will be a stranger in a different way. Under what conditions a noncitizen becomes a citizen, and how foreigners are treated at home and abroad, reveal what the essential bond or stamp of citizenship is. The characteristic attitude among citizens and that toward foreigners and strangers in both classes appear for Aristotle to be mutually reinforcing. This is why it is crucial for him to address the politics of foreign domination, as he does in book 7, not so much for how it intrudes on the lives of those dominated, but for how it distorts the life of the dominators.

In the first part of this chapter I describe one mode of cooperation in Homeric society and propose that Aristotle, in his concern for emotion and tragedy, addresses the problem of the new form of city cooperation between relative strangers and between cities, a problem that tragedy had itself posed, but that Aristotle thought had not been adequately solved. This discussion informs my later interpretation of the role of pity, recognition, and *katharsis*. In contrast to Stephen Salkever's and Carnes Lord's readings of the political meaning of the *Poetics*,[1] I argue that pity, without being a derivative of self-regarding fear, represents an opening for friendship; that the plot device of recognition, or *anagnōrisis*, has particular political significance as the recognition of kinship in strangers, at least as important as the fear of reversal; that *katharsis* is one path to the configuration of the thumotic capacity; and that this can be best seen by examining one of Aristotle's two favorite tragedies, Euripides' *Iphigenia in Tauris*.

## Strangers, *Xenia,* and the Polis

The imagery of strangers is rich in ancient Greek political culture. *Xenos* can mean "foreigner," "stranger," "guest," "host," or "a friend established

---

1. Stephen Salkever, "Tragedy and the Education of the Demos: Aristotle's Response to Plato," in *Greek Tragedy and Political Theory*, ed. J. Peter Euben (Berkeley and Los Angeles: University of California Press, 1986); Carnes Lord, *Education and Culture in the Political Thought of Aristotle* (Ithaca: Cornell University Press, 1982).

through *xenia* or ritualized friendship."[2] Zeus Xenios is protector of the guest-host relationship, itself often part of the greater relationship of *xenia*.[3] Prevalent among the male aristocrats of the Homeric world, *xenia* was a "bond of solidarity manifesting itself in an exchange of goods and services between individuals originating from separate social units."[4] As a method of creating artificial kinship ties it emulated kinship in several details. For example, *xenoi* would name sons after each other or even become foster parents. The outward manifestation of affection between *xenoi* was important, and genuine feeling often resulted. You could depend on your *xenos* to ransom you, to support you with shelter and food, to provide dowries for your daughters, and to celebrate your memory after your death. *Xenia* was a process of turning important strangers into friends, of, as Herman explains, creating cooperation where none would ordinarily or naturally exist. It was a process of creating primitive "political" cooperation that often involved extrakin and extratribal relations and a sharing of resources in a particularly equal fashion. The rise of the polis might be deemed a way for more people to have such sharing of resources and reciprocity relations outside of kin and clan. That is, the drive toward the polis was partly based on the example of *xenia*. At the same time, however, because of its territoriality and greater homogeneity of members, the polis stood in opposition to *xenia*. A Persian and a Greek may have been *xenoi,* but they were not part of the same polis. And, as time went by, by splitting loyalties, *xenia* alliances threatened the polis. Alcibiades' infamous reputation as a traitor is a later misunderstanding of an aristocrat's sustaining his *xenia* ties, while trying to preserve his polis popularity.[5] The city-states attempted to reconcile the conflict of loyalties by establishing *proxenia*, a decree naming a member of another city as *proxenos*, a sort of lobbyist for the granting city in his own community. Often these relations replicated the lines of *xenia* association, since an aristocrat would be asked to nominate a potential *proxenos*, for which role a *xenos* was ably fit. Fifth-century Athens, for example, named ninety-four such *proxenoi*.

2. For this account, I rely on Gabriel Herman, *Ritualised Friendship and the Greek City* (Cambridge: Cambridge University Press, 1987).

3. See Walter Burkert, *Greek Religion: Archaic and Classical* trans. John Raffan (Cambridge: Harvard University Press, 1985), 130 and 248; and Jon D. Mikalson, *Honor Thy Gods: Popular Religion in Greek Tragedy* (Chapel Hill: University of North Carolina Press, 1991), 77ff.

4. Herman, *Ritualised Friendship and the Greek City*, 10.

5. Ibid., 159.

The heroic warrior ethos, in which *xenia* originated, figures promi-
nently in ancient Greek tragedy. Jean-Pierre Vernant has written that
one of the social conditions of fifth-century tragedy was the conflict of
hero and citizen revealed in the opposition of protagonist and chorus.[6]
With tragedy, the hero had become a problem, a subject of debate for a
chorus that expresses anxiety and uncertainty about him. The urge to
grapple with the heroic past was indeed the "mainspring" of tragedy.[7]
One tension between the citizen and the hero was over the hero's often
unrestrained pursuit of personal, usually war related, honor.[8] The city's
attempt to assimilate aristocratic zeal for glory to its own interests is
seen in funeral orations after military expeditions, but it is the city and
its excellences that are celebrated and not that of the individual dead
warriors.[9] Simon Goldhill, who sees tragedy as a "genre of transgression"
in which the "tragic texts seem to question, examine, and often subvert
the language of the city's order," explores a fascinating contrast between
the preplay ceremonies and the text of *Ajax*.[10] He describes four such
ceremonies, but the last, the presentation of state-educated orphans, now
young men, as uniformed soldiers, connecting entry into manhood with
becoming a citizen and warrior, contrasts with the heroic extremism of
Ajax, the Homeric warrior. The ceremonies celebrate the assimilation
of the warrior ethos into the city, whereas the play dissects the threat of
manly heroism to social and political cooperation.

Another tension between the hero and the polis, not as often noted, is
over the terms and types of cooperation, affiliation, and attachment. The
same tension appears in the challenge of gender in tragedy. Both the
hero with his *xenia* relations and the family, with its disputes over
mother and father right displayed in the *Oresteia*, and with its challenge
to political-military values played out in the *Antigone*, continued to

6. Jean-Pierre Vernant and Pierre Vidal-Naquet, *Myth and Tragedy in Ancient
Greece*, trans. Janet Lloyd (New York: Zone Books, 1990), 24–25 and 242.

7. Ibid., 28.

8. Ajax is such a character; see David J. Bradshaw, "The Ajax Myth and the Polis: Old
Values and New," in *Myth and the Polis*, ed. Dora C. Pozzi and John Wickersham (Ithaca:
Cornell University Press, 1991), 99–125; and Wm. Blake Tyrrell and Frieda S. Brown,
*Athenian Myths and Institutions: Words in Action* (New York: Oxford University Press,
1991), 73–98.

9. See Nicole Loraux, *The Invention of Athens*, trans. Alan Sheridan (Cambridge:
Harvard University Press, 1986).

10. Simon Goldhill, "The Great Dionysia and Civic Ideology," in *Nothing to Do with
Dionysos?* ed. John Winkler and Froma Zeitlin (Princeton: Princeton University Press,
1990), 97–129. For similar views see J. Peter Euben, Introduction to *Greek Tragedy and
Political Theory*.

bedevil the polis. We in our own time tend to assume there is an obvious complementarity or symbiosis between families and public spheres, except of course when women are no longer able or willing to devote themselves to childrearing. The polis, with its concentrated and more numerous population, with its aspiration to include more people in cooperation on equal terms, had to develop new terms for attachment with relative strangers as well as new terms for alliance with foreign peoples and cities. One of the problems for the polis was to judge how to establish new ties of cooperation, on what basis, to what ends. This meant, as Herman notes, "new ideals of behavior, new points of reference for interpreting the world, and ... a way of thinking which took the city as its point of departure." Such development in the city "prompted its members to remodel their own personalities to meet these standards."[11]

Aristotelian political theory addresses the problem of the heroic warrior, the more recent problem of the politician seeking public honor, and the equally recent problem of citizens negotiating the character of political cooperation. With the development of the city-state, aristocrats were no longer the only class with their own well-developed ties of resource distribution and security, two tasks accomplished by *xenia*. Cooperation was simultaneously more widely encompassing and more centralized in the city center, and increasingly so in the fifth and fourth centuries. These problems created by these social and political developments required an innovative strategy. All three problems are handled partly through the question of how to organize the political *thumos*. Aristotle's concern for emotion indicates that practical excellence (moral virtue) depends upon right feeling. As a result, questions about how any regime is to be just, well arranged, and sociable require deeper answers than those posed in terms of the right distributive principles, the best relations of production, or the traditions we should emphasize. A deeper answer must investigate the question of "personality" in Herman's terms, of the "self" in modern terms, or of the "soul" in Aristotle's, and especially the place of emotions. Only then can we address the quality of citizenship interaction. In particular, the centrality of emotions helps citizens to determine if, what, and how much they are willing to share with other citizens and strangers. It helps to determine whether citizens are disposed to give time or resources to acts that aid fellow citizens or strangers, and so in what manner they give recognition to others.[12]

11. Herman, *Ritualised Friendship and the Greek City*, 159.
12. Plato himself is concerned about the disintegrative effects of private families and private property among the ruling classes. Yet his goal is less to allow all to flourish and

## Poetics and Politics

In the *Politics*, after considering the nature of the best regime's citizens
(7.7), Aristotle goes on to discuss the education or development of their
nature (7.13–15; 8.1–7). To know how to develop nature with habit and
reason, one must of course know the end of the regime in question. Generally speaking, the regime must aim at living and happiness, which
Aristotle reiterates is the "actualization and complete practice of virtue."
This practice implies not domination and war, since these are highly
restricted accounts of virtue. Rather, the legislator should aim to educate
the citizenry in the activity of leisure, particularly the enjoyment of
music. It is music, rather than letters, drawing, or gymnastics, that is
taught most for the sake of itself. Since music includes tragedy, and Aristotle's treatise on tragedy is concerned both with emotions and with
action and character, it is to the *Poetics* that we must turn to understand
the education of the nature of the citizens, including especially the
*thumos* or emotional capacity of the citizens.

These connections, appearing at the end of the *Politics*, go mostly unexplored by scholars of Aristotle's *Poetics* who treat the text as literary
theory,[13] as a mere systemization of the techniques and motifs of existing
tragedy. Several critics accuse Aristotle of misunderstanding the essence
of tragedy. He is portrayed as wholly insensitive to poetry, as having
removed tragedy "from the realms of madness and criminality," as deny-
ing that "radically irrational energy exists anywhere either in our psyches or in the dynamics of the visible world itself."[14] Or, pronounced in
another way, Aristotle's "rationalistic and ethically ameliorative orientations . . . tame the struggles represented in tragedy."[15]

The critics' entirely apolitical attention to his work and the criticisms of
it are not unrelated. That is, by failing to see the political-ethical context,

---

more to guarantee the rule of reason. Aristotle, who articulates the telos of flourishing on
the shoulders of Plato, appropriately criticizes the *Republic*'s elimination of personal possession and responsibility.

13. G. F. Else, *Aristotle's* Poetics: *The Argument* (Cambridge, Mass.: Harvard University Press, 1957); Stephen Halliwell, *Aristotle's* Poetics (Chapel Hill: University of North
Carolina Press, 1986); Carnes Lord is the noteworthy exception in *Education and Culture*. Oliver Taplin admits that Aristotle was prescriptive not descriptive, in *Greek
Tragedy in Action* (Berkeley and Los Angeles: University of California Press, 1978).

14. Thomas Gould, *The Ancient Quarrel Between Philosophy and Poetry* (New Haven:
Yale University Press, 1992), 264.

15. Michelle Gellrich, *Tragedy and Theory: The Problem of Conflict Since Aristotle*
(Princeton: Princeton University Press, 1988), 159.

they can discern only Aristotle's supposed poetic obtuseness. Indeed, critics are drawn to derision: "On the whole, he [Aristotle] appears to have survived his education."[16] Since Gould thinks Aristotle is constitutionally incapable of understanding poetry, he claims that for Aristotle poets "clean our emotional lives periodically so that we can get on with more important things."[17] This characterization recalls a very traditional interpretation of *katharsis*, following Bernays, as a physical cleansing.[18]

We must place this criticism in the context of the argument of Gould's book as a whole, that the quarrel between poetry and philosophy has roots in a theological or cosmological dispute over whether the universe and the gods are fundamentally just or unjust. Gould argues that Socrates'/Plato's objection to poetry (really tragedy, since Gould does not discuss comedy) arises from its assertion that the gods are unjust, and that we are all potentially victims of cosmic injustice. At the same time, Gould contends that Plato was capable of unique insight into tragedy's appeal.[19] Aristotle, in contrast, utterly failed to understand both the appeal and the danger of tragedy.

Yet Aristotle overlooked the violence, criminality, madness, and supposed irrational energy and fundamental drive to believe in injustice, because he did not see emotions as essentially disrupting or polluting. He was willing to consider them not as a disease but as a healthy part of ethical and political life. So although Plato and Aristotle saw the same appeal to emotions in tragedy, Plato saw this appeal as polluting to the intellect and to the just life, whereas Aristotle saw it as a means of education and political cohesion.

In fact, Gould discusses tragedy only as a psychological question, never as the political question that it was for Plato and Aristotle. Despite his admissions that certain plays such as *Iphigenia in Tauris* reveal a world "congenial to a Socratic," congenial to a believer in rationality and justice and that "the greatest poets all are found to mix 'poetry' and 'philosophy'", Gould claims that philosophy, or the belief in justice, is the enemy of tragedy.[20] Aristotle, he says, chose *Iphigenia*'s plot over *Oedipus the King*'s because it confirms this worldview.[21]

16. Gould, *The Ancient Quarrel*, 258.
17. Ibid., 266.
18. Ibid., 49.
19. Ibid., 85.
20. Ibid., xxii, 257.
21. Ibid., 19.

# Pity

The question of the importance of emotion in tragedy has emerged with a particular forcefulness in recent years. One author complains that much has been written about how tragedy reduces and expels emotion, but little about how it stimulates and sustains emotion.[22] Another claims that criticism's approach to tragedy has had an "intellectualist bias" neglecting its "emotive purposes."[23] Of course, the subject of tragic emotions has existed ever since Plato's critique of them and Aristotle's characterization of tragedy as "the representation of an action which is serious, complete, and of a certain magnitude ... through the arousal of pity and fear effecting the *katharsis* of such emotions" (*Poetics* 1449b25–29).[24] But since perhaps the most influential interpretation of *katharsis* regarded it as purgation of emotions, little later modern work has been done on the point of the positive value of emotion.[25]

Just as the problem of the emotional is now reappearing in commentary on tragedy, appreciation of the *Poetics*'s role in Aristotelian political philosophy has only recently been renewed. Stephen Salkever and Carnes Lord produce two divergent political readings of the *Poetics* that nonetheless agree on the primacy of fear over pity.[26] Salkever maintains that the context for reading the *Poetics* politically should be sought in Aristotle's debate with Plato over the educability of the *demos*. Unlike Plato, Aristotle believes that the *demos* can undergo a *paideia* supplied by tragedy.[27] The nature of this education I shall discuss later; right now I want to consider the emotive means of that teaching. Salkever believes that pity and fear are the only tragic emotions and that they are particularly "humanizing" because they encourage deliberation. Fear is effective this way because of the nature of the audience: "those whose self-understanding and social situation are in a middle position (*hoi metaxu*) between heroic self-sufficiency and wretched desolation." Such people

---

22. W. B. Stanford, *Greek Tragedy and the Emotions* (London: Routledge and Kegan Paul, 1982), 2.

23. Malcolm Heath, *The Poetics of Greek Tragedy* (Stanford: Stanford University Press, 1987), 79.

24. Quotations are from *The* Poetics *of Aristotle: Translation and Commentary*, trans. Stephen Halliwell (Chapel Hill: University of North Carolina Press, 1987).

25. J. Bernays, "Aristotle on the Effect of Tragedy," in *Articles on Aristotle*, vol. 4, ed. Jonathan Barnes, M. Schofield, and R. Sorabji (London: Duckworth, 1979).

26. Stephen Salkever, "Tragedy and the Education of the *Demos*," 274–303; Carnes Lord, *Education and Culture*.

27. Salkever, "Tragedy," 301.

are not subject to excessive anger, either *orgē* or *thumos*; they are not "the very proud, the very angry, and the very manly."[28] Thus, for Salkever, the emotional constitution emerging from tragic spectatorship relies on a low incidence of arrogant anger (note *thumos* is understood as anger) and on a high susceptibility to fear with auxiliary pity.

But it is fear that is central whereas pity is derivative; in fact the "*function or goal of tragedy* is to arouse the sort of fear that makes political deliberation possible" (emphasis added).[29] As Salkever admits, this emphasis on fear can make Aristotle sound much like Hobbes without explaining how Aristotle differs in his view of political emotion. What does distinguish Aristotle, and what Salkever underplays in his account of the *Poetics*, is the role of pity and fellow-feeling.

Similarly, attention to anger and to fear of anger's excesses predominates when Lord analyzes Aristotle's account of tragedy's educational effect. He makes the important connection between *thumos* and *katharsis*, arguing that through *katharsis* tragedy moderates the *thumos*, yet he is incautious about the various meanings of *thumos*. In one instance, he describes *thumos* as connected to the class of passions associated with pain, as having a "simple" meaning of anger. In another instance, he claims that the "spirited passions" include fear, pity, indignation, anger, jealousy, and the love of honor or "passions bearing on men's social and political relationship—moral indignation, friendship, the desire for honor and superiority."[30] And finally, he thinks of *thumos* as a singular drive—the "impulse to protect, preserve, extend, and exalt what is one's own as against what is alien or foreign."[31] Such spiritedness without qualification threatens the "predominance in politics of prudence or reason," but moderate spiritedness is the "reasonable assertion of one's rights and interests."[32] Ultimately, Lord scarcely alludes to the emotional experience of tragedy, preferring to rely on the notion of "moderation" of anger and of the desire for domination in particular. As in Salkever there is little role for pity; it is only because the "gentlemen" of the regime are kept out of trouble by their taste for culture that they cease their marauding.[33]

In order to adust these interpretations, I illustrate the part played by pity and the smaller role played by fear in Aristotle's political theater by

28. Ibid., 295.
29. Ibid., 294 and 295.
30. Lord, *Education and Culture*, 161.
31. Ibid., 195.
32. Ibid., 164 and 193 n. 16.
33. Ibid., 202.

considering a play Aristotle uses as a central example. Aristotle finds that Euripides "makes the most tragic impression of all poets" (*Poet.* 1453a29–30), and in his explanation of the kinds of plot devices that elicit the most emotional reaction, he lists Sophocles' *Oedipus the King* and Euripides' *Iphigenia in Tauris* as containing the most affecting recognition scenes. Far less written about than *Oedipus*, *Iphigenia* is perhaps too strange, a story set in a non-Greek land that practices human sacrifice, a tragedy with a happy ending. To an unusual degree the play makes pity its causal agent and its subject. Pity and fear may have been felt equally by the audience, but pity alone propels the characters' action.

In the play, Euripides imagines what really happened to Iphigenia, the daughter of the Homeric Agamemnon, after she was sacrificed to allay the gods and the winds before the Greeks sailed against Troy. Some versions of the myth say that just as the knife was over Iphigenia's neck, Artemis substituted a deer for the young girl, whisking her away to the barbarian land of Tauris. The play begins with Iphigenia lamenting her fate as a priestess for Artemis, condemned to perform the sacrifices of all foreigners who land in Tauris. Her brother, Orestes, whom she has not seen since he was an infant and whom she believes is dead, arrives in Tauris pursued by Furies after killing their mother, Clytemnestra, but Iphigenia does not recognize him. Just before she is to kill the newly arrived foreigner, Iphigenia discovers that he is her brother; together they devise a plan for escape from the Taurian king, and Athena intervenes to bring about a happy ending.

*Iphigenia* begins with the main character in remorse, accepting what she believes is the extinction of her family line and opening onto a community of grief. Iphigenia has had a dream of her family's house being destroyed by a thunderbolt that she interprets as revealing the death of her brother. Her female assistants ask her: "What care is yours, / O daughter of Agamemnon [?]" She responds, "O my attendant women, hard mourning melodies are my task / discordant signing of sorrows / lyreless complaints / the tears of pity" (137; 143–45).[34] They respond with "I will sing you an answering song, / . . . the melody used in lamentation" (179–83), empathizing with the grief for the serious harm of losing a family line when the last male member has died. Despite their sympathy, Iphigenia reveals herself to be changed by her dream's revelation—she

---

34. Translations, unless otherwise noted, are from Euripides, *Iphigeneia in Tauris*, trans. Richmond Lattimore (New York and London: Oxford University Press, 1973). For the Greek I rely on *Euripides Fabulae*, vol. 2, ed. John Diggle (Oxford: Oxford University Press, 1981). Hereafter cited by line numbers referring to the Greek text.

can no longer give sympathy. "O wretched heart of mine, you were considerate / toward strangers formerly, and always pitied them [*galenos esth'a kai philoiktirmon aei*] / ... But now, by reason of my dream ... you who arrive from this time forth will find me harsh" (344–52). Before her dream, when she obeyed both divine command and ancient Taurian custom to sacrifice foreigners, she felt sorrow for her victims; now, because of her misfortune, her capacity to acknowledge her acts through emotion is hampered. There is no more woe in her for the woe of victims.

Real danger threatens in Iphigenia's sensing that she will be uncompassionate, yet that sense is not realized. When Orestes appears, long before they recognize each other, his first words to Iphigenia—"O woman, why do you lament?" (483, my translation)—tell us that, contrary to her declaration, she in fact shows pity toward the strangers. The danger is past and her return to pity moves their encounter. As she speaks, she evokes first the family he will lose, arbitrary fate, and his distance from home, his alien status in an alien land. But Orestes dismisses this pity, because her emotive acknowledgment of him makes his predicament harder for him. Pity threatens to infect him, to make him a coward, unmanly, to evoke his own feeling in the face of death: "Why, mistress, whoever you are, these words of pity [*ti taut' odurēi*], / thus adding to the pain we must look forward to?" (482–83). Iphigenia does not directly confront Orestes' rejection of her concern; instead, she continues to question him for details of his and Pylades' life, first their names, their relationship, their provenance. Orestes resists being drawn into giving his story since that would lead him into pity and human understanding. Instead of giving his name, he offers, "The right name to call me would be Unlucky Man." Iphigenia replies "Give that name to your fate." Since he wants nothing to do with pity, Orestes retorts, "If we die nameless, no one can insult our names" (503). Instead of revealing his town of origin, he says, "It will do no good to answer. I am going to die" (506). But he cannot utterly withstand Iphigenia's questioning and is drawn at least to disclose some news from Argos, and ultimately that Agamemnon's only son, although far from home, is alive. Through this encounter, where both want to deny pity, Iphigenia because she believes she has suffered her own misfortune and Orestes because he believes it will leave him incapable of facing his fate, the pity still propels them toward recognition. They reach recognition because Orestes remains loyal to his *xenos* Pylades, who has accompanied him on his journey to Tauris. When Iphigenia offers to release Orestes without Pylades if he promises to deliver a letter to Argos, he refuses. Instead, Orestes stays to die, while Pylades will return with the letter to Argos, accepting the risk of being accused of betraying his friend and *xenos* in order to obtain his inheritance through Electra, Orestes' sister and Pylades' wife.

The female attendants point out that both fates constitute serious harms, neither of which is clearly more pitiable. Indeed, the play implies a sort of organization of judgments of pity, just as Aristotle suggests that good men declining and bad men both rising and declining in fortune are not pitiable. Orestes, for example, is pitiable to Iphigenia, for killing his mother (559), while Agamemnon is not pitiable (860–67) partly because he himself was without pity. In contrast to the demands of Orestes not to be pitied, the play emphasizes the efficacy of a related emotion, mutual sympathy in collective efforts. Orestes recognizes the women's strong capacity for pity: in order to convince her female attendants to stay silent about their escape plans, Iphigenia tells them: "We are women, a gender disposed kindly to one another / and most loyal in protecting our common affairs" [*gunaikes esmen, philophron allelais genos / soizein te koina pragmat' asphalestatai*] (1059–61, my translation). Even the strong Orestes cannot escape Tauris by swift running or fighting; he must depend on Iphigenia's clever ruse, after he has depended on her pity.

Thus the play revels in the power of pity and friendship to overcome ignorance and oppression. Fear and anger are less dominant features of the narrative. The one eruption of anger by Thoas at the escape of the two protagonists is quickly stifled by the intervention of Athena. It is no wonder, then, that Aristotle emphasizes fear *and* pity as the most overt audience reactions to tragedy. Aristotle sees a congruence between the pity of the characters and the pity of the audience, and the *Iphigenia*, I propose, he regards as paradigmatic for the role of pity in tragedy and in the emotional constitution of citizens. But even if we have a better grasp of Aristotle's preferred emotional orientation for citizens, how is this orientation, especially the occurrence of pity, effected? Here we must look to his discussion of tragedy's plot techniques.

## Recognition

"Recognition [*anagnōrisis*] is unquestionably the least respectable term in Aristotelian poetics"[35] and by extension in his politics. Scenes in which

35. Terence Cave, *Recognitions: A Study in Poetics* (Oxford: Clarendon Press, 1988), 1.

someone recognizes a long-lost sister, brother, father, mother, friend, lover, are considered the stuff of melodrama and romance. Just as there is little political analysis of poetics, so there has been paltry attention to recognition as an honest dramatic device. If in literary theory and practice, as Terence Cave argues, recognition has become more respectable, there is a similar return to recognition in politics and political theory.

Whereas modern political theory stresses the recognition of individuality, uniqueness, or achievement, Aristotle's handling of recognition involves finding kinship in the identity of the other. The stress is on recognizing someone else rather than winning recognition for yourself, although in recognizing the other you recognize yourself. The failure of recognition is not in being misrecognized, or in not being recognized, but in not recognizing. One may object that the use of recognition, a term from the techniques of tragedy, in a political context has no support in Aristotle even if the tragedy is conceived as offering political lessons or guides. But separating the supposed lesson from the means of its production would be artificial. Nevertheless, there is no simple correspondence between the viewing of tragedies structured by recognitions and political life. The significance can only be disclosed within the context of political *thumos*.

In the *Poetics*, along with the other plot elements of reversal and pathos that induce fear and pity leading to *katharsis*, recognition is "a change from ignorance to knowledge, bringing the characters into either a close bond, or enmity, with one another, and concerning matters which bear on their prosperity or affliction" (*Poet.* 1452a30–31). The fear, pity, and *katharsis* are audience phenomena; they provide the intention, purpose, or telos of the tragic genre. What the audience experiences is crucial for deciding what the best tragedy should be like, but in the first instance recognition is something that occurs for a character. What becomes known is the identity of a person: "recognition involves people," although in the lesser kinds it "can relate to inanimate or fortuitous objects," or to deeds committed (*Poet.* 1452a35). In chapter 14, Aristotle differentiates plays according to the protagonist's extent of knowledge: Medea acts in full knowledge; Oedipus without knowledge; Iphigenia acquires knowledge just as she is about to act. Medea knows who her children are; Oedipus did not know that the man he met on the road was his father and that the man's widow was his mother. Thus what characters know or fail to know is the relatedness, the kinship, of someone to themselves. They mistake them for strangers, whereas their kinship dwells inside.

Also important is the dramatic means employed to achieve recognition. A sign such as a scar, a memory returning, and reasoning may all precipitate recognition, but the best kind occurs as a result of the plot itself. In the *Iphigenia*, one of Aristotle's examples in this passage, it is reasonable that Iphigenia should want to smuggle back home a letter asking for rescue, and through reading aloud the letter she is recognized. The less skillful method of direct questioning allows Iphigenia to recognize her brother, Orestes.

With the best method, characters "undergo" a recognition in much the same way in which spectators undergo a *katharsis*. They are seized by events, seized in a moment of shock when they suddenly know their relation to a stranger, know the story of their own lives. Characters become spectators, seeing the life they have led for the first time. The former story of their lives is revealed as false; now they can proceed on the truth of their relationships, their acknowledgment of kinship.

In *Iphigenia*, the two recognitions of course bring great joy, since both Orestes and Iphigenia had been seeking each other (unlike Oedipus, who had been desperately seeking to stay away from his mother and father); but they also create the occasion for more spectatorship and simultaneously for extraordinary cooperation. Just after their recognition of one another, Iphigenia begins to imagine a narrative of happiness in Argos, but then the narrative of her unhappy false sacrifice at her father's hand intrudes. Orestes becomes a sympathetic spectator: "Oh, I can see you, though I was not even there." (854). Iphigenia wonders how they can escape, how they can create their own ending: "But now, what will be the end of it all? / What chance will come my way?" (873–74). It is now the chorus who become spectators to the unfolding action: "As witness, not from hearsay, I will testify / to these events, marvels and past the power of words" (900–903). Sister and brother tell each other more stories, but the centerpiece is Orestes' recounting of his fate: "I can tell you. Here is how my many toils began" (939). In his tale he reveals that his trial for matricide, narrated in the *Oresteia*, failed to placate all the Furies. In Delphi, Orestes says, Apollo offered him freedom from the persecution of these chthonic goddesses if he would retrieve a wooden statue of Artemis housed in the Taurian temple. Thus brother and sister are both spectators, telling each other tales, reliving what the recognition has shown. As Sheila Murnaghan has argued, tragedy and Aristotle's theory of tragedy are true to each other in their mutual emphasis on the displacement of horror, on the "indirection" with which both represent terrible events.[36]

---

36. Sheila Murnaghan, "Sucking the Juice Without Biting the Rind: Aristotle and Tragic Mimesis," *New Literary History* 26 (Autumn 1995): 755–73.

With the preference for recognitions that avert imminent deeds, with mimesis understood as mediated representation rather than direct enactment, Aristotle turns plays into "representations of spectatorship."[37]

But in Aristotle's conception, the characters are not only spectators; tragedies are after all representations of actions. In *Iphigenia* at least, spectatorship leads to action. Because narratives evoke emotion, spectators act. Because they were brothers "in friendship but not by birth" (498, my translation), Pylades and Orestes embarked on the journey to capture the statue of Artemis for which they have come to Tauris. Because they created a narrative of friendship through *xenia*, they are impelled to act together. But the action at the end of the play is Iphigenia's. With Iphigenia's joy upon their mutual recognition comes fear that they will not escape, so her turn comes for heroism, heroism with the cooperation of her female companions. Although she has already said that the job of escaping is too big even for a man, and that her death would not hurt their family whereas the death of the first son would seal their family's extinction, she is urged by Orestes to come up with a plan. He immediately recognizes the alchemical abilities of women with "Women are terribly clever in inventing schemes [*deinai gar hai gunaikes heuriskein technas*]" (1032), and of their talent for pity with "A woman has the power to work on pity [*echei toi dunamin eis oikton gune*]" (1054). It is as though Iphigenia is sketching a model of cooperation with distinctly political overtones. She appeals to the women, as quoted earlier: "We are women, a gender disposed kindly to one another / and most loyal in protecting our common affairs" (1059–61, my translation). She acts partly by weaving a narrative, using fiction to put on a spectacle for Thoas. She claims that because one of the Greek strangers was discovered to have committed matricide, the statue has been polluted and must be brought along with the strangers to an oceanside purification. This feigned spectacle allows the party to board the Greek ships and escape Thoas's anger. Pointing to this aspect of Euripides' play is obviously not meant to suggest that we can agree with the characters' essential conception of women or that Aristotle had any interest in the gender delineations, but that for Euripides pity and sympathy are recognized by female characters as essential to saving life.

If characters become similar to spectators by undergoing recognition, do spectators undergo recognition? And if so, where does this lead them? I have examined the effect of the recognition on the character in a play

37. Murnaghan, "Sucking the Juice," 770.

and specifically on the characters in *Iphigenia*. Now I want to draw out
the effect of recognition on the play's audience, its true spectators. At
the beginning of the *Poetics*, Aristotle briefly considers the natural foundation for the historical development of tragedy: humans are typically
mimetic animals who take pleasure in recognizing representations of
objects, a pleasure extending to the dramatic representation of human
action. The reason for this propensity is that humans enjoy using their
understanding (*dianoia*) "identifying such-and-such as a man, for instance" (*Poet.* 1448b17). Humans take pleasure in detecting the familiar in the strange; even when we cannot identify an object or person per
se, we take pleasure in the colors or craft work. The natural desire to recognize the familiar supports the more specific enactment of tragic recognition. The theme of familiarity ties together the ontological propensity
for recognition and the characters' recognition of a stranger as kin.
Although general recognition appears as essentially cognitive, spectators
react to its mimesis with emotion, because reversal and recognition are
tragedy's "greatest means of emotional power" (*Poet.* 1450a34). They
react, first of all for Aristotle, with fear and pity, each of which depends
upon a judgment of similarity between the spectator and a character. Yet
as spectators we do not respond primarily to the psychic life of the stage
characters, we do not "identify," but we respond to events, to plot structure, and in this case to very particular plot structures of reversal and
recognition. This reaction is consistent with Aristotle's claim that fine
tragedy as a whole is concerned with action above all, especially above
character, because "happiness and unhappiness rest on action.... The
goal is a certain activity, not a qualitative state; and while men do have
certain qualities by virtue of their character, it is in their actions that
they achieve, or fail to achieve happiness" (*Poet.* 1450a14–20). In their
responses, spectators become almost the characters themselves, but in
ways that differ from a simple identification between them. Spectators,
like characters, are subject to and affected by the turn of events and the
acquisition of sudden new knowledge. Their emotions respond to action
and events just as they were required to respond. I say almost like them
because spectators are both like characters and not like them; they
respond to events with fear as if they were the same and they respond
with pity as if they were different or other (we do not pity ourselves
primarily). In the same way friends, for Aristotle, are other selves, both
other and self (*NE* 1170b7). Our responses are not identical with the
characters partly because the playwright plans the story to lead to
*katharsis*.

Despite ourselves, Aristotle wants us to see, events often bring us to recognition, in *Iphigenia* a recognition that averts catastrophe, in *Oedipus* a recognition of what one has really done and so of what one was and now is consigned to be. The implication is that other sorts of recognitions, those effected through signs such as birthmarks or simply by memory, are contrived and require unusual efforts or tricks. Recognition leads characters to see who a stranger really was, to see their own lives anew, to become a kind of spectator of their own and others' lives, and then to act; for the audience, general recognition is a natural inclination that is reinforced by the recognition undergone by characters through the emotions felt at events enacted.

# Katharsis

In contrast to the tragic emotions and recognition, *katharsis* has been so much discussed that it might easily win the international prize for the secular concept most subject to exegetical interpretation. Almost everyone who has taken up the subject has his or her own view of a word that is most commonly understood as purgation. Stephen Halliwell has been able to discern six broad varieties of *katharsis* interpretations:

1. *Didactic*, emphasizing self-regarding fear over pity
2. *Emotional fortitude*, a 'loosely stoical' view in which the agent is inured to misfortune, and experiences a reduction in emotional susceptibility
3. *Moderation*, in which the experiences and actions one sees in tragedy help to shape future capacities for the same experiences and actions, related to the doctrine of the mean and of habituation
4. *Outlet*, consisting in a pleasurable expending of pent-up emotions
5. *Intellectual*, a clarification, for example a removal of false opinion and so of pity and fear for the tragic agent
6. *Structural*, as an internal feature of the work itself [38]

Recent scholarship including Halliwell's has completely rejected the nineteenth-century preference for the outlet or purgation understanding,

---

38. See Stephen Halliwell's excellent summary in *Aristotle's* Poetics, 350–56. He himself favors the moderation view, which involves "psychological attunement or balance, not one of simple or invariable reduction" (352). It rests on Aristotle's theory of habituation and may result in a "heightened capacity for emotion."

especially because of its ill fit with Aristotle's cognitive view of emotion, but this scholarship has not settled on a consensus that would incorporate the psychological, aesthetic, and political aspects to an equal degree.[39]

Salkever's and Lord's views are distinguished by their attention to the political goals of undergoing *katharsis* but are less well developed on the actual process of *katharsis*, even though they devote more time to it than to pity or recognition. Salkever's view on the process is particularly suggestive, but I discuss both because they reveal how easily one can stray from the emotional nature of tragedy's effects. In Lord's analysis, *katharsis* happens through a partial, rather than total, purgation of pity and fear[40] and later a "purification" rather than a purgation,[41] but this seems to be the result of intellectual reflection. *Katharsis* is said to occur when the audience reacts to the hero, whose story demonstrates the dangerous excesses of spiritedness.[42] Rather than our feeling with the characters, it appears from Lord's language that we learn a lesson cognitively by seeing overly spirited characters punished. What is crucial is not what we feel during the play, but what we apprehend, and later what we do with the apprehension or lesson. We learn to see what in the protagonist's character is responsible for initiating the tragedy; we learn that he or she has the *hamartia* (fault) of an excess of anger or spiritedness.[43] The lesson acts to "fortify the audience" against their own future excesses of spiritedness. Although he mentions that Aristotle acknowledges that the punishment is disproportionate to the vice, Lord does not say how, given the lack of fairness, the lesson is a good one.

Salkever has several alternative ways of describing *katharsis*. First, he lists three lessons learned via *katharsis*, but he then disavows the idea that tragedy is overdidactic, explaining the educative effect as a "focusing of concern rather than a direct teaching or admonition."[44] Or, *katharsis* can be understood in terms of Aristotle's distinction between form and matter as the "unobtrusive imposition of a certain form upon a certain kind of matter (the democratic audience) by encouraging acceptance of a

39. See also the recent views of Jonathan Lear, "Katharsis"; Richard Janko, "From Catharsis to Aristotelian Mean"; Alexander Nehamas, "Pity and Fear in the *Rhetoric* and the *Poetics*"; all in *Essays on Aristotle's* Poetics, ed. Amelie Oksenberg Rorty (Princeton: Princeton University Press, 1992). Martha Nussbaum also discusses *katharsis* in *The Fragility of Goodness* (New York: Cambridge University Press, 1986).

40. Lord, *Education and Culture*, 159.

41. Ibid., 164.

42. Ibid., 173.

43. Ibid., 171.

44. Salkever, "Tragedy," 300.

certain opinion about what is truly fearful."[45] Finally, he offers Aristotle's actuality-potentiality theory as a basis for saying that what needs *katharsis* is not "something requiring purge or lustration, but rather that which is primarily potential and in need of being shaped."[46] Unfortunately, the subject of this *katharsis* is referred to only as "that which lacks *katharsis*," never as anything more specific. The ideas of concern-focusing, form imposition, and actuality-shaping are useful, but not without a clearer understanding of the nature of emotion and the emotional capacity.

Salkever's version of *katharsis* generally corresponds with the intellectual type described by Halliwell, while Lord's mixes the moderation and the intellectual type. Their versions differ from all those Halliwell mentions in their specifically political results and in their reference to particular political classes. Salkever's gains credence from the historical association of tragedy and democracy, while Lord's is more plausible if we stress the *Poetics* as elucidating tragic theater for the *Politics*'s ideal aristocratic regime. Yet this context would mean that the class of the spirited (in Lord's terms) men are equivalent to the entire citizen class as Aristotle describes it in book 8. Who, then, are the nonspirited men? Surely the laborers and agriculturists do not count as a comparison, and neither do the female quasi-citizens. If spiritedness retains the image of the desire for preeminence, among whom of worth would the spirited be preeminent when everyone in the citizen class was spirited—in Lord's terms? Does he mean that only the best, who are also the spirited, will be sophisticated enough to go through the *katharsis* of tragedy, whereas the rest of the audience will gain certain peripheral and more vulgar pleasures? But he does not say this. Neither Salkever nor Lord claims that Aristotle thought tragedy could only effect its *katharsis* in democracies or highly limited democracies equivalent to aristocracies of spirited men. Nor do they claim that different types of *katharsis* fit with different regimes. Neither thinks of *katharsis* as an expulsion of unsalutary emotion, but they also do not consider the experience a positive training in emotion.

Yet all that Aristotle says about *thumos* should make an alternative view more plausible. Since it appears there is a general emotional capacity, *thumos*, one that has an optimum ethical and therefore political arrangement, and since the *Poetics* appears to be a prescriptive work, *katharsis* should be seen as ethical and political configuration or shaping,

45. Ibid., 300.
46. Ibid., 301.

one involving a clear object: the *thumos*.[47] The movement in the *thumos*, the teaching or alteration that the *katharsis* is supposed to accomplish, does not involve the acceptance of any opinion, although emotions can be altered or aroused by opinion, as the *Rhetoric* attests. What we must ask here is: How is virtue or *hexis* learned? How is the *hexis* of *thumos* learned? That is, how is the "condition, either good or bad, in which we are, in relation to the emotions" (*NE* 1105b26), learned? Aristotle's first answer is that moral virtue results from habits (*NE* 2.1). We develop *hexeis* by corresponding activities; we become just by performing just actions, courageous by performing courageous actions. Likewise, we feel appetites and emotions in the right way "by reacting in one way or in another to given circumstances" (*NE* 1103b19).

But we also learn or continue to learn by spectatorship. One of the reasons that even supremely happy people will need friends is that their "moral purpose or choice is to observe actions which are good and which are his own, and such are the actions of a good man who is his friend" (*NE* 1170a3–4). In fact, "we are better able to observe our neighbors than ourselves, and their actions better than our own" (*NE* 1169b34). Virtues and their local applications in the right manner, at the right time, are learned by watching a person of practical wisdom, by being a spectator of another person's actions. Unlike elementary schooling, learned discussions, and philosophy, tragedy appeals to us in our capacity to feel emotion, because that is how we primarily react to other people when we watch the stories of their lives. Philosophy can use this, but by itself rational discussion, even when infused with emotion, cannot substitute for a mimesis of responding to people in actual life. Although there are similarities, watching a tragedy is more concentrated and more structured than watching a person of practical wisdom. We do not learn rules of conduct, but patterns of conduct, patterns of emotion, of what can happen when we feel in this way, at that time, toward this person, on account of this reason. We learn, in other words, emotional scenarios.[48]

---

47. In *The Fragility of Goodness*, Martha Nussbaum likewise stresses the emotions as keys to understanding *katharsis*. On her reading, *katharsis* is a "clarification" through the emotional response of pity and fear of our common vulnerability (390). She adds that it would be a mistake to take this definition as implying an instrumental use of emotion to reach rational enlightenment. Emotions are necessary for perception and good judgment (307–9). My account builds on hers, adding to clarification the notion of emotional shaping, or configuration, through the habituation of emotions.

48. See Ronald de Sousa, *The Rationality of Emotion* (Cambridge: MIT Press, 1990), for an account of "paradigm scenarios"; and Catherine A. Lutz, *Unnatural Emotion: Everyday Sentiments on a Micronesian Atoll and their Challenge to Western Theory*

The distance that mimesis creates, even as it brings us into touch with the other, allows us to reflect on those emotions so that although we may be engulfed by pity, fear, or anger, we start to wonder why this situation, fictional and yet possible, makes us feel this way. We learn that, in a serious consideration of human action, pity is as efficacious and as necessary as fear and that recognition should lead one to feel benevolence. *Katharsis* is that distancing that allows reason and emotion to work closer together in order to reaffirm the efficacy and need for pity and fear as an opening for friendship or metaphorical kinship. As Salkever maintains, *katharsis* is a shaping, but one that acts to shape the general emotional capacity of the spectator through an interplay of distance and presence. *Katharsis* is one means to coax the *thumos* to react habitually well in political situations.

## Lessons and Configuration

So far I have compared the treatment of pity, recognition, and *katharsis* in two prominent commentators with the treatment in the *Poetics* and in the *Iphigenia*. Yet these elements of tragedy converge in the political lessons of tragic spectatorship. Salkever's and Lord's treatment of this final issue is governed by their assumptions about the socioeconomic class of the audience.

Salkever's key premise is that, for Aristotle, tragedy is directed to a moderately democratic audience, for a democratic audience is both most susceptible to and most in need of tragedy. The focusing of concern constituting *katharsis* enables the audience to "act well, or at least not to act badly" by being protected from a universal inclination to act unjustly, and to learn: "First, that serious mistakes are possible, and one must therefore act with caution; second, that wealth, social prestige, and the power to do whatever we want do not necessarily bring happiness, and one must therefore resist the tendency to identify freedom and happiness with power; third, that the familial order is as fragile as it is precious, and so

---

(Chicago: University of Chicago Press, 1988) where she writes: "In each cultural community there will be one or more 'scenes' identified as prototypic or classic or best examples of particular emotions.... The scenes each emotion concept evokes are most typically social scenes involving relations between two or more individuals. The emotions can be seen as sociocultural achievements in the fundamental sense that they characterize and create a relationship between individuals and groups" (211).

requires the support of institutions such as the laws if it is to be maintained."[49] "[T]ragic art is crucial to the successful actualization of a good democracy,"[50] because it reinforces the disposition to respond to threats with deliberation, rather than with resignation or revenge, on the part of those of "mediocre fortune."[51] Again the dominant emotion is fear.

Salkever's emphasis on training for deliberation accords with Carnes Lord's on *phronēsis* (or, as he calls it, political wisdom or prudence), but they clearly differ on the nature of the audience. Lord argues that Aristotle views tragedy as a lesson for aristocrats: "Particularly for gentlemen who are disposed to be susceptible to the spirited passions and to condone and even to admire such susceptibility in others, tragedy provides, as it seems, a salutary demonstration of their dangerous excesses."[52] More positively, tragedy is an "education par excellence of spirited gentlemen in political virtue or prudence."[53]

Thus, Salkever believes tragedy's political lessons are directed toward moderate democrats; in contrast, Lord finds them directed toward moderate aristocrats. Yet the lessons are similar. For the democrat, excessive love of power and wealth are shown to be unstable guides to happiness, while for the aristocrat, the same excessive love of power, glory, and wealth, although euphemistically called spiritedness, is shown to be incompatible with social order. These counsels clearly involve the arousal of fear, for we fear the repercussions of such excesses, but less clearly explain how tragedy involves pity and recognition.

Neglecting pity and recognition has consequences particularly for a feminist reappraisal of Aristotle. Elsewhere Salkever has argued that Aristotle, along with Plato, deprecates the ancient Greek connection of politics, war, and virility.[54] In so doing Salkever opposes the civic republican, and sometimes feminist, interpretation of Aristotle as a proponent of a public, political sphere superior to a private, economic, and familial sphere. Instead, for Salkever, Aristotle counsels "moderate alienation" from politics, minimizing the public sphere of aggression, domination, and spiritedness (*thumos*), while recommending attention to family, personal friends, and philosophy. In Salkever's article on the *Poetics* that I have

---

49. Salkever, "Tragedy," 300.
50. Ibid., 303.
51. Ibid., 295–96.
52. Lord, *Education and Culture*, 173.
53. Ibid., 164
54. See chapter 4 of Stephen Salkever's *Finding the Mean: Theory and Practice in Aristotelian Political Philosophy* (Princeton: Princeton University Press, 1990).

been discussing, he similarly stresses the moderately semipolitical audience. Lord, on the other hand, believes that the aggressive, spirited, and political quest for honor—read virility and masculinity—can be successfully managed but will inevitably persist.

Yet Aristotle accomplishes something more thoroughgoing than either Salkever or Lord propose. He theorizes a way to reorient political life by educating the emotional repertoire of citizens. So virility or spiritedness is no longer a constant, natural feature of political life, however capable of moderation. Nor is the answer immersion in apparently nonpolitical activities or the tragic spectator's experience of fear. Rather Aristotle, after rejecting conventional Greek virility, incorporates a reformed emotional orientation or configuration into the ideal political psyche.

My account, then, of the configuration of Aristotelian political emotion builds on an interpretation of *thumos* as open to such training and on Aristotle's keen sense that the treatment of strangers was the nub of the problem of polis cooperation. Athenian tragedy pondered the problems associated with the development of the polis, overshadowed as it was by the persisting social values of Bronze Age heroic society. Rituals of *xenia* had once provided for cooperation between strangers; now the new institutions of polis cooperation needed refinement. For this task, Aristotle addresses the emotions and tragedy.

If we use the *Iphigenia* to understand the *Poetics*, we have to change our sense of the effect of tragedy on the *thumos* or a person's emotional capacity. Pity in the *Iphigenia* accomplishes the recognition; more pity accomplishes the escape that in turn accomplishes the quelling of anger and the institution of a new ritual. The *hamartia* or mistake is not an excessive anger (Lord) or a failure to fear the mistakes of the powerful (Salkever), but the failure to recognize the kin in the stranger. While we watch *Iphigenia*, the *katharsis* allays our fear of overlooking our kinship, leaving a keenly attuned pity and sympathy as a way of averting disaster. We might be prone to see the scene of encountering strangers in our daily lives as a dangerous moment when we may miss similarity and fail to incorporate these strangers into the system of cooperation supporting the development of the good life. For rulers and citizens these are crucial orientations, for through pity or compassion both must perceive the nature and extent of human suffering, be disposed through recognition to seeing kinship, and act to reinforce the necessary dependency of citizens on one another. While fear and reversal may be half the story, pity and recognition are the other half.

Thus the *thumos* of good Aristotelian citizens, that is, their emotional capacities, should be shaped to feel pity, meaning to feel a kinship with citizens and strangers. Without this configuration of emotional habits, political friendship is very difficult. Among the key institutions that shape the *thumos* are dominant forms of narrative art or cultural production. This lesson is learned through a political reading of the *Poetics* and *Iphigenia in Tauris* in the context of a revised view of *thumos*.

Whether anything Aristotle has to say is particularly relevant to modern liberal democratic politics is a disputable issue.[55] I maintain that Aristotle is unusually able to trace the workings of emotion in political life, not in the service of helping us to become less emotional and so more rational, but to align our rational and emotional political capacities. Where emphasis is put on the rational in political theory and practice, there one will find less response to the needs, welfare, and benefaction for citizen strangers and foreign strangers. Where emphasis is put on the emotions, duly understood as dependent on beliefs and evaluations, culturally learned, there one will find more willingness to learn how to increase mutual benefaction and efforts to augment the welfare of all. So contemporary political thinking that learns from Aristotle would look to analyzing what emotions are at work in the political culture and in particular political issues, analyze how various institutions, not only cultural production of narratives (film and television in our case), but also political rhetoric and structures of political participation, inculcate emotional dispositions, and be ready to argue for good political emotions and those institutions that support them. To show how this could be done is the subject of the following chapter.

---

55. For critics of such relevance, see Stephen Holmes, "Aristippus in and out of Athens," *American Political Science Review* 73 (March 1979): 113–28; and John Wallach, "Contemporary Aristotelianism," *Political Theory* 20 (November 1992): 613–41. For a contrary view, see Stephen Salkever's *Finding the Mean*; and Martha Nussbaum, "Aristotelian Social Democracy," in *Liberalism and the Good*, ed. R. Bruce Douglass, Gerald M. Mara, and Henry Richardson (New York: Routledge, 1990).

# 6

# Gender and Contemporary Political Emotion

In a recent U.S. presidential election season, journalists were busy examining the paradox of an educated and accomplished woman serving as first lady. In a news article on the issue of Hillary Rodham Clinton, Betty Ford's former press secretary postulated this view of the relationship between a president and a first lady: "I look at the roles as a head-heart distinction. The President is elected. He's the head. The East Wing is the heart. For an Administration to be successful, it has to have both. When Rosalyn Carter sat in at a Cabinet meeting, there was a lot of criticism, and rightly so. It was the wrong symbolism. It made people wonder, 'Where's the heart? Where's the compassion?' She was doing something she wasn't elected to office to do."[1] This extraordinary, blunt quotation demonstrates four elements of a cultural consensus on the emotional. The first and least surprising element is the split between reason and

---

1. Felicity Barringer, "Hillary Clinton's New Role: A Spouse or a Policy Leader?," *New York Times*, November 16, 1992, A1, A14.

emotion, or between the head and the heart. Not only do the anatomical metaphors of the head and the heart clearly separate and demarcate reason and emotion, but this language proceeds to give meaning to two apparently separate social and political roles.

Second, the split in reason and emotion, in head and heart, in president and first lady, is a gender split. Without explicitly pointing to the association, the problem in the quotation is the problem of the woman, her crossing of boundaries, her emotion infecting the head.

Third, the quotation associates the heart with altruistic or agreeable emotions. Similarly the phrase "Have a heart!" is a command or plea, depending on one's perspective, to show mercy, or compassion, or some other "soft" or caring emotion. It is does not command someone to rouse their anger.

Fourth, the view of the world expressed in the quotation evinces a fear of women relinquishing their duties of the heart and their practice of love. If the woman joins the scene of deliberation and decision making, the heart, the compassion, may altogether disappear. While an administration needs both head and heart, as the former press secretary says, the first lady works more as the chief liaison to heartful charities than as an equal commander of administrative activities. The president rules over the political sphere of tough bargaining, power plays, of calculating support and standing firm. And while the actual practice of politics depends on calculative rationality, although often it uses manipulative emotion, it serves to secure, at least in the liberal tradition, rational self-interest and rational autonomy.

This divide between head and heart, reason and emotion—especially emotions such as compassion—structures not just presidential decision making, but more fundamentally what counts as politics. This divide also determines what amounts to a good political theory by reinforcing gendered categories. In fact, discourses on emotion have been called a politics of gender by other means.[2] This present book is about the role of emotions in politics, as well as the meaning of the political once we theoretically recognize emotions working at the center of politics, rather than agreeably sitting in the other wing. At the core of this book has been the argument that we should return to a close examination of Aristotle's understanding of emotional capacity, or *thumos*, as a way of retrieving political emotion. I found in my own reading that when political theorists

2. Catherine Lutz, "Engendered Emotion: Gender, Power, and the Rhetoric of Emotional Control in American Discourse," in *Language and the Politics of Emotion*, ed. Catherine A. Lutz and Lila Abu-Lughod (Cambridge: Cambridge University Press, 1990).

have paid attention to this aspect of his work, Aristotle has been incorrectly amalgamated with Plato on the question of the meaning and the political role of emotion; they have been taken to mean the same thing by *thumos*. As a result, in political theory, it is Plato's views that have predominated, over Aristotle's substantially different ones. And while classicists have surely been more sensitive to the complexity of *thumos*, the aims of their discipline have not encouraged them to detail the significance of this concept for political theory.

Retrieving an early version of a theory of political emotion may be of historical interest, but it does not automatically suggest itself as an adequate contemporary theory. We must admit that time has added new questions and answers to Aristotle's views. Indeed, to comprehend adequately both our broadly social and narrowly intellectual inheritance and current position in relation to political emotion, I believe that it is impossible to proceed without engaging, first, an empirical aspect of the emotion-inculcating political institutions and, second, some aspects of the feminist contribution to political theory. In this chapter I proceed by interpreting the emotional dynamics of U.S. Senate debates about welfare reform over two days in 1995. I then use this example as a common reference point to compare liberal, Aristotelian, and care feminist psychological and justificatory approaches to issues of welfare. Although I could have chosen a different example, for many institutions could be analyzed for their implicit scenarios of political emotion, this example best captures what is politically at stake in domestic politics for citizens enmeshed and schooled in their regimes' emotional dispositions. For the purposes of this chapter the liberal approach is a negative contrast because its strategy is to cultivate rational self-interested dispositions through various political institutions and through rationalist moral justification. I focus on care feminism because, out of the abundance of feminist theorizing, it best incorporates attention both to emotion and to political issues with especially wide ramifications in our political culture. In fact, many feminist theorists have contributed to the ongoing reevaluation of the place of emotion in ethics and in philosophy generally. This literature is quite varied, so a comprehensive survey is beyond the scope of this book. In many cases, however, these contributions fail to analyze emotion explicitly or in detail, but rather imply a different status of the emotional and affective capacities of humans.[3] I argue that while care

3. Mary Daly, *Gyn/Ecology: The Metaethics of Radical Feminism* (Boston: Beacon Press, 1978), and *Pure Lust: Elemental Feminist Philosophy* (Boston: Beacon Press, 1984); Susan Griffin, *Woman and Nature* (New York: Harper and Row, 1980); Joan Cocks,

feminism is clearly a radical refocusing of political attention, it harbors a number of deficiencies related to issues surrounding political emotion, some of which lessen its impact in terms of its own goals, others of which damage its ability to offer an admirable vision of the good political society. Ultimately, I offer an approach to political emotion that is inspired by both Aristotle and feminist theory.

Invoking Aristotle and feminism in one sentence may still be startling to some. In the early days of feminist writing on the tradition of political theory, this would have seemed a chimerical or treacherous suggestion. Aristotle was a masculinist, articulating for ages to come the biological and moral inferiority of women and constructing a philosophy and politics based on the renunciation of the feminine. But since I began this project more nuanced and favorable views have appeared, and on the topic of emotion Aristotle is recognized as a crucial forerunner. This is not to say that he has been made over into a fashionably outfitted feminist, nor that with newfound finesse he could be. Still, this book builds on an incipient demasculinization of Aristotle.[4] While there are good reasons for categorizing Aristotle as misogynist, there are others equally as good for discovering in him sources of resistance to dominant gender modes of his time and ours. The expansion of *thumos* should be seen as part of Aristotle's critique of traditional Greek masculinity. In earlier writers such as Homer and Plato, *thumos* most characterizes the warrior, battle is its paradigmatic stage, anger or indignation its most active emotions. In contrast, Aristotle's expansion diminishes its militaristic and masculinist overtones. This shift hardly transforms Aristotle into a protofeminist.

---

"Wordless Emotions: Some Critical Reflections on Radical Feminism," *Politics and Society* 13, no. 1 (1984): 27–57; Alison Jaggar, "Love and Knowledge: Emotion in Feminist Epistemology," in *Gender / Body / Knowledge: Feminist Reconstructions of Being and Knowing*, ed. Alison Jaggar and Susan Bordo (New Brunswick: Rutgers University Press, 1989); Arlie Russell Hochschild, *The Managed Heart: Commercialization of Human Feeling* (Berkeley and Los Angeles: University of California Press, 1983); Genevieve Lloyd, *The Man of Reason: "Male" and "Female" in Western Philosophy*, 2d ed. (Minneapolis: University of Minnesota Press, 1993). For additional citations, see Chapter 1, note 53.

4. The collection of essays *Feminist Interpretations of Aristotle*, ed. Cynthia Freeland (University Park: Pennsylvania State University Press, 1998), explores some of this issue. See also the revisionist views of Deborah Achtenberg, "Aristotelian Resources for Feminist Thinking," and Marcia Homiak, "Feminism and Aristotle's Rational Ideal," both in *Feminism and Ancient Philosophy*, ed. Julie K. Ward (New York: Routledge, 1996); Martha Nussbaum, "Aristotle, Feminism, and Needs for Functioning," *Texas Law Review* 70 (1992): 1019–28; Stephen Salkever in chapter 4 of *Finding the Mean: Theory and Practice in Aristotelian Political Philosophy* (Princeton: Princeton University Press, 1990); and Arlene Saxonhouse, *Women in the History of Political Thought: Ancient Greece to Machiavelli* (New York: Praeger, 1985).

Instead, I contend that thinking *through* Aristotle on these matters can alter our view of the authoritative place of rationality in the philosophical tradition and illuminate emotional aspects of political life silenced and buried by modern history.

# The Rhetoric of Welfare Reform

As a step toward such a theory of political emotion, I would like to demonstrate what an analysis of political emotion relevant to the issue of care feminism would look like by examining the 1995 U.S. congressional debates surrounding "welfare reform." In the spirit of Aristotle's *Rhetoric,* I analyze how Democrats and Republicans deploy emotions to persuade their audiences, and how they draw on cultural scenarios or narratives of political emotion. Saying that they deploy emotion does not mean that their rhetoric is necessarily manipulative, nor that "rational" speeches would be superior. In persuasion, rationality cannot be divorced from emotion, nor should it be. Emotions contain either rational or irrational judgments; their rationality or irrationality must be judged in their particular contexts.[5] Without emotion in political speech and ethical reflection we would loose both the motivation to achieve our ends and perception of the moral problem. Following Aristotle, then, I do not criticize the debates for being emotional, but only use them to show the power of the emotional narratives manifest in political speech and to argue for a political philosophy that theorizes such compelling emotional persuasion.

In 1995, the United States Senate debated welfare reform, specifically the "Work Opportunity Act," a bill proposed to eliminate the federally guaranteed Aid to Families with Dependent Children (AFDC) by allowing states to run their own programs financed partly through federal block grants. The Democratic rival bill, "Work First," was distinguished by its guarantees of child care to employed mothers on AFDC.

Anyone examining the emotional texture of this debate cannot help but immediately notice the almost universal proclamation of the welfare system's failure. Slade Gorton called welfare a "disastrous failure for the American social condition."[6] Kay Bailey Hutchinson concluded that "we

---

5. For a recent version of this argument, see Douglas Walton, *The Place of Emotion in Argument* (University Park: Pennsylvania State University Press, 1992).
6. *Congressional Record,* August 7, 1995, S11752.

have failed miserably."[7] "Taxpayers and those we serve agree this system has failed," according to Bob Dole. Equally, for the democratic Tom Harkin, "today's system is broken."[8] What do these words of failure and brokenness seek to arouse, but despair? Not despair simply, but managed despair, for the idea is to call up the enormity of the past aspiration, its disappointment, and the handiness of the immediately available legislative solutions. The senators can admit to an American failure, can evoke despair for unified solutions, but struggle to reign in the despair with their rhetorical work.

Next, we are asked to quake with imaginative fear. Welfare for Kay Bailey Hutchinson is a "self-perpetuating monster" in whose "coils" we find AFDC mothers and children "lured down a dead end street."[9] We are not exactly asked to sympathize with these victims—Hutchinson does not narrate the experience and feeling of any particular family on AFDC. Rather, the non-AFDC audience is made to feel the monster and its coils, the alien of the federal government in our midst, perhaps in our bellies. Fear is meant to drive us under the program-cutting knife.

If managed despair and imaginative fear are not enough, the senators embolden their audience with excessive pride, the relish of telling people what to do, and sexual dread. All three give life to the specters of dependency and illegitimate or out-of-wedlock births. Spencer Abraham focuses our attention on the 400 percent increase in illegitimate births since 1960 and its source in welfare programs. "We all want to reduce out-of-wedlock births," he reminds us.[10] Joseph Lieberman counsels us to focus on the "causes of welfare-dependency and especially on out-of-wedlock births where no father has assumed responsibility."[11] These comments are just a sampling, since, as is well known, a considerable effort has been launched to reinvigorate the appellations "illegitimate" and "out-of-wedlock." Moral condemnation of the self-defeating results of sexuality appeals to the pride or moral righteousness of those who consider themselves moral and sexually continent. Vicariously, the audience can send a message to the sexually incontinent, can order and direct with the long arm of social policy. The pleasures of moralism are offered here in abundance, because moralism on sexual issues is the most pleasurable kind.

Finally, and most revealingly, the senators often speak about two

8. Ibid., S11760.
9. Ibid., S11753.
10. *Congressional Record*, August 8, 1995, S11818.
11. Ibid., S11834.

characters—one represents their audience, the other the object of a tale of woe. One is called "taxpayer," the other "welfare recipient." The taxpayer has been mildly compassionate, long suffering, and now cruelly abused. Possessing the good of a honest day's work and individual responsibility, he or she can now bestow these on the welfare class. This is a taxpayer who has watched as the federal government's leniency has created a "monster."

The welfare recipient is both victim and perpetrator, trapped in the system's coils, failing to exercise responsibility, self-reliance, or self-sufficiency. According to the senators, welfare expanded not only because government was lenient, but because recipients astutely exploited the government's leniency. They failed to work, had more children, children out of wedlock, and acquiesced in the undermining of paternal authority. This division of taxpayer and recipient encourages animosity and resentment. Two sets of people are divided by the widest gulf—one who supports the nation, the other who simply lives on its product; one gives, the other takes; one is a worker, the other is a parasite. Such is the contemporary cardinal emotional scenario of political anger surrounding welfare.

## Liberal Political Emotion

The most influential competitor to feminist interpretations of political culture is the reigning liberal political tradition. Although in recent years many scholars have challenged the hegemony of liberal discourse in the heritage of United States politics, normative liberal theorists still largely work within a traditional liberal framework. In what way, then, can liberal political psychology account for the senatorial rhetoric of welfare reform? In the past, liberal psychology has been easy to caricature, primarily because twentieth-century liberal theorists neglected their classical seventeenth-century inheritance. This, at least, is the argument of Stephen Holmes's *Passions and Constraints*, in which he contends that early liberal theorists had a rich, complex political psychology, centered on the fragility of reason and the rarity of interest calculations.[12] No liberal conceived of human beings as driven overwhelmingly by rational egoism. Instead, Holmes argues that for liberals "[o]rdinary human

12. Stephen Holmes, *Passions and Constraint: On the Theory of Liberal Democracy* (Chicago: University of Chicago Press, 1995).

motivation ... is shot through with habit and passion, custom and impulse. The rational assessment of costs and benefits has a real but modest and episodic role in shaping human behavior. Reason's importance varies enormously from context to context and is seldom the only decisive factor."[13] For Locke, Hobbes, Hume, Kant, Smith, and Mill, humans are driven by a multitude of selfless, noncalculating, irrational passions as diverse and contentious as cruelty, pride, megalomania, desire for glory, envy, fear, and sometimes even pity and affection. To cure the disease of the passions, liberals typically promote calculating self-interest as moral reform because a people devoted to economic advancement "will, for the most part, rationally pursue self-preservation oblivious to the siren song of aristocratic glory and religious redemption."[14] In the liberal vision, nurturing the motivation of "rational self-interest" requires an assiduous transformation of social manners and institutions.[15] To that psychological end they promote first a commercial society, second, individualism, and third, constitutional and democratic deliberative institutions, including a wall between church and state.

Notice that although Holmes defends liberalism from the charge that it as a reductionist psychology, that in particular it promotes antisocial, atomistic, self-centered lives, he still argues that rational self-interest is the aspiration if not the reality of liberalism. In some ways it does not make much difference to our policies and deliberations whether liberalism's intellectual acuity can be successfully defended; as liberals we would still recommend what the critics of liberalism believe liberalism simply assumes. Whether rational self-interest is prescription or description might matter if we wished to ascertain how hard liberals must work to transform a typical person's psyche, but assumptions underlying our deliberations and the policies recommended would look pretty much the same.

The gaping emotional absence in the middle of Holmes's account becomes most obvious when he confirms welfare rights as a part of the tradition of classical liberalism. Although he concedes that there is no necessary relationship between liberalism and support for welfare rights, he contends that early liberals did and would have no problem supplying such support. Yet, unaccountably, he omits any references to the passions. Whereas at the beginning of the book liberalism is vividly defended for its psychological acumen, now not a word is said on the

13. Ibid., 267.
14. Ibid., 25.
15. Ibid., 26.

subject of what political psychology would foster social welfare. Such an omission encourages us to wonder how well liberalism can deal with the passions of welfare politics.

Following Holmes's model of liberal political psychology, we should expect various liberal institutions to have done the psychological work of inculcating rational self-interest in the populace and its representatives. Moreover, we might expect those given the responsibility for deliberating and persuading in legislatures to approach issues with the intention of eliciting self-interest and quelling the relevant disagreeable passions. In fact, if we examine actual debates, we see that the psychological work done in these debates is not the inculcation of rational self-interest, but the specifically emotional work of reinforcing narratives of what I will call managed despair, imaginative fear, bourgeois anger, and sexual dread. These disagreeable political emotions are enhanced rather than dispelled by appeals to rational self-interest, and thus Holmes's model fails to describe what happens in this case. Much of Holmes's model depends on the unexamined contrast between emotion and reason. Rational self-interest can oppose disagreeable passions so successfully because it is supposed to be the other of emotion. But the dichotomy is false. It is apparent from the story of the rise of "interest," as Albert Hirschman tells it, that rational self-interest is itself an emotion, albeit disguised in the mystifying costume of reason. Of course, this is only one case, and I look at the emotional work done not by the institutions Holmes describes, but by oratory within one such institution. Yet I believe that this case is a significant one because it engages the deep assumptions about how liberal citizens see themselves as related to one another. Furthermore, insofar as we think of this legislative assembly as an institution, oratory is an integral part of it.

In the paradigmatic strategy of liberal political theory, then, self-interest calms the passions. And in the Senate debates, too, self-interest is not missing. The very word "taxpayer" must recall the monetary interest of the audience. Welfare reform is clearly first and foremost in the interest of the taxpayer—AFDC payments infringe on the income the taxpayer has earned. But this self-interest, rather than calming, dampening, or offsetting the passions, is strangely in collusion with them. The words of the Senators invoke managed despair, imaginative fear, excessive pride, the relish of telling people what to do, animosity, and resentment. Such passions, which in liberal psychology ordinarily opposed self-interest, feed on and are directed by self-interest.

Liberal political psychology, therefore, fails to achieve its purpose of calming disagreeable passions. Self-interest inspires rather than tames socially harmful dispositions. The emotional narrative of John Locke's civil contractor continues to inhabit contemporary politics, generating new narratives of good and evil. In Locke's *Second Treatise*, fear, anxiety, and discomfort, mixed with rational calculations of the advantages of establishing a common authority, propel the naturally acquisitive human into political society. Because humans were materially independent before the establishment of political society, political society is unnecessary to human advancement, according to Locke, except as protection against the tyrannical and criminal incursions of other people. No motives of benevolence and compassion are necessary for, or characteristic of, political society. In fact, for Locke the purpose of the good society *eliminates* the emotions of fear and anxiety he does discuss.

Liberal political psychology of the kind that Holmes adumbrates echoes through recent liberal strategies for justifying welfare policies. Since liberals hope that rational self-interest will save us from pernicious passionate enthusiasms of various kinds, their moral justifications often employ premises assuming rational agency.[16] But these approaches neglect the emotional conditions required for moral arguments. In so doing their stress on individual autonomy and rationality conflict with the apparent dependency and slavishness in welfare recipients.

## Aristotelian Political Emotion

Aristotle, as I have shown, was moving in the direction of considering *thumos* as a general emotional capacity. This move enabled him to see that on another view politics required less the protection of the boundaries of one's honor and material wealth than the active involvement in providing the conditions of happiness for others as part of noble action in general.

In Aristotle's political philosophy we sample the relationship between a social understanding of emotion and the education of emotion through inculcation into an idea of the good life. With Aristotle's view of emotion, unlike Rousseau's for example, we have access to the context for individual

16. John Rawls, *A Theory of Justice* (Cambridge, Mass.: Harvard University Press, 1971); Raymond Plant, Harry Lesser, and Peter Taylor-Gooby, eds., *Essays on the Normative Basis of Welfare Provision* (Boston: Routledge and Kegan Paul, 1980); Jeff Reiman, *Justice and Moral Philosophy* (New Haven: Yale University Press, 1990).

emotion. The regime or way(s) of life promoted by a regime are the first influences on the scenarios and variations of emotions. The regime itself through its symbolic language will function by arousing and quelling certain emotions. Political oratory, tragedy, and the institutional activities of citizenship all inculcated (and sometimes manipulated) political emotion. The best political emotional disposition, the political *thumos*, was a balance between anger, fear, pity, and affection. Judicious anger supports the desire for freedom and independence. Fear checks the overweening inclinations of anger. Pity opens the doors to recognizing kinship between oneself and others. Affection supports regularized benefaction giving meaning and pleasure to our dependence on one another. But it should not be forgotten that the characteristic work or *ergon* of the human being is activity of the soul in conformity with the rational element. At its best, the soul's reason, emotion, desire, and pleasure are aligned.

The lessons of Aristotle's approach to political emotion could be summarized in this way:

(1) Political emotion is political in the sense that there exist paradigm scenarios of political involvement and affect, just as there are such scenarios of how we meet companions. Such scenarios can be found in political theories as well as in popular culture, including film, television, and political performances of culturally significant holidays and rituals. Perhaps no scenario can be said to be the one unique scenario of contemporary political emotion, but political culture gains whatever unity it has in part from prominent paradigm scenarios. Interpreting these scenarios gives us important insight into how political regimes work, how they generate loyalty, how they create images of the relationship between citizens, how they manage what goods we expect from political community and what we are willing to give to community and other individuals.

(2) A good politics depends in large part on being able to encourage good emotional dispositions, to harmonize with good rational judgments. Emotions can be addressed only through agent-centered ethics and politics. In contrast, rule-centered ethics relies either on a set of specific instructions (which might of course have commands for feeling certain emotions) or, more typically, on a rational content-neutral rule used as a procedure to test maxims of action. Agent-centered ethics addresses the character of a person, his or her typical motivations, responses, and therefore his or her emotions. In its political application, agent-centered ethics raises issues of the good—substantive public purposes such as cultural achievement, international domination, or economic prosperity. It asks which of these purposes are to become a regime's guiding purpose(s). It

also asks smaller, but no less relevant, questions such as how the regime should support the individual capacity to achieve the best life, however construed.

(3) Since virtues or excellences include action and emotions learned by habitual performance, actions and emotions will be learned through social institutions. Habit does not refer to mere repetition of individualized behavior, but to repetition of action, gesture, and feeling of an exemplary person. But the idea of such a person creates institutions, as if she herself had left tracks and furrows in which we can approximate her action and emotions. A political theory incorporating political emotion will examine institutions for their contribution to good political emotional dispositions.

(4) Just as there is a certain organization to the virtues, oriented around the life of the mind or politics for example, so there is a certain organization of emotions that supports the virtues. *Thumos* refers to that particular psychic capacity for emotion that will be organized by the virtues and by institutions. Each regime will offer an answer to the question of what constitutes human happiness and who is the exemplary good person and so will answer what virtues of emotions and acts are required. It should be noted that although I have argued that we must appreciate the historical variability of emotional norms, scenarios, and styles, and so it would seem that all we can do is to leave *thumos* to the ancient Greeks, in fact the idea of *thumos* is not so utterly culturally and historically distant from us that we cannot conceive it as a partial model for our own times. J. Peter Euben has insisted on both the historical distinctiveness of Greek tragedy and its usefulness for the present, writing that Greek tragedies "dramatize the limits of our political discourse, disclosing the exclusions it sustains and the parts of our lives it misdescribes or fails to recognize."[17] This point well suits the history of Greek *thumos*.

For Aristotle, justification of emotional dispositions and welfare practices relies on his conception of *eudaimonia*, happiness or flourishing. As Aristotle understands flourishing, it is the active, well-developed use of our rational and emotional capacities accompanied by external goods such as moderate wealth, family, and friends. Aristotle articulates this well-developed use of our capacities through a list of virtues or excellences, both moral and intellectual. So the flourishing person actively uses what Aristotle calls theoretical wisdom when contemplating philosophical

17. J. Peter Euben, *The Tragedy of Political Theory: The Road Not Taken* (Princeton: Princeton University Press, 1990), 48–49.

issues, practical wisdom when considering how to achieve flourishing in general, and the moral virtues including courage, friendship, generosity, and justice when living through everyday life. In other words, to be a good person means far more than refraining from harming someone else; it also means positive action both in one's own life and toward others. It means seeking out situations where you will have to use your intellectual capacities or display your moral courage or generosity. And because, as I mentioned, we have not only rational but also emotional capacities, themselves intertwined, and because moral virtues such as courage are ways of feeling before they are ways of acting (with the help of practical wisdom), a good life requires not only acting but feeling the proper emotions "at the right object, in the right way, and at the right time" (*NE* 1119b18–20).

Look at the two virtues relevant to welfare—generosity and friendship. Part of human flourishing is having learned how to feel generous and affectionate and how to desire the good of your friends, and then to engage in those activities that enable you to exercise the actions and emotions associated with generosity and friendship. A generous and friendly person then seeks to express these virtues by acts and emotions of generosity and friendship.

For Aristotle the sphere of moral action was first and foremost politics, with its political friendship between citizens, and then personal friendship. If this is the case, the political regime in which we live first should be oriented to enabling as many people as possible to live well and should establish practices and institutions of benefaction. Like those who want to abolish all forms of social provision, Aristotle believed that to some extent people's needs are met in the household—but by women who had no part in the public world and by slaves who were incapable of public life. Yet he still believed that participation in politics meant providing for the material as well as the mental flourishing of other citizens. I think we should learn from Aristotle that the elimination of public practices of benefaction would entail the removal of more people from public life, women especially, and that even if such public practices were removed, then men would still be needy for help from other men. Notice that political practices create the opportunities for expression of these virtues; welfare practices, at their best, provide those opportunities.

Notice again that this account of flourishing values, not just our rational agency or our ability to choose for ourselves, for which liberty will be needed, but also our emotional agency. To speak this way about emotion may be strange to many of us because we have a tendency to believe that emotions are uncontrollable, individual, subjective phenomena. Yet for Aristotle and the growing number of contemporary theorists I described in Chapter 1, emotions are complex composites of factual beliefs, moral evaluations, physical sensations, and social narratives. They are as much socially learned as they are dependent on individual history and biological inheritance. On this account, a political regime is judged partly by how it inculcates emotions. If a regime devotes itself to the military virtues of courage above all else, as some ancient city-states were, then it will have stunted its citizens' emotional capacities.

## Care Feminism and Feminist Political Emotion

One substantive, prescriptive feminist ethical and political theory that in some measure formulates a connection between emotion and political life is the ethic of care and care feminism. The catalyst for this burgeoning discussion in feminist moral and political theory was Carol Gilligan's work on moral development among women that theorized the existence of an "ethic of care."[18] The reigning model of moral development was based entirely on studies of men, and then later when applied to women, left them generally at lower levels of development. In a series of studies that emphasized questions of how participants defined moral problems rather than questions that ask participants to solve hypothetical moral dilemmas, Gilligan claimed to have discovered a coherent alternative conception of morality with its own sequence of development. The reigning model of how people do and should think morally presented a hierarchy of six stages divided into three levels rising from the "preconventional" through the "conventional" to the "postconventional, autonomous, or principled level." At the highest stage, moral thinking is "defined by the decision of conscience in accord with self-chosen ethical principles appealing to logical comprehensiveness, universality, and consistency. These principles are abstract and ethical (the Golden Rule, the categorical imperative); they are not concrete moral rules such as the Ten Commandments."[19] In contrast, Gilligan suggested a three-stage approach that rises from an initial stage of selfishness, where decisions are based

18. Carol Gilligan, *In a Different Voice: Psychological Theory and Women's Development* (Cambridge, Mass.: Harvard University Press, 1982).
19. Lawrence Kohlberg, *The Philosophy of Moral Development: Moral Stages and the Idea of Justice* (San Francisco: Harper and Row, 1981), 19.

on a concern for the self and not for others, to the second stage of self-sacrifice, where decisions are based on a notion of responsibility to others and on whether an action ensures care for the dependent and unequal (conventional maternal and feminine morality), to the final stage of maturity where decisions are based on care both for others and for self. The mature self is recognized as interdependent and becomes universal in its condemnation of exploitation and hurt.

In countering Kohlberg's model, Gilligan intended to recover the dignity of women's moral deliberation and to suggest that the gender divide in occupations and ways of life had consolidated into two different and distinct modes of moral deliberation, one of which was conveniently derided and ignored by moralists and moral philosophers alike. If she seemed to some readers to be perpetuating the traditional, age-old stereotype of the kind-hearted, compassionate woman and the just, rule-bound man, or at least the fact of some gender difference, Gilligan herself asserted that "the contrasts between male and female voices are presented here to highlight a distinction between two modes of thought and to focus a problem of interpretation rather than to represent a generalization about either sex. In tracing development, I point to the interplay of these voices within each sex."[20] Although she ultimately left the ideal moral character unarticulated, Gilligan concluded, "Development for both sexes would therefore seem to entail an integration of rights and responsibilities through the discovery of the complementarity of these disparate views."[21]

Despite this nod to integration, Gilligan chiefly intended to chart an alternative developmental scale and an alternative mature morality. In her most succinct statement of this alternative morality, the different voice, Gilligan wrote that "the moral problem arises from conflicting responsibilities rather than from competing rights and requires for its resolution a mode of thinking that is contextual and narrative rather than formal and abstract. This conception of morality as concerned with the activity of care centers moral development around the understanding of responsibility and relationships, just as the conception of morality of fairness ties moral development to the understanding of rights and rules."[22]

The meaning of the terms needing explication—care, responsibility, and context—are not explicitly defined or well explored in Gilligan's book.

20. Gilligan, *In a Different Voice*, 2.
21. Ibid., 100.
22. Ibid., 19.

She is not, after all, composing a systematic ethical theory, but sorting and interpreting what she hears in interviews. The scattered nature of much of the comments that would interest an ethical philosopher make the job of characterizing the ethic of care difficult. Moreover, only two particular ethical dilemmas are discussed—a hypothetical example that asks whether a man should steal an exorbitantly expensive drug for his dying wife and real-life examples of women deliberating about abortion.

The ethic of care encompasses three goods, a process of deliberation, and an imperative. The first and most important good is care for others. A caring person, engaged in ongoing relationships, attends to the needs of others, particularly need for compassion from strangers, for nursing from close friends and relatives, the need to be respected and valued by at least some others, the need for commitment to relationships. Because there are both physical and emotional needs, there are physical and emotional acts of care. The second good is the protection of relationship, attachment, or connection between people. The third good is care for the self, meaning care for one's own autonomy, for one's own goals, and for respecting one's own responsibility for decisions that one makes either consciously or de facto.

In the deliberative process of the care ethic, a person typically asks for more information, for more context, and for how such a conflict became possible and adjudicates the various responsibilities of care—in the Heinz example, a spouse's for his or her ailing partner, and a pharmacist's for a seriously ill stranger. Whereas the boy interviewed sees the Heinz dilemma as a conflict of the right to life and the right to property and sees the solution as the precedence of the first right over the second, the girl has a less clearly defined procedure. Since neither the option of stealing nor letting the wife die without the medicine is acceptable, she searches for a third way. She finds "the puzzle in the dilemma to lie in the failure of the druggist to respond to the wife," so that the solution lies in more dialogue between the pharmacist and Heinz. The problem for the girl, according to Gilligan is "a fracture of human relationship that must be mended with its thread."[23]

Finally, the ethic of care endorses a basic command or principle that according to Gilligan distinguishes it from other moral theories. Whereas mainstream liberalism expects us chiefly to respect the negative rights of others—as Gilligan writes, "to respect the rights of others and thus to protect from interference the rights to life and self-fulfillment"—the

23. Ibid., 28, 31.

women interviewed tended to express a "moral imperative ... to care, a responsibility to discern and alleviate the 'real and recognizable trouble' of this world."[24]

Gilligan's formulation of this "ethic of care" has inspired a great deal of fascinating work on what the ethic of care might be, whether it has predecessors in the history of moral theory, how different or complementary it might be to an "ethic of justice," and many more specific questions.[25] And like other moral philosophies that have long been used as guides to political theory, the ethics of care has inspired its own corresponding political theory.

Care political theories contest the vaunted aim of securing freedom and autonomy through political and civil rights, in favor of care as an equally important, if not more important, value. According to Virginia Held, a good feminist society would model relations among its members on the cooperation of mother and child and it would recognize the "creation and nurturing of the next generation as [its] most central task."[26] Joan Tronto poses her concern more broadly: "What would it mean in the late twentieth-century American society to take seriously, as part of our definition of a good society, the values of caring—attentiveness, responsibility, nurturance, compassion, meeting others' needs—traditionally associated with women and traditionally excluded from public consideration?"[27] While Grace Clement also elaborates an ethics of care for public use, she ultimately sees a justice ethic and a care ethic as partners, checking each other's excesses, joined into one unified account of moral reasoning and one policy-making guideline.[28] For all three theorists, the concern is not how to distribute goods such as freedom, wealth, and income, but the pervasive, taken-for-granted acts and gestures of calming, cheering, cooking, feeding, washing, driving, sending, picking up, (the list is, as the work is, potentially endless) for someone else—in other words, care.

Care ethics and care politics represent one of the few modern political theories whose adherents are courageous enough to support an emotive

---

24. Ibid., 100.

25. See especially Eve Kittay and Diana Meyers, eds., *Women and Moral Theory* (Totowa, N.J.: Rowman and Littlefield, 1987) and Eve Browning Cole and Susan Coultrap-McQuin, eds., *Explorations in Feminist Ethics: Theory and Practice* (Bloomington: Indiana University Press, 1992).

26. Virginia Held, *Feminist Morality* (Chicago: University of Chicago Press, 1993), 159.

27. Joan Tronto, *Moral Boundaries: A Political Argument for an Ethic of Care* (New York: Routledge, 1993), 3.

28. Grace Clement, *Care, Autonomy, and Justice: Feminism and the Ethic of Care* (Boulder: Westview Press, 1996).

disposition rather than counseling the practice of rationality refined away from emotion. What is fascinating about care feminism is the two-pronged idea of care itself. For care is both a feeling, or emotion, or attitude, and a certain kind of activity. It is in fact an ambiguous word, able to signify the mental state or the practical action, and thus liable to be misinterpreted as only one of these, especially as merely a feeling. So care feminism has labored to make us see the work in caring, the time, the physical acts, the concentration needed for good caring. Care is therefore not merely a natural reflex, but a practice deserving elaboration in a theory of its own. For Tronto, it is the *"species activity that includes everything that we do to maintain, continue, and repair our 'world' so that we can live in it as well as possible.* That world includes our bodies, our selves and our environment."[29] As a practice it has four stages—caring about, taking care of, care-giving, care-receiving—each of which requires a necessary quality from the caregiver: attentiveness, responsibility, competence, responsiveness. To identify the distinguishing qualities of care, Clement proposes that caregivers usually work in the context of personal relations, aim to promote the well-being of the receiver, and act with concern for the receiver even if the work is done as a paying job. And Held, although she does not define caring in general, identifies the practice of mothering as a paradigmatic example. From their work one can learn about the successes and the dangers of care; one can use it as a kind of ethical handbook of care.

Any theory of political emotion should take into account the way in which care feminism has delineated a practice that depends for its successful completion and for its renewal on a disposition to feel certain kinds of emotion. Tronto explicitly restricts caring to that practice encompassing both the disposition and the activity, thereby ensuring that care politics will encompass emotion. Too often we separate emotion, practices, and institutions. If one believes that emotions are essentially irrational and turbulent, then one will likely claim that practices and institutions are far better guided by reason. Here, in care feminism, we have a convincing discussion that does not suppress the emotional conditions of an important social practice. But perhaps more important, care feminism identifies practice and an emotional repertoire that all previous political philosophy simply mostly ignored because the tradition of philosophy did not include any of the varied experience of women.

If we return to the Senate debate example and the liberal emotional

---

29. Tronto, *Moral Boundaries*, 103.

paradigm, we should see that care feminism reveals just how marginalized benevolent and caring emotions are. Although Holmes notes that the liberals recognized benevolence, sympathy, affection, attachment and love, he, like liberalism itself, does little or nothing with these emotions. Instead, liberalism focuses disproportionately on the "disagreeable" passions, especially factionalism and religious enthusiasm. In contrast, despite the emphasis on practice, care feminism suggests the need to sustain and cultivate the "agreeable" emotions as motivations and ways of thinking in both private and public life. Care feminism raises the expectation that properly arranged programs and practices will elicit feelings of responsibility, concern, and affection both among family members and between personal friends and strangers.

While care feminism, then, provides an example of a theory ostensibly committed to an emotional disposition and more capable of dealing with the Senate example, it nevertheless harbors two problems relevant to the issues of this book. First, it lacks a theory of emotion able to explain how social emotions and dispositions attain dominance and how they vary historically and culturally and, most important, how political relationships depend on emotional dispositions. In other words, care feminism fails to emphasize adequately the subject of emotion, and thereby fails to appreciate just how specifically emotional habits, narratives, and styles of contemporary U.S. culture work against care. Second, it floats adrift, moorless, without focused attention on justifying its commitment to care. Although for many, including a good number of feminists, the act of building foundations has been vehemently discredited as a skill necessary for political theory, others have been equally indisposed to abandon some, however qualified, evaluation of political theories based on their deep assumptions about human psychology and happiness.

To start with the first problem: Held, Tronto, and Clement all acknowledge that care is partly an emotional concept and that care ethics requires emotion for motivation, for understanding the particularities of a care situation, and for discovering what kind of care is needed and how it should be provided. Held is especially sensitive to the numerous ways in which emotion enters the issues she cares about. Yet their focus is explicitly *not* on emotion. Tronto, more strongly than Held and Clement, wants to discourage our seeing care as an issue of emotional life. Her focus, she writes, is on the *practice* of caring defined quite broadly as an activity that maintains, continues, and repairs.[30] If instead we conceive of care as

30. Ibid., 103.

a disposition only without the element of activity or a practice, we risk sentimentalizing and privatizing care. We trivialize and neglect care insofar as we associate it with emotion.[31]

Now I do not want to distort Tronto's point; she explicitly says that she does not mean to shun the dispositional or emotional part of care, but that on her analysis the politics and culture of the late twentieth century, particularly in the United States, require the revaluation of care by disclosing it as practice and labor. I agree that in order to talk intelligibly to most men in contemporary institutions, and to raise women's own estimations of their caring skills, this practical aspect of care should be stressed. Yet notice how this emphasis on practice can have the effect of minimizing even further the "unacceptable," the apparently nugatory emotional aspects of care. But, more important, such an emphasis may prevent us from gaining a bird's-eye view over the variety of emotional stances and repertoires playing out in political life.

Alongside care feminists' argument that care should be understood first as practice and labor, and then in Tronto's terms as a political concept, I believe we should at the same time stress that care does include emotion and dispositions to emotion, and that to address these issues requires analysis of the emotional culture that constitutes or shapes our sense of the most significant practices in human life. But this would not mean arguing about a powerful, evanescent, subjective, unreliable thing called emotion. After all, emotions are, as I have argued following Aristotle and more recent theorists, cognitive, social, and often predictable. Emotional life itself can be seen as a sort of practice. Here we might recall Aristotle's claim that an active life is not, as most Greek men thought, a life of political ruling and dominating others, but that philosophy and contemplation equally deserve recognition as activities. Here Aristotle is deflating the pretensions of the masculinist culture of his time. While many Greek men, such as Thucydides' Pericles, thought that the best life for a man was active engagement in politics and war, but that the best life for a woman was silence in the household, Aristotle ingeniously severs the link between external acts and activity. Internal movements may also count as a form of activity. With such argumentative maneuvers, Aristotle engages the pretensions of elite ancient Greek masculinist culture.

But whereas Aristotle may simply be friendly to the view that feeling and displaying emotion is a form of praxis, feminist-inspired work explicitly articulates this position. Arlie Hochschild writes that service

31. Ibid., 118–19.

professions often require workers to do "emotional labor," the labor of arranging one's own emotions to suit employer or social guidelines.[32] Cheshire Calhoun has suggested using this term to refer to labor done to and for others, especially the "management of others' emotions—soothing tempers, boosting confidence, fueling pride, preventing frictions, and mending ego wounds."[33] Although for Calhoun this work is typically expected of women in the household, it is performed in a variety of sites. In one of her examples, the workplace is the site for one colleague's dispelling the embarrassment of another by a simple joke. Friendships, in which a friend asks the other friend for moral advice, again illustrate emotional labor. In her third example, the university is the site in which a teacher transforms a student's view of sexual harassment, so moving the student from passivity to anger.

Now it might be objected that these acts of dispelling embarrassment, giving advice, transforming someone's opinion are all acts of care, rather than emotional labor. Emotional labor then is just a form of care. The relationships of colleague, friend, teacher, and student are best fulfilled with some degree of caring. In each case people act through words and gestures to help other people cultivate an emotion they had trouble feeling on their own. But these are all caring acts whatever emotion they involve. Moreover, care is the larger category whereas such emotional labor is a subcategory. Surely care might include both physical and emotional care, and in cases where physical care is not needed, emotional care is what is at issue.

I would argue, however, that even Calhoun's notion of "emotional labor" does not extend far enough. While she enlarges emotional labor from its concentration on a single person managing his or her own emotions to one person shaping another's emotions, I suggest that we consider not only how individuals in intimate relationships perform emotional labor but how political oratory, political institutions, and even works of political theory do emotional labor. In addition, we should consider how emotional labor in this extended sense is done not only for the purpose of making people simply feel better, but also with the effect of inducing negative emotions or of reconstituting or reconfiguring emotions we already

32. Arlie Hochschild, *The Managed Heart*. A related notion is "sex-affective production" found in Ann Ferguson, *Blood at the Root: Motherhood, Sexuality, and Male Dominance* (London: Pandora Press, 1989), and *Sexual Democracy: Women, Oppression and Revolution*. (Boulder: Westview, 1991).

33. Cheshire Calhoun, "Emotional Labor," in Cole and Coultrap-McQuin, *Explorations in Feminist Ethics,* 118.

have. Even in Calhoun's examples, the teacher induces what might be understood as a negative emotion, especially given the emotional norms for women. While it is women's emotional labor in these personal, "dyadic" settings, as Calhoun calls them, that alerts us to the neglected importance of such labor, we should consider how emotional labor occurs in larger settings.

In fact, the analysis of such labor is exemplified in Aristotle's work. After all, the *Poetics* details the emotional labor of tragedy, and literary critics since Aristotle have often expanded his sense of the emotional effects of the arts. So, too, the *Rhetoric* partly details the knowledge a political speaker needs to persuade (not merely manipulate) an audience's emotions. For many reasons, political science neglects this tradition, or rather has convinced itself of the power of duly defined rationality to explain and model political behavior. Such rationality has been formed by a long tradition of political theory and discourse that appeals to and propagates, as the natural motivational stance of political agents, a calculating self-interest or self-preference. The power of feminist care theory resides in its portrayal of an alternative emotional/rational orientation, but in addition it can point the way to more general ideas of how emotional culture affects the plausibility, the persuasiveness, of care ethics.

So while Tronto outlines a theory of care practice with four stages and four elements, and Clement argues for the mutual support of care and autonomy and for welfare policies that aim to advance citizen's abilities both to be autonomous and to care, I believe that we need to understand the operations of political emotion, the emotional labor that is done in the traditional male public sphere. I realize that there is a difference between the unheralded labor of individual women and the "labor" of institutions, theories, or of men themselves, all of whom might not deserve credit partly because they have rejected the responsibility for such labor. Yet I maintain that the crucial point is to extend a concept derived from reflecting on the experience of some women to the broader cultural arena. Care feminism could be seen as part of a theory of political emotion that can help to explicate the sites, manner, and extent of the provision or denial of care. At the same time, I believe we should consider how such a theory of political emotion exceeds the issue of care. After all, feminism itself has goals other than expanding the role of care. Indeed, if initially feminism was a call and then a movement for women to gain equality with men by means of the traditional liberal freedoms and ideals, it has been transformed into a variety of more radical demands, including raising care as a political issue. These more radical demands demonstrated how much feminism was inevitably about changing sensibilities and emotional orientations of various kinds. Although the reclamation of emotion is more central to feminism than to other political movements, since praising the normality and the indispensability of emotion to intellectual, political, and social life helps to dispel various dichotomies that support sharp gender distinctions, other political issues and movements may be equally amenable to analysis derived from a theory of political emotion.

What this means it that once issues of care are set into a more comprehensive account of emotion and political emotion, we will be in better shape to see how various institutions both manifest and perpetuate the legitimating emotional scenarios and repertoires. In addition, we will be sensitive to other emotions, to the work of emotions both agreeable and disagreeable, both morally central and morally peripheral Care focuses on love, sympathy, concern and compassion. Modern Western political theorists, when not assuming rational actors, spoke of fear, anxiety, and greed. Aristotle, as I have noted accords efficacy to a variety of emotions, but also endorses a normative commitment to friendship and anger, pity and fear. But with a theory that looks widely at emotions, we can examine emotions that Aristotle may have neglected. Take grief, for example. As part of a more comprehensive theory of political emotion one could evaluate public institutions for how well they engage political grief. In an article that suggests this approach in terms of the politics of immigration, Bonnie Honig reads the biblical Book of Ruth as "an account of the institutional and cultural conditions for the proper work of mourning."[34] Applying the story's lessons to contemporary immigration, Honig identifies secondary associations that do not require national citizenship and sister city cooperations as institutions that can facilitate "mourning, empowerment, solidarity, and agency." Along the same lines, we could ask how well we respond to historical tragedies. The Washington Holocaust Museum may be a particular effective education for grief. Aids activists have been particularly inventive in organizing political grief.[35] In contrast, the United States has never had a national slavery museum or other public institutions to elicit and nurture grief over such a long-running inhumanity. South Africa's Truth and Reconciliation Commission might provide a fruitful subject for exploring how temporary institutions can

34. Bonnie Honig, "Ruth, the Model Emigrée: Mourning and the Symbolic Politics of Immigration," *Political Theory* 25, no. 1 (1997): 131.

35. See the comments of Ann Cvetkovich in her introduction to her *Mixed Feelings: Feminism, Mass Culture, and Victorian Sensationalism* (New Brunswick: Rutgers University Press, 1992).

handle grief attendant on recent political injustices. Women have been often historically responsible for grieving rituals, which certainly fall under a broad idea of care, but without focusing on the public shaping and construction or neglect of such political emotion, we would miss a great part of its role in harnessing political power and creating public values.

The second problem with care feminism in the three authors I have examined is that it lacks a sustained, convincing justification of the ethics it supports and often of the practices that it praises. A full justification would require evaluating normatively to what extent a social and political structure should be organized to nurture particular capacities of human beings, what emotional dispositions are beneficial in a political regime, and under what conditions a regime should cultivate emotions other than those implicit in care, emotions such as anger, grief, envy, and fear. [36]

It is a bit startling in Clement's detailed comparison of the ethic of care and the ethic of justice to find so few comments about virtue ethics. In her introduction, Clement briefly answers the objection that the ethic of care is just a fashionably dressed-up version of Aristotelian or Humean ethics by claiming that both these traditions do not confront the gender coding in ethics. Of course, this is right in one sense, as Aristotle suggests that women have different and perhaps lesser virtues. But as several scholars have argued, he also challenges the overly masculinist interpretations of virtue by criticizing the fourth-century Greek male's obsession with war and domination. For some, the construction of the Aristotelian philosophical or contemplative ideal of life is just another, albeit new, masculinist paradigm; for others, it is precisely the feminine that is invoked to construct this life. However this debate concludes, why not deal with care feminism in relationship to these theories if they do have substantial similarities? [37]

For this second flaw in care feminism, Aristotle allows us to resist a

36. For an account of the good of disagreeable emotions, especially hatred and rage, see Cynthia Burack, *The Problem of the Passions*.

37. For two works that address this connection see Aafke E. Komter, "Justice, Friendship and Care: Aristotle and Gilligan—Two of a Kind?," *The European Journal of Women's Studies* 2, no. 2 (1995): 151–69; Ruth Groenhout, "The Virtue of Care: Aristotelian Ethics and Contemporary Ethics of Care," in *Feminist Interpretations of Aristotle*, ed. Cynthia A. Freeland, 171–200 (University Park: Pennsylvania State University Press, 1998). For a critical view, see Susan J. Hekman, *Moral Voices and Moral Selves: Carol Gilligan and Feminist Moral Theory* (University Park: Pennsylvania State University Press, 1995), 34–40.

narrow enthusiasm for care and compassion and to contemplate the ultimate justification for particular configurations of emotional and practical dispositions. He supplies a genuine evaluative language of human capacities, excellences, and flourishing capable of sorting through our various social and political emotions. In his commendation of pity and fear, his identification of the failure to recognize kinship as a central failing of political emotion, Aristotle ends a debate with the Platonic and Homeric configurations of *thumos*. Anger in particular was overemphasized in these configurations. For Aristotle, while anger remains necessary, and expected as a guarantee of independence and pursuing what is rightly one's own, excessive use of it in domination of other peoples contravenes the essence of a good political regime.

Care feminism, perhaps for strategic reasons, excessively values caring to the detriment of other humanly valuable practices—artistic and intellectual achievement, for example. Held's focus on the relations of mother and child leads to her claim that of "all the human capacities, it is probably the capacity to create new human beings that is most worth celebrating" and that the "central task" of a society should be the "creation and nurturing of the next generation."[38] Even if a good feminist regime must revere the labor of nurturing or caring more than most historical regimes have done, it is unclear why it should be central and how it can be reconciled with other potential aims such as economic prosperity, ecological health, and protection of human rights, among other ends.

Should, however, feminists use not just the form of Aristotelian philosophical argument but also its content, not just the search for contemporary configurations of political emotion, but Aristotle's own preferred configuration? Again, it is impossible to even begin a persuasive argument in this space, but let me suggest for the moment that they should. Where would this lead? Using my account of the *Poetics*, a feminist political theorist should ask: how do we beget public institutions that encourage public benevolence and public recognition of essential similarity?[39]

---

38. Held, *Feminist Morality*, 81 and 159.

39. This suggestion might be startling in the midst of a trend in feminist theory, and to some extent in feminist practice, that converges on "difference" rather than similarity. Feminists have argued that 1970s American feminism neglected race, class, and ethnic difference, with some additionally arguing that the category "woman" itself is part of a heterosexual matrix, without a stable, unified content. In effect, the experience and hopes of women are so different that the future existence of "feminism" itself is questioned. Although I believe that this is a deeply important issue, in this space I can only say that a compromise must be struck. Some issues, "welfare" for example, require both respect for differential needs and a capacity to feel the moral impact of these needs. This capacity, in

How can recognition and *katharsis* happen in apparently nonnarrative institutions? Although our current connotations of pity make it seem a sign of superiority and a mere aesthetic indulgence without consequence, some such disposition is indispensable to any moral action, as I believe care feminists have insisted. Whether we call it pity, compassion, sympathy, empathy, goodwill, friendship, or a disposition of care, one of these configurations of the recognition of kinship with strangers must underlie both a good feminist regime and specifically an understanding of welfare. On the other hand, this emotion/practice is not sufficient for a flourishing life or regime. Fear, anger, envy, curiosity, or wonder may all in some form need their recognized place. Here, then, Aristotle is clearly a friend of care feminism, but one who considers an expanded spectrum of morally and politically necessary emotions and suggests possible avenues of renewed justification.

In a concerted attack on youth culture, American universities and feminism, Allan Bloom writes:

> And here is where the whole business turns nasty. The souls of men—their ambitious, warlike, protective, possessive character —must be dismantled in order to liberate women from their domination. Machismo—the polemical description of maleness or spiritedness which was the central *natural* passion in men's souls in the psychology of the ancients, the passion of attachment and loyalty—was the villain, the source of difference between the sexes.... With machismo discredited the positive task is to make men caring, sensitive, even nurturing, to fit the restructured family.... Men tend to undergo this re-education somewhat sullenly but studiously, in order to avoid the opprobrium of the sexist label and to keep peace with their wives and girlfriends. And it is indeed possible to soften men. But to make them "care" is another thing, and the project must inevitably fail.[40]

As must be now apparent to the reader, when Bloom invokes a monovocal ancient Greek psychology, he is mistaken; when he portrays spiritedness

---

turn, arises from emotively crossing perceptions of difference to find similarity. For support, I recommend Anne Phillips's cogent "Universal Pretensions in Political Thought," in *Destabilizing Theory: Contemporary Feminist Debates*, ed. Michelle Barrett and Anne Phillips (Stanford: Stanford University Press, 1992).

40. Allan Bloom, *The Closing of the American Mind* (New York: Simon and Schuster, 1987), 129.

or *thumos* as the natural essence of possessive manliness, he is misinformed; when he divides harsh masculine emotions from soft feminine ones, he is merely parochial. Indeed, oddly for a man who attacks the German degradation of American universities, Bloom surreptitiously echoes Nietzsche. For it was Nietzsche's contention that the liberal democratic culture of the West was lachrymose and brimming with pity: "Here everyone helps everyone else, here everyone is to a certain degree an invalid and everyone a nurse. This is then called 'virtue'—: among men who know a different kind of life it would be called something else: 'cowardice,' perhaps, 'pitiableness,' 'old woman's morality.'"[41] Even though Bloom does not condemn liberalism in such ravishing terms, liberalism's enervating tendencies must be propped up by reinvigorated masculinity; feminism, the rational heiress of liberalism, connives in its undoing. The same strains can be heard in Harvey Mansfield's recent pieces on our dire cultural situation.[42]

A crucial misstep was made and will continue to be made if we accept the existing interpretations of ancient *thumos*. If we cannot see how expansive *thumos* becomes with Aristotle, and how our classical heritage, despite the fame of its rationalism, houses a significant role for emotion, we will continue to be blind to the emotional dimensions of political life and their need to be normatively theorized. Although those commentators who have taken an interest in *thumos* have shown how anger and desire for honor or recognition motivate political actors, their narrow understanding of *thumos* has prevented them from contemplating other emotional alternatives. Once we see that *thumos* is the capacity for emotion requiring and inevitably bearing the imprint of the political regime in which a person lives, we can compare a wide variety of alternatives, and not be restricted to a particularly masculinized version of the goods and feelings of political life. Once we realize that the history of political philosophy has immanent within itself one version of a theory of political emotion, the way for further research is opened not only into the post-Aristotelian development of emotion but also in contemporary positive theory.

I have argued over the course of this study that Aristotle is a fertile source for reflection on the emotional components of political life. He is so because of his suggestive transformations of *thumos*. In my narrative, the

---

41. *Twilight of the Idols*, trans. R. J. Hollingdale (New York: Penguin, 1982), 90.

42. Harvey Mansfield, "Some Doubts About Feminism," *Government and Opposition* 32, no. 2 (September 1997): 291–300; and "Why a Woman Can't Be More Like a Man," *Wall Street Journal*, November 3 1997, A22.

word *"thumos"* originally referred to an organ in the Homeric body filled with a variety of emotions, but because the most typical Homeric body was a warrior's, anger predominated. When Plato, following Socrates, asked what kind of life is worth living and who is the just man, *thumos* became part of a unified, although not always harmonious, soul. Plato's pupil Aristotle reopened *thumos* to a variety of emotions as the general capacity to experience emotion and a desire for social relationships.

Although this history of *thumos* holds many pleasures for the scholar of Greek cultural history, its significance is not in historical nuance, but in its intersection with the formation of central philosophical understandings of reason and political motivation. The dominance of motivations formulated from rational choice theory or from Marxist views of class interest are so rigid that the work on classical conceptions of spiritedness along with the feminist turn to an ethic of care are passages to more complex portraits of the mutual influence of individual action, character or psychology, and political institutions.

I have also remarked on the features of the contemporary sense of emotion in politics. Because "interest" escaped its origins as an emotion, gaining explanatory authority by its alliance with reason, our more personal, and thereby truly political, convictions are systematically obscured, blinding us to the emotional dispositions expected of us whether by fellow citizens, by political representatives, or by political scientists. If we return interest to its proper place as one among many possible emotional orientations, we will gain flexibility, verisimilitude, and deeper meaning in our accounts of political life. What both feminism and retrospectively Aristotle request is for us to feel pleasure and pain at different situations than we did before, to feel sympathy and anger in new ways, at different objects, and to be guided by an overall disposition more alive to the kinships between us. The subject of political emotion, saved from the romanticists and the psychological scientists, can now be recovered by political philosophy to better capture the stakes and possibilities of political life. Without such a theory of political emotion, we are at the mercy of late twentieth-century purveyors of the elixir of spirited manliness.

# Bibliography

Achtenberg, Deborah. "Aristotelian Resources for Feminist Thinking." In *Feminism and Ancient Philosophy*, ed. Julie K. Ward. New York: Routledge, 1996.

Antony, Louise M. and Charlotte Witt, eds. *A Mind of One's Own: Feminist Essays on Reason and Objectivity*. Boulder: Westview Press, 1992.

Ackrill, J. L. "Aristotle on *Eudaimonia*." In *Essays on Aristotle's Ethics*, ed. Amelie Oksenberg Rorty. Berkeley and Los Angeles: University of California Press, 1980.

Adkins, A. W. H. *From the Many to the One*. Ithaca: Cornell University Press, 1970.

———. *Merit and Responsibility*. New York: Oxford University Press, 1960.

———. *Moral Values and Political Behaviour in Ancient Greece*. New York: Norton, 1972.

Agonito, Rosemary. *History of Ideas on Women*. New York: G. P. Putnam, 1977.

Ahrensdorf, Peter J. "The Question of Historical Context and the Study of Plato." *Polity* 27, no. 1 (Fall 1994): 113–35.

Annas, Julia. *An Introduction to Plato's Republic*. Oxford: Clarendon Press, 1981.

Aries, Phillipe. *The Hour of Our Death*. New York: Oxford University Press, 1991.

Aristotle. *The Complete Works of Aristotle: The Revised Oxford Translation*. Edited by Jonathan Barnes. Princeton: Princeton University Press, 1984.

———. *De Anima*. Edited by David Ross. Oxford: Oxford University Press, 1956.

———. *Eudemian Ethics*. Translated by H. Rackham. Cambridge: Loeb Classical Library, 1935.

———. *Nicomachean Ethics*. Translated by H. Rackham. Cambridge: Loeb Classical Library, 1939.

———. *Nicomachean Ethics*. Translated by Martin Ostwald. New York: Macmillan, 1962.

———. *Nicomachean Ethics*. Translated by Terence Irwin. Indianapolis: Hackett, 1985.

————. *The Poetics of Aristotle: Translation and Commentary*. Translated by Stephen Halliwell. Chapel Hill: University of North Carolina Press, 1987.

————. *Politics*. Translated by Carnes Lord. Chicago: University of Chicago Press, 1984.

Armon-Jones, Claire. "The Thesis of Constructionism." In *The Social Construction of Emotions*, ed. Rom Harre, 32–56. Oxford: Basil Blackwell, 1986.

Arthur, Marilyn B. "The Divided World of Iliad 6." In *Reflections of Women in Antiquity*, ed. Helene P. Foley. New York: Gordon and Breach, 1981.

————. "Early Greece: The Origins of the Western Attitude Towards Women." In *Women in the Ancient World: The Arethusa Papers*, ed. John Peradotto and J. P. Sullivan. Albany: State University of New York Press, 1984.

Averill, James R. "The Acquisition of Emotions in Adulthood." In *The Social Construction of Emotions*, ed. Rom Harre, 56–78. Oxford: Basil Blackwell, 1986.

Baier, Annette. "The Need for More Than Justice." *Canadian Journal of Philosophy* suppl. vol. 13 (1987): 14–56.

Barber, Benjamin. *Strong Democracy*. Berkeley and Los Angeles: University of California Press, 1984.

Barker, Ernst. *The Political Thought of Plato and Aristotle*. New York: Dover, 1959.

Barker-Benfield, G. J. *The Culture of Sensibility: Sex and Society in Eighteenth-Century England*. Chicago: University of Chicago Press, 1992.

Barringer, Felicity. "Hillary Clinton's New Role: A Spouse or a Policy Leader?" *New York Times*, November 16, 1992, A1, A14.

Bartky, Sandra Lee. "Shame and Gender." In *Femininity and Domination: Studies in the Phenomenology of Oppression*, 83–98. Thinking Gender. New York: Routledge, 1990.

Bauman, Zygmunt. *Modernity and the Holocaust*. Ithaca: Cornell University Press, 1989.

Benhabib, Seyla. "The Generalized and the Concrete Other: The Kohlberg-Gilligan Controversy and Feminist Theory." In *Feminism as Critique*, ed. Seyla Benhabib and Drucilla Cornell. Minneapolis: University of Minnesota Press, 1987.

Benjamin, Jessica. *The Bonds of Love: Psychoanalysis, Feminism, and the Problem of Domination*. New York: Pantheon Books, 1988.

Bernadette, Seth. *Socrates' Second Sailing*. Berkeley and Los Angeles: University of California Press, 1991.

Bernays, J. "Aristotle on the Effect of Tragedy." In *Articles on Aristotle*, vol. 4, ed. Jonathan Barnes, M. Schofield and R. Sorabji. London: Duckworth, 1979.

Berns, Laurence. "Spiritedness in Ethics and Politics: A Study in Aristotelian Psychology." *Interpretation* 12 (1984): 335–48.

Bickford, Susan. "Beyond Friendship: Aristotle on Conflict, Deliberation, and Attention." *Journal of Politics* 58, no. 2 (1996): 398–421.

Bloom, Allan. *The Closing of the American Mind*. New York: Simon and Schuster, 1987.

————. "Interpretive Essay." Translated by Allan Bloom. In *The Republic of Plato*. New York: Basic Books, 1968.

Blum, Lawrence A. *Friendship, Altruism, and Morality*. Boston: Routledge and Kegan Paul, 1980.

Blundell, Mary Whitlock. *Helping Friends and Harming Enemies: A Study in Sophocles and Greek Ethics.* Cambridge: Cambridge University Press, 1990.

Bolotin, David. "The Critique of Homer and the Homeric Heros in Plato's *Republic.*" In *Political Philosophy and the Human Soul,* ed. Michael Palmer and Thomas L. Pangle, 83–93. Lanham, Md: Rowman and Littlefield, 1995.

Bordo, Susan R., *The Flight to Objectivity: Essays on Cartesianism and Culture.* Albany: State University of New York Press, 1987.

Bottomore, Tom, ed. *A Dictionary of Marxist Thought.* Cambridge: Harvard University Press, 1983.

Bradshaw, David J. "The Ajax Myth and the Polis: Old Values and New." In *Myth and the Polis,* ed. Dora C. Pozzi and John Wickersham. Ithaca: Cornell University Press, 1991.

Bremmer, Jan. *The Early Greek Concept of the Soul.* Princeton: Princeton University Press, 1983.

Brown, Wendy. *Manhood and Politics: A Feminist Reading in Political Theory.* Totowa, New Jersey: Rowman and Littlefield, 1988.

———. "'Supposing Truth Were a Woman . . .': Plato's Subversion of Masculine Discourse." *Political Theory* 16, no. 4 (November 1988): 594–616.

Burack, Cynthia. *The Problem of the Passions: Femnism, Psychoanalysis, and Social Theory.* New York: New York University Press, 1994.

Burkert, Walter. *Greek Religion: Archaic and Classical.* Translated by John Raffan. Cambridge: Harvard University Press, 1985.

Butler, E. M. *The Tyranny of Greece.* New York: Macmillan, 1935.

Calhoun, Cheshire. "Emotional Labor." In *Explorations in Feminist Ethics: Theory and Practice,* ed. Eve Browning Cole and Susan Coultrap-McQuin. Bloomington: Indiana University Press, 1992.

Calhoun, Cheshire, and Robert C. Solomon. "Introduction." In *What is an Emotion? Classic Readings in Philosophical Psychology,* ed. Cheshire Calhoun and Robert C. Solomon. New York: Oxford University Press, 1984.

———, eds. *What is an Emotion? Classic Readings in Philosophical Psychology.* New York: Oxford University Press, 1984.

Campbell, Sue. *Interpreting the Personal: Expression and the Formation of Feelings.* Ithaca: Cornell University Press, 1997.

Cassirer, Ernst. *The Question of Jean-Jacques Rousseau.* 2d ed. Trans. Peter Gay. New Haven: Yale University Press, 1989.

Casswell, Caroline. *A Study of Thumos in Early Greek Epic.* Leiden: E. J. Brill, 1990.

Cave, Terence. *Recognitions: A Study in Poetics.* Oxford: Clarendon Press, 1988.

Charney, Ann P. "Spiritedness and Piety in Aristotle." In *Understanding the Political Spirit,* ed. Catherine Zuckert. New Haven: Yale University Press, 1988.

Chodorow, Nancy. *The Reproduction of Mothering: Psychonalysis and the Sociology of Gender.* Berkeley and Los Angeles: University of California Press, 1978.

Claus, David B. *Toward the Soul: An Inquiry Into the Meaning of Psuche Before Plato.* New Haven: Yale University Press, 1981.

Clement, Grace. *Care, Autonomy, and Justice: Feminism and the Ethic of Care.* Boulder: Westview Press, 1996.

Cocks, Joan. "Wordless Emotions: Some Critical Reflections on Radical Femi-
    nism." *Politics and Society* 13, no. 1 (1984): 27–57.
Code, Lorraine. *What Can She Know? Feminist Theory and the Construction of
    Knowledge*. Ithaca: Cornell University Press, 1991.
Cole, Eve Browning, and Susan Coultrap-McQuin, eds. *Explorations in Femi-
    nist Ethics: Theory and Practice*. Bloomington: Indiana University Press,
    1992.
Cook, Fay Lomax, and Edith J. Barrett. *Support for the American Welfare State:
    The Views of Congress and the Public*. New York: Columbia University
    Press, 1992.
Cooper, John M. "Aristotle on the Forms of Friendship." In *Reason and Emotion*,
    312–35. Princeton: Princeton University Press, 1999.
———. "Political Animals and Civic Friendship." In *Friendship: A Philosophi-
    cal Reader*, ed. Neera Kapur Badhwar, 303–26. Ithaca: Cornell University
    Press, 1993.
Cropsey, Joseph. *Political Philosophy and the Issues of Politics*. Chicago: Uni-
    versity of Chicago Press, 1977.
Crotty, Kevin. *The Poetics of Supplication: Homer's Iliad and Odyssey*. Ithaca:
    Cornell University Press, 1994.
Cvetkovich, Ann. *Mixed Feelings: Feminism, Mass Culture, and Victorian Sen-
    sationalism*. New Brunswick, N.J.: Rutgers University Press, 1992.
Daly, Mary. *Gyn / Ecology: The Metaethics of Radical Feminism*. Boston: Beacon
    Press, 1978.
———. *Pure Lust: Elemental Feminist Philosophy*. Boston: Beacon Press, 1984.
Damasio, Antonio R. *Descartes' Error: Emotion, Reason, and the Human Brain*.
    New York: G. P. Putnam's Sons, 1994.
de Sousa, Robert. *The Rationality of Emotion*. Cambridge: MIT Press, 1990.
Dinnerstein, Dorothy. *The Mermaid and the Minotaur: Sexual Arrangements
    and Human Malaise*. New York: Harper and Row, 1976.
DiStephano, Christine. *Configurations of Masculinity: A Feminist Perspective
    on Political Theory*. Ithaca: Cornell University Press, 1991.
Dodds, E. R. *The Greeks and the Irrational*. Berkeley and Los Angeles: Univer-
    sity of California Press, 1968.
Dover, K. J. "The Portrayal of Moral Evaluation in Greek Poetry." *Journal of
    Hellenic Studies* 103, no. 83 (1983): 35–48.
Downs, Anthony. *An Economic Theory of Democracy*. New York: Harper, 1957.
Dubois, Page. *Centaurs and Amazons*. Ann Arbor: University of Michigan
    Press, 1982.
Dziob, Anne Marie. "Aristotelian Friendship: Self-Love and Moral Rivalry."
    *Review of Metaphysics* 46 (1993): 781–801.
Ehrenreich, Barbara, and Janet McIntosh. "The New Creationism." *The
    Nation*, June 9 1997, 11–16.
Else, G. F. *Aristotle's Poetics: The Argument*. Cambridge: Harvard University
    Press, 1957.
Etzioni, Amitai. *The Moral Dimension*. New York: Free Press, 1988.
Euben, J. Peter, ed. *Greek Tragedy and Political Theory*. Berkeley and Los Ange-
    les: University of California Press, 1986.
———. *The Tragedy of Political Theory: The Road Not Taken*. Princeton: Prince-
    ton University Press, 1990.

Euripides. *Euripides Fabulae*. Vol. 2. Edited by John Diggle. Oxford: Oxford University Press, 1981.

———. *Iphigeneia in Tauris*. Translated by Richard Lattimore. New York and London: Oxford University Press, 1973.

Ferguson, Ann. *Blood at the Root: Motherhood, Sexuality, and Male Dominance*. London: Pandora Press, 1989.

———. *Sexual Democracy: Women, Oppression and Revolution*. Boulder: Westview, 1991.

Finley, M. I. *The World of Odysseus*. New York: Penguin, 1979.

Firestone, Shulamith. *The Dialectic of Sex: The Case for Feminist Revolution*. New York: William Morrow, 1970.

Flax, Jane. "Political Philosophy and the Patriarchal Unconscious: A Psychoanalytic Perspective on Epistemology and Metaphysics." In *Discovering Reality: Feminist Perspectives on Epistemology, Metaphysics, Methodology, and Philosophy of Science*, ed. Sandra Harding and Merrill B. Hintikka, 245–81. Boston: D. Reidel, 1983.

Fortenbaugh, W. W. *Aristotle on Emotion: A Contribution to Philosophical Psychology, Rhetoric, Poetics, Politics, and Ethics*. London: Duckworth, 1975.

Foucault, Michel. *The History of Sex, Vol. 1: An Introduction*. Translated by Robert Hurley. New York: Vintage Books, 1980.

Franks, Robert. *Passions Within Reason: The Strategic Role of the Emotions*. New York: W. W. Norton, 1988.

Freeland, Cynthia, ed. *Feminist Interpretations of Aristotle*. University Park: Pennsylvania State University Press, 1998.

Fukuyama, Francis. *The End of History and the Last Man*. New York: The Free Press, 1992.

Gaskin, Richard M. "Do Homeric Heros Make Real Decisions?" *Classical Quarterly* 40, no. 1 (1990): 1–15.

Gellrich, Michele. *Tragedy and Theory: The Problem of Conflict Since Aristotle*. Princeton: Princeton University Press, 1988.

Gill, David. "Two Decisions: *Iliad* 11.401–22 and *Agamemnon* 192–230." In *Studies Presented to Sterling Dow on His Eightieth Birthday*, ed. Alan J. Boegehold, 125–34. Durham: Duke University, 1984.

Gilligan, Carol. *In a Different Voice: Psychological Theory and Women's Development*. Cambridge: Harvard University Press, 1982.

Goldhill, Simon. "The Great Dionysia and Civic Ideology." In *Nothing to Do with Dionysos?* ed. John Winker and Froma Zeitlin. Princeton: Princeton University Press, 1990.

Goleman, Daniel. *Emotional Intelligence*. New York: Bantam Books, 1995.

Gosling, J. C. B. *Plato*. London: Routledge and Kegan Paul, 1973.

Gould, Thomas. *The Ancient Quarrel Between Poetry and Philosophy*. Princeton: Princeton University Press, 1990.

Griffin, Susan. *Woman and Nature*. New York: Harper and Row, 1980.

Griffiths, Morwenna. "Feminism, Feelings and Philosophy." In *Feminist Perspectives in Philosophy*, ed. Morwenna Griffiths and Margaret Whitford, 131–51. Bloomington and Indianapolis: Indiana University Press, 1988.

———. *Feminisms and the Self: The Web of Identity*. New York: Routledge, 1995.

Griswold, Charles L., ed. *Platonic Writings, Platonic Readings*. New York: Routledge, 1988.

Groenhout, Ruth. "The Virtue of Care: Aristotelian Ethics and Contemporary Ethics of Care." In *Feminist Interpretations of Aristotle*, ed. Cynthia A. Freeland, 171–200. University Park: Pennsylvania State University Press, 1998.

Grube, G. M. A. *Plato's Thought*. Boston: Beacon Press, 1958.

Gutzwiller, Kathryn J., and Ann Norris Michelini. "Women and Other Strangers: Feminist Perspectives in Classical Literature." In *(En)Gendering Knowledge*, ed. Joan E. Hartman and Ellen Messer-Davidow, 1993.

Halliwell, Stephen. *Aristotle's Poetics*. Chapel Hill: University of North Carolina Press, 1986.

Hamilton, Alexander, James Madison, and John Jay. *The Federalist Papers*. New York: Mentor, 1961.

Harré, Rom, ed. *The Social Construction of Emotions*. Oxford: Basil Blackwell, 1986.

Hartsock, Nancy C., M. *Money, Sex, and Power: Toward a Feminist Historical Materialism*. Boston: Northeastern University Press, 1985.

Havel, Václav. *Summer Meditations*. Translated by Paul Wilson. New York: Alfred A. Knopf, 1992.

Heath, Malcolm. *The Poetics of Greek Tragedy*. Stanford: Stanford University Press, 1987.

Hegel, Wilhelm Friedrich. *Philosophy of Right*. Translated by T. M. Knox. New York: Oxford University Press, 1967.

Hekman, Susan J. *Moral Voices, Moral Selves: Carol Gilligan and Feminist Moral Theory*. University Park: Pennsylvania State University Press, 1995.

Held, Virginia. *Feminist Morality: Transforming Culture, Society, and Politics*. Chicago: University of Chicago Press, 1993.

Herman, Gabriel. *Ritualized Friendship and the Greek City*. Cambridge: Cambridge University Press, 1987.

Hirschman, Albert O. *The Passions and the Interests*. Princeton: Princeton University Press, 1977.

———. *Shifting Involvements: Private Interest and Public Action*. Princeton: Princeton University Press, 1982.

Hirschmann, Nancy. *Rethinking Political Obligation: A Feminist Method for Political Theory*. Ithaca: Cornell University Press, 1992.

Hobbes, Thomas. *Leviathan*. Edited by Edwin Curley. Indianapolis: Hackett, 1994.

Hochschild, Arlie Russell. *The Managed Heart: Commercialization of Human Feeling*. Berkeley and Los Angeles: University of California Press, 1983.

Holmes, Stephen. "Aristippus in and Out of Athens." *American Political Science Review* 73 (March 1979): 113–28.

———. *Passions and Constraints: On the Theory of Liberal Democracy*. Chicago: University of Chicago Press, 1995.

Homer. *The Iliad of Homer*. Translated by Richmond Lattimore. Chicago: University of Chicago Press, 1951.

———. *The Iliad*. Translated by A. T. Murray. Loeb Classical Library. Cambridge: Harvard University Press, 1978.

Homiak, Marcia. "Feminism and Aristotle's Rational Ideal." In *Feminism and Ancient Philosophy*, ed. Julie K. Ward. New York: Routledge, 1996.

Honig, Bonnie. "Ruth, the Model Emigrée: Mourning and the Symbolic Politics of Immigration." *Political Theory* 25, no. 1 (1997): 112–35.

Honneth, Axel. "Integrity and Disrespect: Principles of a Conception of Morality Based on the Theory of Recognition." *Political Theory* 20 (1992): 187–200.

Honor, Hugh. *Neo-Classicism*. New York: Penguin, 1977.

Howe, Neil, and Philip Longman. "The Next New Deal." *Atlantic Monthly*, April 1992, 88–99.

Hutter, Horst. *Politics as Friendship: The Origins of Classical Notions of Politics in the Theory and Practice of Friendship*. Ontario: Wilfrid Laurier University Press, 1979.

Ignatieff, Michael. *The Needs of Strangers*. New York: Penguin, 1982.

Irwin, T. H. "Aristotle's Defense of Private Property." In *A Companion to Aristotle's Politics*, ed. David Keyt and Fred D. Miller Jr., 200–225. Cambridge: Blackwell, 1991.

Irwin, Terence. *Plato's Ethics*. Oxford: Oxford University Press, 1995.

———. *Plato's Moral Theory*. Oxford: Clarendon Press, 1977.

Jaeger, Werner. "A New Greek Word in Plato's Republic." *Eranos* 44 (1946): 123–30.

Jaggar, Alison. "Love and Knowledge: Emotion in Feminist Epistemology." In *Gender/Body/Knowledge: Feminist Reconstructions of Being and Knowing*, ed. Alison Jaggar and Susan Bordo. New Brunswick, N.J.: Rutgers University Press, 1989.

Janko, Richard. "From Catharsis to Aristotelian Mean." In *Essays on Aristotle's Poetics*, ed. Amelie Oksenberg Rorty. Princeton: Princeton University Press, 1992.

Keller, Evelyn Fox. *Reflections on Gender and Science*. New Haven: Yale University Press, 1985.

Kern, Stephen. *The Culture of Love: Victorians to Moderns*. Cambridge: Harvard University Press, 1992.

Keyt, David, and Fred D. Miller Jr., eds. *A Companion to Aristotle's Politics*. Cambridge: Basil Blackwell, 1991.

King, Katherine Callen. *Achilles: Paradigms of the War Hero from Homer to the Middle Ages*. Berkeley and Los Angeles: The University of California Press, 1987.

Kitayama, Shinobu, and Hazel Rose Markus, eds. *Emotion and Culture: Empirical Studies of Mutual Influence*. Washington, D.C.: American Psychological Association, 1987.

Kittay, Eve Feder, and Diana Meyers, eds. *Women and Moral Theory*. Totowa, N.J.: Rowman and Littlefield, 1987.

Klosko, George. *The Development of Plato's Politics*. New York: Methuen, 1986.

Kohlberg, Lawrence. *The Philosophy of Moral Development: Moral Stages and the Idea of Justice*. Essays on Moral Development, vol. 1. San Francisco: Harper and Row, 1981.

Komter, Aafke E. "Justice, Friendship and Care: Aristotle and Gilligan—Two of a Kind?" *The European Journal of Women's Studies* 2, no. 2 (1995): 151–69.

Kosman, L. A. "Being Properly Affected: Virtues and Feelings in Aristotle's Ethics." In *Essays on Aristotle's Ethics*, ed. Amelie Oxsenberg Rorty. Berkeley and Los Angeles: University of California Press, 1980.

Lang, Mabel L. "From War Story Into Wrath Story." In *Ages of Homer: A Tribute to Emily Townsend Vermeule*, ed. Jane B. Carter and Sarah P. Morris. Austin: University of Texas Press, 1995.

Lear, Jonathan. *Aristotle: The Desire to Understand*. New York: Cambridge University Press, 1988.

———. "Katharsis." In *Essays on Aristotle's Poetics*, ed. Amelie Oksenberg Rorty. Princeton: Princeton University Press, 1992.

Levy, Robert I. "Emotion, Knowing, and Culture." In *Culture Theory: Essays on Mind, Self, and Emotion*, ed. Richard A. Shweder and R. A. Levine, 214–37. New York: Cambridge University Press, 1984.

Lloyd, Genevieve. *The Man of Reason: "Male" and "Female" in Western Philosophy*. 2d. ed. Minneapolis: University of Minnesota Press, 1993.

Lloyd-Jones, Hugh. *The Justice of Zeus*. 2d. ed. Berkeley and Los Angeles: University of California Press, 1983.

Locke, John. "Second Treatise." In *Locke's Two Treatises on Government*, ed. Peter Laslett. New York: Mentor, 1960.

Long, A. A. "Morals and Values in Homer." *Journal of Hellenic Studies* 90 (1970): 121–39.

Loraux, Nicole. *The Invention of Athens*. Trans. Alan Sheridan. Cambridge: Harvard University Press, 1986.

Lord, Carnes. "Aristotle's Anthropology." In *Essays on the Foundations of Aristotelian Political Science*, ed. Carnes Lord and David O'Connor, 49–73. Berkeley and Los Angeles: University of California Press, 1991.

———. *Education and Culture in the Political Thought of Aristotle*. Ithaca: Cornell University Press, 1982.

———, and David K. O'Connor, eds. *Essays on the Foundations of Aristotelian Political Science*. Berkeley and Los Angeles: University of California Press, 1991.

Lutz, Catherine A. "Engendered Emotion: Gender, Power, and the Rhetoric of Emotional Control in American Discourse." In *Language and the Politics of Emotion*, ed. Catherine A. Lutz and Lila Abu-Lughod, 69–91. New York: Cambridge University Press, 1990.

———. *Unnatural Emotions: Everyday Sentiments on a Micronesian Atoll and Their Challenge to Western Theory*. Chicago: University of Chicago Press, 1988.

Lutz, Catherine A. and Lila Abu-Lughod. "Introduction." In *Language and the Politics of Emotion*, ed. Catherine A. Lutz and Lila Abu-Lughod. New York: Cambridge University Press, 1990.

Lutz, Catherine, and Geoffrey M. White. "The Anthropology of Emotions." *Annual Review of Anthropology* 15 (1986): 405–36.

Lynch, John P., and Gary B. Miles. "In Search of *Thumos*: Toward an Understanding of a Greek Psychological Term." *Prudentia* 12 (1980): 3–9.

Lyons, William. *Emotion*. London: Cambridge University Press, 1980.

MacIntyre, Alasdair. *Whose Justice? Which Rationality?* South Bend: University of Notre Dame, 1988.

Mansbridge, Jane. "Expanding the Range of Formal Modeling." In *Beyond Self-Interest*, ed. Jane Mansbridge. Chicago: University of Chicago Press, 1990.

Mansfield, Harvey. "Some Doubts About Feminism." *Government and Opposition* 32, no. 2 (September 1997): 291–300.

———. "Why a Woman Can't Be More Like a Man." *Wall Street Journal*, November 3, 1997, A22.

Mara, Gerald. "The Near Made Far Away: The Role of Cultural Criticism in Aristotle's Political Theory." *Political Theory* 23 (1995): 280–303.

Marx, Karl. "Economic and Philosophical Manuscripts of 1844." In *The Marx-Engels Reader*, 2d ed., ed. Robert C. Tucker. New York: W. W. Norton, 1978.

Mayer, John D., and Peter Salovey. "What is Emotional Intelligence?" In *Emotional Development and Emotional Intelligence*, ed. Peter Salovey and David J. Sluyter. New York: Basic Books, 1997.

McKerlie, Dennis. "Friendship, Self-Love, and Concern for Others." *Ancient Philosophy* 11, no. 1 (1991): 85–101.

Meyers, Diana Tietjens, ed. *Feminists Rethink the Self*. Boulder: Westview Press, 1997.

Mikalson, Jon D. *Honor Thy Gods: Popular Religion in Greek Tragedy*. Chapel Hill: University of North Carolina Press, 1989.

Monroe, Kristin Renwick. *The Heart of Altruism: Perceptions of a Common Humanity*. Princeton: Princeton University Press, 1996.

Morris, Ian. "The Use and Abuse of Homer." *Classical Antiquity* 5, no. 1 (1986): 81–138.

Morsbach, H., and W. J. Tyler. "A Japanese Emotion: *Amae*." In *The Social Construction of Emotions*, ed. Rom Harré. Oxford: Basil Blackwell, 1989.

Morton, F.L. "Sexual Equality and the Family in Tocqueville's *Democracy in America*." *Canadian Journal of Political Science* 17 (1984): 310–24.

Mulgan, Richard. *Aristotle's Political Theory*. Oxford: Oxford University Press, 1977.

Murnaghan, Sheila. "Sucking the Juice Without Biting the Rind: Aristotle's Poetics and the Nature of Tragic Mimesis." *New Literary History* 26 (Autumn 1995): 755–73.

Murphy, N. R. *The Interpretation of Plato's* Republic. Oxford: Oxford University Press, 1951.

Murray, Oswyn. *Early Greece*. Atlantic Highlands, N.J.: Humanities Press, 1980.

Nagy, Gregory. *The Best of the Achaeans: Concepts of the Hero in Archaic Greek Poetry*. Baltimore: Johns Hopkins University Press, 1979.

Nehamas, Alexander. "Pity and Fear in the *Rhetoric* and the *Poetics*." In *Essays on Aristotle's Poetics*, ed. Amelie Oksenberg Rorty. Princeton: Princeton University Press, 1992.

Nichols, Mary. *Citizens and Statesmen: A Study of Aristotle's Politics*. Savage, Md.: Rowman and Littlefield, 1992.

———. "Spiritedness and Philosophy in Plato's *Republic*." In *Understanding the Political Spirit*, ed. Catherine Zuckert. New Haven: Yale University Press, 1988.

Nietzsche, Friedrich. *Twilight of the Idols*. Translated R. J. Hollingdale. New York: Penguin Books, 1982.

Nussbaum, Martha. "Aristotelian Social Democracy." In *Liberalism and the Good*, ed. R. Bruce Douglass, Gerald M. Mara and Henry Richardson. New York: Routledge, 1990.

———. *Aristotle's De Motu Animalium: Text with Translation, Commentary, and Interpretive Essays*. Princeton: Princeton University Press, 1978.

————. "Aristotle, Feminism, and the Needs for Functioning." In *Feminist Inter-pretations of Aristotle*, ed. Cynthia A. Freeland, 248–59. University Park: Pennsylvania State University Press, 1998.

————. "Emotions as Judgments of Value." *Yale Journal of Criticism* 5, no. 2 (1992): 201–11.

————. *The Fragility of Goodness: Luck and Ethics in Greek Tragedy and Phi-losophy*. New York: Cambridge University Press, 1986.

————. "Human Functioning and Social Justice: In Defense of Aristotelian Essentialism." *Political Theory* 20, no. 2 (May 1992): 202–46.

————. *Love's Knowledge: Essays on Philosophy and Literature*. New York: Oxford University Press, 1990.

————. "Nature, Function, and Capability: Aristotle on Political Distribution." *Oxford Studies in Ancient Philosophy* suppl. vol. 1 (1988): 145–83.

————. *Poetic Justice: The Literary Imagination and Public Life*. Boston: Bea-con Press, 1995.

————. *The Therapy of Desire: Theory and Practice in Hellenistic Ethics*. Prince-ton: Princeton University Press, 1994.

Nussbaum, Martha C., and Jonathan Glover, eds. *Women, Culture and Develop-ment: A Study of Human Capabilities*. New York: Oxford University Press, 1995.

Nussbaum, Martha C., and Amartya Sen, eds. *The Quality of Life*. New York: Oxford University Press, 1992.

Oakley, Justin. *Morality and the Emotions*. New York: Routledge, 1992.

Okin, Susan. *Women in Western Political Thought*. Princeton: Princeton Uni-versity Press, 1981.

————. *Justice, Gender, and the Family*. New York: Basic Books, 1989.

————. "Reason and Feeling in Thinking About Justice." *Ethics* 99, no. 2 (1989): 229–49.

Orwin, Clifford. "Rousseau and the Discovery of Political Compassion." In *The Legacy of Rousseau*, ed. Clifford Orwin and Nathan Tarcov, 296–320. Chicago: University of Chicago Press, 1997.

O'Connor, David K. "Two Ideals of Friendship." *History of Philosophy Quarterly* 7, no. 2 (1990): 109–22.

Padel, Ruth. *In and Out of the Mind: Greek Images of the Tragic Self*. Princeton: Princeton University Press, 1992.

Pakulak, Michael. "Friendship and the Comparison of Goods." *Phronesis* 37, no. 1 (1992): 111–30.

Pangle, Thomas L. "The Political Psychology of Religion in Plato's Laws." *Amer-ican Political Science Review* 70, no. 4 (1976): 1059–77.

Penner, Tony. "Thought and Desire in Plato." In *Plato: A Collection of Critical Essays*, ed. Gregory Vlastos. Notre Dame: University of Notre Dame Press, 1978.

Pfister, Joel, and Nancy Schnog, eds. *Inventing the Psychological: Towards a Cultural History of Emotional Life in America*. New Haven: Yale Univer-sity Press, 1997.

Phillips, Anne. "Universal Pretensions in Political Thought." In *Destabilizing Theory: Contemporary Feminist Debates*, ed. Michelle Barrett and Anne Phillips. Palo Alto: Stanford University Press, 1992.

Pinch, Adela. "Emotion and History: A Review Article." *Comparative Studies in Society and History* 37 (1995): 100–109.

———. *Strange Fits of Passion: Epistemologies of Emotion, Hume to Austen*. Stanford: Stanford University Press, 1996.

Plant, Raymond, Harry Lesser, and Peter Taylor-Gooby, eds. *Essays on the Normative Basis of Welfare Provision*. Boston: Routledge and Keegan Paul, 1980.

Plato. *Plato: Complete Works*. Edited by John Cooper. Indianapolis: Hackett, 1997.

———. *The Republic of Plato*. Translated by Allan Bloom. New York: Basic Books, 1968.

Pomeroy, Sarah. *Goddesses, Whores, Wives, and Slaves: Women in Classical Antiquity*. New York: Schocken Books, 1975.

Price, A. W. *Love and Friendship in Plato and Aristotle*. Oxford: Clarendon Press, 1989.

———. *Mental Conflict*. New York: Routledge, 1995.

Rapaport, Elizabeth. "On the Future of Love: Rousseau and the Radical Feminists." In *Women and Philosophy: Toward a Theory of Liberation*, ed. Carol C. Gould and Marx W. Wartofsky, 185–205. New York: G. P. Putnam's Sons, 1976.

Rawls, John. *A Theory of Justice*. Cambridge: Harvard University Press, 1971.

Reddy, William. "Against Constructionism: The Historical Ethnograpy of Emotions." *Cultural Anthropology* 38, no. 3 (1997): 327–40.

Redfield, James M. *Nature and Culture in the Iliad: The Tragedy of Hektor*. Chicago: University of Chicago Press, 1975.

Reeve, C. D. C. *Philosopher Kings: The Argument of Plato's Republic*. Princeton: Princeton University Press, 1988.

Reiman, Jeff. *Justice and Moral Philosophy*. New Haven: Yale University Press, 1990.

Reiner, Paula. "Aristotle on Personality and Some Implications for Friendship." *Ancient Philosophy* 11, no. 1 (1991): 67–84.

Robinson, T. M. *Plato's Psychology*. 2d. ed. Toronto and Buffalo: University of Toronto Press, 1995.

Rorty, Amelie Oksenberg, ed. *Essays on Aristotle's Poetics*. Princeton: Princeton University Press, 1992.

———, ed. *Essays on Aristotle's Rhetoric*. Berkeley and Los Angeles: University of California Press, 1996.

———, ed. *Explaining Emotions*. Berkeley and Los Angeles: University of California Press, 1980.

Rosaldo, Michelle Z. "Toward an Anthropology of Self and Feeling." In *Culture Theory: Essays on Mind, Self, and Emotion*, ed. R. A. Shweder and R. A. LeVine, 137–57. Cambridge: Cambridge University Press, 1984.

Rousseau, Jean-Jacques. *Emile or On Education*. Translated by Allan Bloom. New York: Basic Books, 1979.

———. *The First and Second Discourses*. Edited by Roger D. Masters. Translated by Roger D. and Judith R. Masters. New York: St. Martin's Press, 1964.

Rowe, C. J. "The Nature of Homeric Morality." In *Approaches to Homer*, ed. Carl A. Rubino and Cynthia W. Shelmerdine, 248–75. Austin: University of Texas Press, 1983.

Russo, Joseph, and Bennett Simon. "Homeric Psychology and the Oral Epic Tradition." *Journal of the History of Ideas* 29 (1968): 483–98.

Sale, William Merritt. "The Government of Troy: Politics in the *Iliad*." *Greek, Roman, and Byzantine Studies* 35 (Spring 1994): 5–102.

Salkever, Stephen G. *Finding the Mean: Theory and Practice in Aristotelian Political Philosophy*. Princeton: Princeton University Press, 1990.

———. "Freedom, Participation, and Happiness." *Political Theory* 5, no. 3 (1977): 391–413.

———. "Tragedy and the Education of the Demos: Aristotle's Response to Plato." In *Greek Tragedy and Political Theory*, ed. J. Peter Euben. Berkeley and Los Angeles: University of California Press, 1986.

———. "Who Knows Whether It's Rational to Vote?" *Ethics* 90 (January 1980): 203–17.

Sansone, David. "The Sacrifice Motif in Euripides' *IT*." *TAPA* 105 (1975): 275–91.

Saxonhouse, Arlene. "Family, Polity, and Unity: Aristotle on Socrates' Community of Wives." *Polity* 15, no. 2 (1982): 202–19.

———. *Fear of Diversity: The Birth of Political Science in Ancient Greek Thought*. Chicago: University of Chicago Press, 1992.

———. "From Tragedy to Hierarchy and Back Again: Women in Greek Political Thought." *American Political Science Review* 80, no. 2 (June 1986): 403–18.

———. *Women in the History of Political Thought: Ancient Greece to Machiavelli*. New York: Praeger, 1985.

———. "Thymos, Justice, and Moderation of Anger in the Story of Achilles." In *Understanding the Political Spirit*, ed. Catherine Zuckert. New Haven: Yale University Press, 1988.

Schein, Seth L. *The Mortal Hero: An Introduction to Homer's Iliad*. Berkeley and Los Angeles: University of California Press, 1984.

Scheman, Naomi. "Anger and the Politics of Naming." In *Engenderings: Constructions of Knowledge, Authority, and Priviledge*, 11–21. Thinking Gender. New York: Routledge, 1993.

———. "On Sympathy." In *Engenderings: Constructions of Knowledge, Authority, and Priviledge*, 11–21. Thinking Gender. New York: Routledge, 1993.

Schnog, Nancy. "On Inventing the Psychological." In *Inventing the Psychological*, ed. Pfister and Schnog, 3–16. New Haven: Yale University Press, 1997.

Schollmeier, Paul. *Other Selves: Aristotle on Personal and Political Friendship*. Albany: SUNY Press, 1994.

Schroeder, Donald N. "Aristotle on the Good of Virtue Friendship." *History of Political Thought* 13, no. 2 (1992): 203–18.

Schwartz, Barry. *The Battle for Human Nature: Science, Morality, and Modern Life*. New York: W. W. Norton, 1986.

Schwarzenbach, Sibyl. "On Civic Friendship." *Ethics* 107, no. 1 (1996): 97–128.

———. "A Political Reading of the Reproductive Soul in Aristotle." *History of Philosophy Quarterly* 9, no. 2 (1992): 243–64.

Scully, Stephen. *Homer and the Sacred City*. Ithaca: Cornell University Press, 1991.

Sears, David O., and Carolyn L. Funk. "Self-Interest in Americans' Political Opinions." In *Beyond Self-Interest*, ed. Jane Mansbridge. Chicago: University of Chicago Press, 1990.

Seery, John Evan. "Politics as Ironic Community: On the Themes of Descent and Return in Plato's Republic." *Political Theory* 16, no. 2 (1988): 229–56.

Sen, Amartya. "More Than 100 Million Women Are Missing." *New York Review of Books*, December 20, 1990, 61–66.

———. "Rational Fools: A Critique of the Behavioral Foundations of Economic Theory." In *Beyond Self-Interest*, ed. Jane J. Mansbridge, 25–43. Chicago: University of Chicago Press, 1990.

Shanley, Mary Lyndon, and Carole Pateman, eds. *Feminist Interpretations and Political Theory*. University Park: Pennsylvania State University Press, 1991.

Sharples, R. W. "'But Why Has My Spirit Spoken with Me Thus?': Homeric Decision-Making." *Greece and Rome* 30, no. 1 (April 1983): 1–7.

Sherman, Nancy. *The Fabric of Character: Aristotle's Theory of Virtue*. New York: Oxford University Press, 1989.

———. *Making a Necessity of Virtue: Aristotle and Kant on Virtue*. New York: Cambridge University Press, 1997.

Shorter, Edward. *The Making of the Modern Family*. New York: Basic Books, 1975.

Smith, M. B. "A Map for the Analysis of Personality and Politics." *Journal of Social Issues* 24, no. 1 (1968): 15–28.

Snell, Bruno. *The Discovery of the Mind: The Greek Origins of European Thought*. Translated by T. G. Rosenmeyer. New York: Harper and Row, 1960.

Solomon, Robert. *A Passion for Justice: Emotions and the Origins of the Social Contract*. Reading, Mass.: Addison-Wesley, 1990.

———. *The Passions: The Myth and Nature of Human Emotion*. New York: Anchor, 1977.

Spacks, Patricia Meyer. *Boredom: The Literary History of a State of Mind*. Chicago: University of Chicago Press, 1996.

Spelman, Elizabeth V. "Good Grief, It's Plato!" In *Feminists Rethink the Self*, ed. Diana Tietjens Meyers. Boulder: Westview Press, 1997.

———. "The Heady Political Life of Political Compassion." In *Reconstructing Political Theory*, ed. Mary Shanley Shanley and Uma Narayan, 128–43. University Park: Pennsylvania State University Press, 1997.

———. "The Virtue of Feeling and Feeling of Virtue." In *Feminist Ethics*, ed. Claudia Card, 213–32. Lawrence: University of Kansas Press, 1991.

Stanford, W. B. *Greek Tragedy and the Emotions*. London: Routledge and Kegan Paul, 1982.

Stearns, Carol Z., and Peter N. Stearns, eds. *Emotion and Social Change: Toward a New Psychohistory*. New York: Holmes and Meier, 1988.

Stearns, Peter N. *American Cool: Constructing a Twentieth-Century Emotional Style*. New York: New York University Press, 1994.

Stearns, Peter N. and Carol Z. Stearns. "Emotionology: Clarifying the History of Emotions and Emotional Standards." *American Historical Review* 90 (October 1985): 813–36.

Stone, Lawrence. *The Family, Sex, and Marriage in England 1500–1800*. New York: Harper and Row, 1977.

Strauss, Leo. *The City and Man*. Chicago: University of Chicago Press, 1964.

———. *Liberalism Ancient and Modern*. New York: Basic Books, 1968.

———. *Natural Right and History*. Chicago: University of Chicago Press, 1953.

———. *What is Political Philosophy? and Other Studies*. Glencoe, Ill.: Free Press, 1959.

Sullivan, Shirley Darcus. "How a Person Relates to *Thumos* in Homer." *Indogermanische Forschungen* 85 (1985): 138–50.

———. *Psychological Activity in Homer: A Study of Phren*. Ottawa: Carleton University Press, 1988.

Swanson, Judith. "Aristotle on Liberality: Its Relation to Justice and Its Public and Private Practice." *Polity* 27, no. 1 (1994): 3–23.

———. *The Public and the Private in Aristotle's Political Philosophy*. Ithaca: Cornell University Press, 1992.

Taplin, Oliver. *Greek Tragedy in Action*. Berkeley and Los Angeles: University of California Press, 1978.

Taylor, Charles. "The Politics of Recognition." In *Multiculturalism and "The Politics of Recognition,"* ed. Amy Gutman. Princeton: Princeton University Press, 1992.

———. *Sources of the Self: The Making of the Modern Identity*. Cambridge: Harvard University Press, 1989.

Teske, Nathan. *Political Activists in America: The Identity Construction Model of Political Participation*. New York: Cambridge University Press, 1997.

Tessitore, Aristide. "Making the City Safe for Philosophy: *Nicomachean Ethics*, Book 10." *American Political Science Review* 84 (1990): 1252–62.

———. *Reading Aristotle's Ethics: Virtue, Rhetoric, and Political Philosophy*. Albany: State University of Albany Press, 1996.

Thomas, C. G. "The Roots of Homeric Kingship." *Historia* 15 (1966): 387–400.

Thomas, Laurence. *Living Morally: A Psychology of Moral Character*. Philadelphia: Temple University Press, 1989.

Tronto, Joan. "Beyond Gender Difference to a Theory of Care." *Signs* 12 (1987): 644–63.

———. *Moral Boundaries: A Political Argument for An Ethic of Care*. New York: Routledge, 1993.

Tuana, Nancy, ed. *Feminist Interpretations of Plato*. University Park: Pennsylvania State University Press, 1994.

Tyrrell, Wm. Blake, and Freida S. Brown. *Athenian Myths and Institutions: Words in Action*. New York: Oxford University Press, 1991.

Unger, Roberto Managabeira. *Passion: An Essay on Personality*. New York: Free Press, 1984.

Vander Waerdt, P. A. "The Peripatetic Interpretation of Plato's Tripartite Psychology." *Greek, Roman, and Byzantine Studies* 26 (1985): 283–302.

Vernant, Jean-Pierre, ed. *The Greeks*. Translated by Charles Lambert and Teresa Lavender Fagan. Chicago: The University of Chicago Press, 1995.

———. *Mortals and Immortals*. Edited by Froma I. Zeitlin. Princeton: Princeton University Press, 1991.

———. *The Origins of Greek Thought*. Ithaca: Cornell University Press, 1982.

Vernant, Jean-Pierre and Pierre Vidal-Naquet. *Myth and Tragedy in Ancient Greece*. Translated by Janet Lloyd. New York: Zone Books, 1990.

Vetlesen, Arne Johan. *Perception, Empathy, and Judgment: An Inquiry Into the Preconditions of Moral Performance*. University Park: Pennsylvania State University Press, 1994.

Vlastos, Gregory. "Was Plato a Feminist?" In *Feminist Interpretations of Plato*, ed. Nancy Tuana. University Park: Pennsylvania State University Press, 1994.

Voegelin, Eric. *Plato and Aristotle*. Vol. 3 of *Order and History*. Baton Rouge: Louisiana State University Press, 1957.

Wallach, John. "Contemporary Aristotelianism." *Political Theory* 20 (November 1992): 613–41.

Walton, Douglas. *The Place of Emotion in Argument*. University Park: Pennsylvania State University Press, 1992.

Ward, Julie K., ed. *Feminism and Ancient Philosophy*. New York: Routledge, 1996.

Weil, Simone. "The *Illiad* or The Poem of Force." In *Simone Weil: An Anthology*, ed. Sian Miles. New York: Weidenfield and Nicholson, 1986.

Wilkes, K. V. "Psuche Versus the Mind." In *Essays on Aristotle's De Anima*, ed. Martha C. Nussbaum and Amelie Oksenberg Rorty. New York: Oxford University Press, 1992.

Williams, Bernard. *Shame and Necessity*. Berkeley and Los Angeles: University of California Press, 1993.

Williams, Carolyn D. *Pope, Homer, and Manliness: Some Aspects of Eighteenth Century Classical Learning*. New York: Routledge, 1993.

Yack, Bernard. *The Problems of a Political Animal: Community, Justice and Conflict in Aristotelian Political Thought*. Berkeley and Los Angeles: University of California Press, 1993.

Young, Iris Marion. *Justice and the Politics of Difference*. Princeton: Princeton University Press, 1990.

Zanker, Graham. *The Heart of Achilles: Characterization and Personal Ethics in the Iliad*. Ann Arbor: The University of Michigan Press, 1994.

Zeitlin, Froma I. "Playing the Other: Theater, Theatricality, and the Feminine in Greek Drama." In *Nothing to Do With Dionysos?* ed. John J. Winkler and Froma I. Zeitlin. Princeton: Princeton University Press, 1990.

Zuckert, Catherine. "On the Role of Spiritedness in Politics." In *Understanding the Political Spirit: Philosophical Investigations from Socrates to Nietzsche*, ed. Catherine Zuckert, 1–29. New Haven: Yale University Press, 1988.

———, ed. *Understanding the Political Spirit: Philosophical Investigations from Socrates to Nietzsche*. New Haven: Yale University Press, 1988.

# Index